Teaching Children and Adolescents Physical Education

FOURTH EDITION

George Graham, PhD
Pinehurst, NC

Eloise Elliott, PhD
West Virginia University

Steve Palmer, PhD
Northern Arizona University

**HUMAN
KINETICS**

Library of Congress Cataloging-in-Publication Data

Names: Graham, George, 1943-
Title: Teaching children and adolescents physical education / George Graham,
     PhD, Eloise Elliott, PhD, West Virginia University, Steve Palmer, PhD,
     Northern Arizona University.
Description: Fourth Edition. | Champaign : Human Kinetics, [2016] |
     Previously published: Champaign, IL : Human Kinetics, 2008, under title
     Teaching children physical education. | Includes bibliographical
     references and index.
Identifiers: LCCN 2016007127| ISBN 9781450452939 (print) | ISBN 9781492528647
     (e-book)
Subjects: LCSH: Physical education teachers--Training of--United States. |
     Physical education for children--Study and teaching--United States.
Classification: LCC GV363 .G68 2016 | DDC 613.7/042--dc23 LC record available at http://lccn.loc.gov/2016007127

ISBN: 978-1-4504-5293-9 (print)

The web addresses cited in this text were current as of February 2016, unless otherwise noted.

Acquisitions Editor: Scott Wikgren; **Developmental Editor:** Jacqueline Eaton Blakley; **Managing Editors:** Carly S. O'Connor and Derek Campbell; **Copyeditor:** Patsy Fortney; **Indexer:** Dan Connolly; **Permissions Manager:** Dalene Reeder; **Senior Graphic Designer:** Nancy Rasmus; **Cover Designer:** Keith Blomberg; **Photographs (cover):** © Human Kinetics; **Visual Production Assistant:** Joyce Brumfield; **Senior Art Manager:** Kelly Hendren; **Associate Art Manager:** Alan L. Wilborn; **Illustrations:** © Human Kinetics, unless otherwise noted; **Printer:** Walsworth

We thank Boise State University, North Junior High School, Riverside Elementary, Heritage Middle School, Lake Hazel Middle School, and Kuna High School in Boise, Idaho, for assistance in providing the locations for the video shoot for this book.

The video contents of this product are licensed for educational public performance for viewing by a traditional (live) audience, via closed circuit television, or via computerized local area networks within a single building or geographically unified campus. To request a license to broadcast these contents to a wider audience—for example, throughout a school district or state, or on a television station—please contact your sales representative (**www.HumanKinetics.com/SalesRepresentatives**).

Printed in the United States of America   10 9 8 7 6 5 4 3 2

The paper in this book is certified under a sustainable forestry program.

Human Kinetics
Website: www.HumanKinetics.com

United States: Human Kinetics
P.O. Box 5076
Champaign, IL 61825-5076
800-747-4457
e-mail: info@hkusa.com

Canada: Human Kinetics
475 Devonshire Road, Unit 100
Windsor, ON N8Y 2L5
800-465-7301 (in Canada only)
e-mail: info@hkcanada.com

Europe: Human Kinetics
107 Bradford Road
Stanningley
Leeds LS28 6AT, United Kingdom
+44 (0)113 255 5665
e-mail: hk@hkeurope.com

For information about Human Kinetics' coverage in other areas of the world,
please visit our website: www.HumanKinetics.com

E5942

To my special family, Teresa, Nick, Tommy, Jackie, Verenda, Austin, Carter, Savanna, Lois, and Natalie. I am a lucky guy!

—George

To my grandkids, Quinn Eloise and Spencer Michael, who bring me so much love and sunshine and give me great pleasure and inspiration when I see them enjoying hours of physical activity every day.

—Eloise

To Jennie for her support and my sons, Evan, Scott, and Troy, for their inspiration.

—Steve

Contents

Preface   vii

Acknowledgments   xiii

Accessing the Web Resource   xvii

1 Successful Teaching   1

The Teacher, Not Only the Content 2 • How Teaching Physical Education Differs From Teaching in the Classroom 3 • Analogies of Teaching 4 • Changing and Dynamic Nature of Teaching 5 • Difficulty of Describing Good Teaching 5 • Challenge of Teaching Physical Education 6 • The Teacher Makes the Difference 8 • Pedagogy Toolbox 10 • Working Definition of *Successful* 10 • Summary 13

2 Creating a Positive Learning Environment   15

Teacher Expectancy 17 • Teacher Stereotypes 18 • Creating an Emotionally Safe Environment 19 • Determining Management Protocols 19 • Teaching Behavior Protocols 28 • Summary 32

3 Long-Term Planning   35

Need for Planning 38 • Tendencies to Avoid Planning 43 • Planning Formats and Components 44 • Summary 50

4 Writing the Lesson Plan   53

Writing the Daily Lesson Plan 54 • Lesson Purpose: Learnable Pieces 54 • Developing the Content 55 • Major Parts of a Lesson Plan 56 • Lesson Components 70 • Adapting Lessons for Students With Special Needs 71 • Teaching With a Purpose 73 • Summary 74

5 Teaching From the Lesson Plan   77

Student Centered Versus Subject Centered 78 • Observation Techniques 80 • Four Key Content Development Questions 82 • Observing Individuals 83 • Observing Classes for Content Development 83 • Fun 90 • Summary 91

6 Getting the Lesson Started   93

Instant Activity 94 • Communicating the Purpose of the Lesson 97 • Traditional Ways to Start a Lesson 101 • Summary 103

7 Instructing and Demonstrating   105

Instructing 106 • Demonstrating 112 • Pinpointing 114 • Checking for Understanding 115 • Closure 116 • Play-Teach-Play 117 • Using Video Technology 119 • Analyzing Students' Use of Time 120 • Summary 122

8 **Motivating Students to Practice**   **125**

Three Keys to Motivating Youngsters 126 • Eight Techniques for
Motivating Students 132 • Developing Realistic Expectations 142 •
Teacher as Cheerleader 144 • Summary 145

9 **Providing Feedback**   **149**

Types of Feedback 150 • Analyzing Your Feedback 155 • Research on
Physical Education Teacher Feedback 158 • Summary 159

10 **Minimizing Off-Task Behavior and
Discipline Problems**   **161**

Why Do Students Act Out? 162 • Strategies for Minimizing
Off-Task Behavior 162 • Discipline Systems 167 • Characteristics of
Effective Discipline Systems 173 • Disciplinary Confrontation 175 •
Summary 177

11 **Building Critical Thinking Skills**   **181**

Value of Critical Thinking Experiences 182 • Convergent Problem
Solving 184 • Divergent Problem Solving 186 • Verbal Problem
Solving 187 • Necessary Teacher Characteristics 188 • Direct or
Indirect: Which Approach Is Best? 193 • Summary 193

12 **Building Positive Feelings**   **195**

Inappropriate Practices 196 • Intentional and Ever Present 200 •
Techniques and Strategies 201 • Testing 208 • Understanding
Feelings 209 • Learned Helplessness 211 • Concluding
Thoughts 211 • Summary 212

13 **Assessing and Reporting Student Progress**   **215**

Why Assess? 216 • What to Assess? 217 • Alternative
Assessment 218 • Evaluating Assessment Data 226 • Standardized
Assessments 230 • Reporting and Grading 231 • Summary 235

14 **Continuing to Develop as a Teacher**   **239**

Stages of Teaching 240 • Techniques for Continuing to Improve
as a Teacher 244 • Seven Habits of Highly Effective Teachers 251 •
What Type of Teacher Will You Become? 251 • Parting Thoughts 252 •
Summary 253

Index   255

About the Authors   261

Preface

We hope you are reading this book because you are a physical education teacher or plan to become one. If you are hoping to find some fun games or activities, ways to improve fitness, or simply ways to keep classes busy, happy, and well behaved for 30 minutes or so, then you probably won't like this book. This book is for teachers who want their students to learn sport skills and movement and fitness concepts while developing positive attitudes toward physical activity.

The first three editions of this text were written by George Graham and focused solely on children's physical education. This fourth edition has been expanded to focus on K-12 physical education. For this edition, George is fortunate to be joined by two of his former students, Eloise Elliott and Steve Palmer, who were public school teachers before earning their PhDs and moving to universities. Their teaching and research continue to be focused on K-12 students and teachers.

One of the truisms in life is that if you can't throw and catch a ball, you probably won't enjoy sports that require those two skills (such as softball, basketball, and ultimate). Teaching is similar. If you don't learn the skills for teaching effectively, then you probably won't enjoy or be successful at teaching. This book is not about *what* to teach but rather *how* to teach. During our years of observing and working with physical educators, we have encountered countless teachers who were searching for the perfect games or activities, ones that classes would enjoy and also learn from. All too often, however, they were not able to find the perfect game because their students would not listen long enough or carefully enough to understand how to play the game. Thus the perfect game often disintegrated into confusion, uncertainty, and even chaos. This book is different because it focuses solely on the teaching, or pedagogical, skills used by successful physical education teachers.

Our text is written from the perspective of a teacher as opposed to that of a university professor. We have done this for several reasons. The first is that our entire careers have been focused on physical education—and especially those who teach it! We have worked hard to stay connected to K-12 schools and teachers. It is all too easy to be at a university and lose touch with the realities of teachers' lives and forget what it's like to teach several hundred youngsters a day with barely enough time to eat lunch and use the restroom. Many states have implemented high-stakes testing with public accountability. Consequently, in addition to everything else they do, some physical educators have to justify their programs more than ever before. While this is not part of their job description, it is a wearying, time-consuming, and often frustrating part of teaching physical education as we move further into the 21st century.

We are in the midst of a full-blown obesity epidemic. Experts are predicting that, for the first time ever, this generation of children might live shorter lives than their parents. Thus, in addition to high-stakes testing, many schools are increasingly focused on the health of children.

We have been fortunate throughout our careers to be surrounded by excellent physical education teachers who have both inspired and impressed us with their teaching skills and effectiveness with youngsters. They are truly geniuses with kids! And they are all unique. We list some of their names in the acknowledgments because we have learned so much from them and, even though they might not know it, their teaching is reflected throughout the book.

We also rely on the teaching research completed in the last 50 years or so and apply it to teaching physical education so that it will be valuable to undergraduates as well as those already teaching. As you will see, some of the studies are recent. Other studies were completed some time ago but are included because their findings and insights remain relevant to teaching today.

This book is unique in that it focuses on the teaching process—the skills and techniques that successful teachers use to make their classes more interesting and appropriate. Future teachers will find the book helpful because it describes and analyzes many of the teaching skills and techniques used by veteran teachers. Topics such as motivation, minimizing discipline problems, and structuring successful learning environments will be of particular interest to novice teachers.

Experienced teachers, in contrast, will discover that some of the techniques they already use are named and described in the book. Our hope is that veteran teachers will also be challenged to consider some new techniques for structuring their classes, developing lessons, and adjusting tasks for individuals—ideas that will benefit them and their students. We have learned a lot about teaching in the past five decades, and the veterans will find this information both useful and informative.

Features

Teaching cannot be reduced to a simple formula. There are always decisions to be made—quickly and frequently. Learning to make those decisions can be done only on your feet. You can read about what teachers do, but until you are actually in the eye of the hurricane, it is difficult to grasp the complexity of choices confronting a teacher. In this book, we explain the decision-making process by separating it into various chapters. Realistically, parts of every chapter in the book will be used in virtually every lesson that is taught. To help you better understand and integrate these concepts, we have included several features to encourage the type of thinking that teachers do during a lesson.

Chapter Introductions

Each chapter begins with a brief introduction that sets the stage. This is helpful for connecting one chapter to another and also for understanding the teaching skills and techniques that are discussed in that chapter.

Chapter Objectives

Each introduction includes a series of objectives that highlight the key points in that chapter. Some textbooks use the word *student* instead of *teacher*. We have used *teacher* instead of *student* because those who are interested in this book are, or will become, teachers.

Mini-Stories

Because this book is intended for both experienced and beginning teachers, we include many practical examples in the form of mini-stories and insights throughout the text. This feature makes the book applicable in the real world and reinforces the concept that teaching physical education is a dynamic experience that requires adapting and thinking on your feet. Stated differently, teaching situations are sometimes messy, requiring changes on the fly. These mini-stories are highlighted in boxes to let you know that they represent actual experiences that one of us had when teaching physical education. Our initials are included in each story so you will be able to tell which of us is telling that story.

A sample mini-story follows:

Magic Cue

A popular misconception about teaching physical activity is that there is a magic cue. If you can just find that cue, the learner will instantly improve and become proficient. Golfers are notorious for trying to discover the magic cue. In reality, we know that the cue might be appropriate but that one single trial is not enough to make a cue a habit. It won't automatically help the first time it is explained and demonstrated. When I (GG) was learning to downhill ski, for example, the cue that initially helped me the most was to keep my weight forward. But the first time I heard that cue and concentrated on it, I didn't magically ski the hill without falling. Fortunately, my instructor kept repeating it, and eventually I incorporated the cue into my motor pattern and began to fall less and less (Schmidt & Wrisberg, 2008).

Tech Tips

Since the third edition was published there have been scores of new technologies being used by physical educators. In this edition you will find some great examples of how technology is enhancing physical education programs. Many of these ideas are being used by Misti Wajciechowski and Matthew Pomeroy, two teachers who have technology expertise and who were gracious enough to share their ideas with us for inclusion in this edition.

A sample tech tip follows:

TECH TIPS Organize Your Planning

One challenge as a teacher is having the time to plan your entire year, by grade level, while coordinating with all of the other school activities. Use a website such as Portaportal or even Pinterest to keep your entire unit resources in one space for access wherever you are!

Our technology integration experts remind us of some considerations to help integrate technology successfully into your physical education program:

- Do not use technology in physical education classes for the sake of using technology—use it to enhance the learning experience (i.e., make content more rich and exciting, formatively assess each student quickly and more frequently, give higher-quality and more specific feedback, create summative assessment experiences, allow for greater individuality and student-centered learning opportunities).
- Use technology to help you, the teacher (i.e., get more information about your students that you can store and access after the lesson, gain a better understand of each student's knowledge level, better adjust upcoming lesson content).

- If using smart devices, or any technology, make sure that all students have access to one. If students are being permitted to use their own devices and all students do not have one, then design activities that can be done as a group or in pairs.

Be warned that some of the apps and ideas come with a fee or are initially free and then require a fee for upgrades. Additionally, at the time of writing this new edition, the apps described were all available from Google Play or iTunes. It is likely, however, that some apps may no longer be available by the time you look for them. You may find something newer and better is now available. The idea is to look for a way that you can more effectively help students learn.

Web Resource With Video Examples

The previous edition included a DVD with video examples of K-5 teachers demonstrating many of the skills with their classes. This new edition retains the previous edition's video examples and adds many new examples from physical education classes at the secondary level. The video content is now available on a web resource accessed by pass code (see "Accessing the Web Resource") along with many assessments and other forms from the book that can be downloaded in Microsoft Word or PDF format. The web resource is accessible at www.HumanKinetics.com/TeachingChildrenAndAdolescentsPhysicalEducation.

Throughout the text we call your attention to places where video content is available to illustrate the skills when they are being used by K-12 teachers. It looks like this:

Establishing Protocols   The web resource provides brief videos of several teachers working to establish protocols with their students. You will find these examples especially useful for understanding how successful teachers establish their protocols.

As you view the video vignettes, you might notice that the clothing worn by the teachers and the children seems outdated. Some of the lessons were taught years ago. Some of the examples used by the teachers might be old, too (such as when they name professional athletes). Try not to let that distract you. The teaching skills used then are every bit as relevant today.

As you view the sample videos, remember that these are taken from actual lessons and thus may not be perfect—but they will enhance your understanding of how the skills might be used in your teaching.

Links to National Standards and Grade-Level Outcomes

In 2014 the Society of Health and Physical Educators (SHAPE America) published a revised set of national physical education standards along with grade-level outcomes. As you read previously, this book is about the process of teaching, not what to teach (the content). Throughout the book, however, we use content examples to explain the teaching process. In chapters 4 and 5 on planning, for example, we use examples from the grade-level outcomes to indicate how a teacher might decide what content to include in the curriculum. In all of these examples we have indicated the code that identifies the grade-level outcome from the national standard. For example, in chapter 4 we discuss the process of deciding on lesson objectives. The example we use is teaching youngsters to strike an object (ball, shuttlecock) with a paddle. To show you where the content came from in the national standards, we include the following code: (S1.E24.2). This indicates that the outcome is from Standard 1, example 24, grade level 2). All of the standards and grade-level outcomes are on SHAPE America's website at shapeamerica.org.

Reflection Questions

Each chapter concludes with a series of questions for reflection. Because teaching cannot be reduced to a precise formula, the questions help you think about the teaching process and the reasons you teach the way you do. They will also lead you to question some of the ways physical education has been taught in the past—find the good points and remodel those practices that may be counterproductive for children.

Good teachers have a sense of wonder about their teaching. They question whether their techniques worked, how something could have been better, what would happen if another element were introduced, why one way is better than another, whether there are other ways to do something in less time, and how to gain the interest of more students. We hope the reflection questions will deepen your sense of wonder about teaching.

Chapter Summary and References

Each chapter concludes with a summary or parting thought and a list of the references cited in that chapter.

Overview of Chapters

One of the challenges of writing a book on the process of teaching is figuring out how to describe a process that is intertwined, complex, and nonlinear. When you break out various teaching skills, you tend to oversimplify their use because they are removed from the dynamic context of a lesson. Realistically, however, there is no choice in a book. The video vignettes and questions for reflection will restore a sense of context and complexity to the variety of skills that you use to create stimulating lessons for students. Furthermore, after the introductory chapter, chapters are arranged in chronological order, based on the points at which various teaching skills and techniques might be used in a lesson.

Chapter 1 presents discussions of the purpose, challenges, and rewards of physical education described in realistic settings. The chapter concludes with a description of the knowledge that successful teachers of physical education have and how it looks when translated into practice. The important message of chapter 1 is that this book is about how to teach (that is, the process); it is not a description of activities and games that teachers might use in instructing youngsters.

Discipline and off-task behavior are often primary concerns of teachers. Chapter 2 describes how you can minimize discipline problems by developing management routines (protocols) that prevent off-task behavior from the first day of the school year.

Long-term planning, the subject of chapter 3, and short-term (lesson) planning described in chapter 4 are probably not a favorite subject, but it is a necessary one. These chapters feature ideas for planning and sequencing lessons and also for developing yearly and daily plans that are sequential and developmentally appropriate and accommodate various levels of skill and knowledge among students.

One of the premises of this book is that good teachers recognize the differences in youngsters—that one class of eighth-graders is different from the next, and that within any eighth-grade class, there is a wide range of abilities and interests. This student-centered approach to teaching requires that you be able to observe and interpret the movement of youngsters and then adapt the lessons accordingly. Chapter 5 describes how to teach the lesson using the lesson plan. Strategies for observing and analyzing youth as they move are provided. Questions regarding when you should change from one task to another and what to do when individuals need to continue working on a task but want to do something else are featured.

A successful beginning to a lesson is often the prelude to a worthwhile class. Chapter 6 discusses this aspect of teaching. Chapter 7 analyzes the ways in which you can provide instruction and use demonstrations to help children better understand and retain important concepts.

A worthwhile topic for discussion among any group of teachers is motivating students. Chapter 8 suggests ways to do this and emphasizes intrinsic rather than extrinsic motivation techniques.

Chapter 9 concerns when and how you can provide feedback that is consistent with the focus of the lesson.

Despite all of your good intentions and preparations, some kids will manage to be off task. Chapter 10 describes how successful teachers deal with these problems.

Chapter 11 examines the teaching skills of asking questions and setting problems for students to solve, emphasizing the importance of cognitive understanding.

Chapter 12 focuses on the affective domain and suggests ways in which you can help students feel good about themselves and about physical activity. Chapter 13 provides a contemporary perspective on assessing (testing) students in schools.

Chapter 14 is the conclusion, covering the importance of teachers' continuing to learn and develop professionally to avoid becoming stagnant and out of touch.

eBook
available at
HumanKinetics.com

Acknowledgments

Since I semiretired in 2010, I have had the opportunity to think a lot about my career. It started in the public schools of California and Oregon. From there I moved to teaching at the Universities of Georgia and South Carolina and Virginia Tech and Penn State. Throughout my career I spent time every semester working with teachers and kids in the schools so that I would not forget the realities of teaching K-12 physical education. I feel a warm glow when I think about all the teachers I have been fortunate to work with over the years who have, knowingly or unknowingly, contributed to what I have written in the pages that follow.

The most influential people are the elementary school teachers I have been associated with and who continue to inspire and motivate me. Even though I am now miles away from them, I think of teachers such as Liz Johnson, Sean Fortner, John Pomeroy, Rosa Edwards, Larry Satchwell, and Casey Jones. I don't think they have any idea how good they are with kids! They are no different from athletes at the height of their game: They make teaching appear so easy, yet they have worked incredibly hard for years to arrive at the top of their profession. Had I not been able to work with teachers like them, this book would be very different. Though too few recognize these teachers' excellence, they are truly touching the lives of the thousands of youngsters they work with throughout their careers. I am also grateful to the elementary school physical educators in State College, Pennsylvania, who have been so supportive: Andy Lloyd, Sharn Nicholson, Becky Ferguson, and Ann Frederick.

I want to express my appreciation to the last "block" of undergraduate students I was fortunate to work with at Penn State. They were and continue to be dedicated, curious, bright, and a whole lot of fun. A few of them I have kept in contact with, including Danielle Hewitt (who was especially helpful at the beginning of this revision with insights related to middle and high school physical education), Jess Chez Levy, Matt Beck, Katie Madden, Doug Miller, John Schwartz, Nicole Danielle, Katy Hess, Kendal Elizabeth, Ryan McGee, Michael Joseph, Morgan Leigh, and Katie McMurdy Rudolph. I never wanted to leave teaching, but you and the spirit of your block made the transition a whole lot easier because I knew that the profession was in good hands.

I have been challenged the most by my graduate students, who asked such penetrating and complex questions in their quest to become outstanding college professors and researchers. I learned more from them than they'll ever know, and I am grateful for their questions—and apologize for my inability to answer so many of them. But, as I hope they have learned, the most important part of the journey is asking the right questions.

My thinking and writing have been influenced by several professionals who have remained in contact with me and continue to ask the right questions, albeit from a distance most of the time. They include Mark Manross, Christine Hopple, Marina Bonello,

Missy Parker, Tom Ratliffe, Ken Bell, Kim Oliver, and Lisa Witherspoon. I also want to acknowledge two university professors who have inspired me for many years with their work ethic, dedication to the profession, and quest to remain on the cutting edge in their thinking and writing even though they are now retired: Daryl Siedentop and Larry Locke.

I am delighted that two of my former doctoral students, Eloise Elliott and Steve Palmer, agreed to coauthor this fourth edition of the book as we expand to a K-12 focus. They are dedicated professionals who also have a passion for supporting K-12 teachers and improving their programs.

—George Graham

The experiences throughout my career that have been most influential on my knowledge about teaching, and teaching physical education, have been my work with K-6 students for many years in the public schools in Mercer County, West Virginia; the hundreds of undergraduate physical education teacher education majors whom I taught at Concord University (CU) in Athens, West Virginia; and my doctoral program at Virginia Tech. As a professor instructing many undergraduate PETE students at CU, I was fortunate to work with two K-5 teachers who allowed me to see high-quality PE in action and allowed me the opportunity to train my students with the best role models. Thanks to Aleta Jo Crotty and Patrick Haye for providing positive physical education to students and, therefore, to my preservice teachers.

At Virginia Tech I was fortunate to learn from the best: Dr. George Graham, who continues to inspire me to teach others what high-quality physical education looks like and how to be an effective teacher. Thanks to George for the opportunity and honor to cowrite this fourth edition with Steve. And my fellow doctoral students at VT continue to amaze me with their work. I am fortunate to call them my friends.

In my current position at West Virginia University, my colleagues and doctoral students motivate me, give me new opportunities to learn, and keep me in touch with K-12 physical education. Special thanks to Sean Bulger and Emily Jones for their dedication to the profession and to our team efforts in creating a more physically active culture in schools. And thanks to Luciana Braga for allowing me to be a mentor and now a colleague in creating new opportunities for K-12 students and for teaching university students the importance of pedagogy.

—Eloise Elliott

My contributions to this text would not have been possible without the help, support, and experiences working with students and school and university colleagues. Many of the stories and examples that found their way into the pages of this text are from elementary, middle school, and university students. I'm grateful to the wonderful teachers and administrators who have been so supportive throughout my time at Northern Arizona University: Tari Popham, Holly Jones, Steve Boadway, Theresa Freas, KC Hershey, Donald Penny, Jana Fix, Maureen Landrith, and many others who have always been willing to avail their classes for research and practicum. I also acknowledge my university colleagues, Erica Pratt and Tiffany Kloeppel, for their feedback and suggestions on new secondary content added to this edition.

Finally, I thank George Graham for inviting me to help with this text revision. I am honored to work with George and Eloise on such a tremendous resource for new and current physical education teachers. George, you are a fabulous mentor and friend and I'm grateful for having the opportunity to work with and learn from you.

—Steve Palmer

All three of us (George, Eloise, and Steve) would like to offer a special thanks to Dr. Ken Bell, professor at Boise State, who is the executive producer organizing and coordinating shooting the videos that accompany this text. It's a testament to Ken's work and the quality of the Boise State PETE program that there are so many good teachers we were able to work with. Thanks also to those teachers we filmed: Jake Miller, John Bale, Amanda Muri, Mandy Horning, Mike Cummings, and Kristi Lund. They have developed high-quality physical education programs for youngsters. We appreciate their allowing us to intrude on their schools to film them in action.

We especially acknowledge two teachers who integrate technology into their physical education programs and have written the technology tips that you will find throughout the book: Misti Wajciechowski and Matthew Pomeroy. The practical ideas are ones that Misti and Matt have found to work in their PE classes.

Finally, we acknowledge the folks at Human Kinetics who have worked so hard and so well to bring this fourth edition to press. First, special thanks to Scott Wikgren, vice president and director of the Health, Physical Education, Recreation and Dance Division, for his support, keen insights, and willingness to go to bat for this book. He has worked hard for many years to advance the new physical education. He knows and values good physical education and is doing his part to spread the word. We express our appreciation to Jackie Blakley, developmental editor of the fourth edition. Jackie kept us in line and maintained patience throughout the process. She has been a pleasure to work with. We are also grateful to the others who worked on this edition: managing editor Derek Campbell, graphic designer Nancy Rasmus, permission manager Dalene Reeder, and the rest of the Human Kinetics team.

Accessing the Web Resource

Throughout *Teaching Children and Adolescents Physical Education, Fourth Edition,* you will notice references to a web resource. This online content is available to you for free upon purchase of a new print book or an e-book. All you need to do is register with the Human Kinetics website to access the online content. The following steps will explain how to register.

The web resource offers video demonstrations of teaching techniques and practices described in the book. In addition, it features blank versions of some forms described in the book that you might find helpful to have in electronic format. We are certain you will find that the real-world video examples will enhance your understanding of what it is to be a master teacher, and the blank forms will make it easier for you to begin to put your own mastery into practice.

Follow these steps to access the web resource:

1. Visit www.HumanKinetics.com/TeachingChildrenAndAdolescentsPhysicalEducation.

2. Click the fourth edition link next to the corresponding fourth edition book cover.

3. Click the Sign In link on the left or top of the page. If you do not have an account with Human Kinetics, you will be prompted to create one.

4. After you register, if the online product does not appear in the Ancillary Items box on the left of the page, click the Enter Pass Code option in that box. Enter the following pass code exactly as it is printed here, including capitalization and all hyphens: **GRAHAM-E8N-WR**

5. Click the Submit button to unlock your online product.

6. After you have entered your pass code the first time, you will never have to enter it again to access this online product. Once unlocked, a link to your product will permanently appear in the menu on the left. All you need to do to access your online content on subsequent visits is sign in to **www.HumanKinetics.com/TeachingChildrenAndAdolescentsPhysicalEducation** and follow the link!

Click the Need Help? button on the book's website if you need assistance along the way.

Successful Teaching

After reading this chapter, you should be able to do the following:

- Explain why teaching physical education is characterized as a dynamic, constantly changing process.
- Discuss both the obstacles and the benefits of teaching physical education.
- Explain the concept of orchestration as it relates to the selection and use of teaching skills.
- Describe the distinction between content (what is taught) and the process of teaching (pedagogy).
- Delineate the major components of successful physical education teaching.

Filmmaker Woody Allen famously added to George Bernard Shaw's line about teaching, "And those who can't teach, teach physical education." We do have teachers in our profession who can't (or don't) teach (obviously, some of them taught Woody Allen!). As an unfortunate result, a number of adults in the United States recall physical education (PE) classes as painful, humiliating, and virtually worthless experiences.

Fortunately, that is changing. Today, we have a new breed of physical educators in the United States who are revolutionizing the way physical education is taught. These revolutionaries teach physical education in ways that make even students who aren't fond of physical activity look forward to physical education with enthusiasm. These teachers care as much about the low-skilled, sensitive, unconfident student as they do about the aggressive, athletic student. And they have found ways to make their classes both pleasant and worthwhile for all students—the low skilled and the high skilled, and all those in between.

This book describes and analyzes the techniques, behaviors, skills, and approaches used by successful teachers to develop and teach lessons that are developmentally appropriate—and that result in enjoyable and beneficial learning experiences.

The Teacher, Not Only the Content

When I (GG) think back on all of the teachers who taught me throughout my school years, several come immediately to mind—the good ones and the not-so-good ones. One of the teachers who pops into memory is my high school trigonometry teacher. I had decided in elementary school that math was not one of my academic strengths (and my math grades supported my belief). I struggled through required math courses from year to year—until I took a trigonometry course in my senior year. I vividly remember the first day. The teacher informed us that our text would be a college-level trigonometry book. I thought, *I am in big trouble in this course.* Surprisingly, that wasn't so. Although the topic and the textbook were difficult for me, my trig teacher made the material very interesting, and I actually did quite well. Despite my negative attitude at the beginning of the semester, I almost enjoyed learning math.

Obviously, it wasn't the subject—trigonometry—that encouraged me to do better than I had expected. It was the teacher—the way he explained concepts, took time with us, never made us feel foolish, structured the content, answered questions with understandable examples, arranged for us to succeed in small steps, and did a plethora of other small things that, when totaled, were the earmarks of a highly effective teacher of trigonometry.

Fortunately, this book isn't about trigonometry. It's about teachers and the kinds of things they do (or don't do) that make learning attainable and enjoyable for students. Trigonometry, reading, and physical education can all be taught in ways that are exciting and educational. However, they can also be taught in ways that are boring, confusing, and distasteful. We are not just concerned with the content to be taught. We are also concerned with teachers and all of the things they do that make students' attempts to learn the material productive and stimulating—so that they learn and enjoy the process.

That might sound as if we are suggesting that the content—and your knowledge of the content—is unimportant. That isn't true. To be a good teacher, you must know your subjects thoroughly (Ward, 2013) so that you can teach in ways that are engaging and productive for your students. My high school trigonometry teacher understood the subject well, which enabled him to develop lessons that were interesting, enjoyable, and productive.

The distinction between knowing what to teach (the content or curriculum) and knowing how to teach (the process or the pedagogy of the teacher) is an artificial one. Content and pedagogy cannot be separated. They are interwoven. But in studying and understanding the process of teaching, this artificial distinction is nevertheless helpful. The chapters that follow describe many of the teaching skills and techniques used by successful K-12 teachers, along with practical examples of how to use them to create lessons and programs.

Because physical education is a unique subject in schools, teachers use orchestrations of skills that are somewhat different from those used by their colleagues in the classroom. This book delineates many of the teaching skills employed by successful physical education teachers and the ways they are used in realistic teaching situations.

How Teaching Physical Education Differs From Teaching in the Classroom

Teaching any subject is challenging. Teaching physical education may be the most challenging. Here are a few reasons: The students are moving rather than anchored in desks; a teacher might work with 5-year-olds during one lesson and with 11-year-olds a few minutes later; the range of content covers the entire spectrum of physical activity; and facilities and equipment are often less than ideal. No doubt you can add to this list.

In addition to these factors, the pace is frenetic, often with 30 or more students active at once. Larry Locke (1975), in his now-classic description of a children's physical education lesson, captured the complexity and pace of teaching with a vibrant accuracy that is hard to find in written descriptions. Because this book is about teaching physical education in the real world, it seems appropriate to begin by setting the stage with his description of a two-minute observation of a class of 34 fourth-grade children during a gymnastics unit.

Teacher is working one on one with a student who has an obvious neurological deficit. She wants him to sit on a beam and lift his feet from the floor. Her verbal behaviors fall into categories of reinforcement, instruction, feedback,

and encouragement. She gives hands-on manual assistance. Nearby two boys perched on the uneven bars are keeping a group of girls off. Teacher visually monitors the situation but continues work on the beam. At the far end of the gym a large mat is propped up so that students can roll down it from a table top, and the mat is slowly slipping closer to the edge. Teacher visually monitors this but continues work on the beam. Teacher answers three individual inquiries addressed by passing students but continues as before. She glances at a group now playing follow the leader over the horse (this is off-task behavior) but as she does a student enters and indicates he left his milk money the previous period. Teacher nods him to the nearby office to retrieve the money and leaves the beam to stand near the uneven bars. The boys climb down at once. Teacher calls to a student to secure the slipping mat. Notes that the intruder, milk money now in hand, has paused to interact with two girls in the class and, monitoring him, moves quickly to the horse to begin a series of provocative questions designed to reestablish task focus. (Locke, 1975)

This two-minute vignette suggests how complex teaching is—and that's only 120 seconds out of 17,000 the teacher spent that day actually teaching.

Ten Thousand Students

A physical educator typically teaches several hundred students a week—let's assume 350. Over a 30-year career, that adds up to over 10,000 youngsters. And many teachers work with 500 to 600 students a week! In this business a single successful physical educator can truly make a difference in the lives of many youth.

Analogies of Teaching

Teaching is complex. Sometimes it may feel as though you are in the eye of a hurricane. Balls, students, and ideas are whirling everywhere with no apparent order—but all demand immediate attention.

Teaching has also been likened to a three-ring circus. The teacher is in the center ring—as the circus master. From this central position, the teacher simultaneously directs all three rings and attempts to maintain a pace and variety that hold the interest of the audience.

A third teaching analogy is that the teacher is like a composer and conductor of a symphony. There are many ways to arrange and blend the instruments in an orchestra: the strings, the brass, the woodwinds, the percussion instruments. Some extraordinary works of music are dominated by violins, violas, and cellos. Oboes, bassoons, and flutes are featured in other pieces. Marches and military music are dominated by brass and percussion instruments. The fascinating part of listening to and watching a symphony orchestra is observing the myriad ways the pieces of the orchestra blend in harmony to form enjoyable, often memorable, works of music.

That is how we see successful physical education teachers. They are artists, able to use teaching skills to develop and orchestrate lessons that are both absorbing and beneficial to students of all ages and abilities. As is true of music, there is no single way to organize and teach a lesson.

Changing and Dynamic Nature of Teaching

There is no predetermined formula that you can follow precisely to become a successful teacher. Teaching is too unpredictable. One eighth-grade class is not identical to another. Students are different on Monday morning than they are on Friday afternoon. So are teachers! Our understanding of teaching has increased over the years, but knowing what skills, strategies, and tactics to use when and with whom is still an artistic decision that varies from class to class and from teacher to teacher.

True teaching, as distinguished from rolling out the ball, is not like working on an assembly line—it's constantly changing and dynamic. Schon (1990) used the phrase "indeterminate zone of practice" to describe the uncertainty and ambiguities teachers face. Some professions appear to be driven by rules: When this happens, do this; when that happens, do that. Although one may try to reduce teaching to a precise science or formula, there is a substantial degree of artistry and judgment involved in every lesson.

A person isn't simply born an artist—or a teacher. There are techniques to learn and concepts to understand. Painters, for example, might learn painting techniques for use with watercolors, oils, and pastels. In addition, they need to understand and express concepts through their chosen media: harmony of color and light, shading, combining colors to create hues and tones, perspective, form, unity, and abstraction. Artists select from among these skills and concepts to express their desired meanings.

Good teachers follow an approach similar to that of good artists. They acquire a range of skills and techniques, not necessarily at a university, which then allows them to develop and teach lessons that are meaningful and worthwhile. Although some of the skills are learned consciously, others seem to be acquired subconsciously. Regardless of how the skills are acquired, successful teachers possess a repertoire of abilities from which they select to consistently and intentionally provide their students with developmentally appropriate experiences in physical activity (Graham et al., 1992; Stork & Sanders, 1996).

Our scientific understanding of the skills and techniques used by expert teachers continues to grow (Borich, 2013; Brophy & Good, 1986; Rink, 2003, 2013; Siedentop & Tannehill, 2000; Silverman, 1991). We are learning more about what good teachers do (and don't do) with youth, and discussions continue regarding how to evaluate teaching (Metzler, 2014; Rink, 2013; Ward, 2013). As in virtually any profession, however, knowing when and how to use this information requires an artistic decision.

Difficulty of Describing Good Teaching

Try to tell someone how to juggle—without demonstrating. Finding the right words and phrases might be difficult. You might be an excellent juggler but find words inadequate tools for helping someone else learn the skill. Like juggling, teaching physical education is a process that is easier to observe than to describe. Good teachers are artists, but they have a hard time describing what they do. We can recognize a good teacher when we see one, but it's much harder to explain why that teacher is so much better than another teacher.

In this book we break the complex teaching process into small parts to offer a more penetrating analysis and deeper understanding. This is possible on paper—but not with 30 students on the playground or in the gym. Writing (and reading) about teaching is a luxury because it lets us pause and reflect on the aspects of teaching: how they're used, why they're used, and how they might be used differently in different settings.

When we're teaching, we don't have the opportunity to say to a class every few seconds, "Freeze. I want to spend three minutes thinking about what I am going to do next as a teacher." In writing, however, we can describe the challenges of teaching—and how they are met by good teachers—at a more leisurely pace than the frenetic, urgent one described by Locke (1975) earlier in this chapter.

Challenge of Teaching Physical Education

Teaching any subject in American schools today is a challenge, even when viewed from the perspective of the written word that can be frozen in time. All teachers face obstacles; they also feel great satisfaction when they do their jobs well.

Obstacles

In a single day, an elementary school physical education teacher typically works with 7 to 12 classes of children. The ages might range from 5 to 11; the physical abilities may range from poor to excellent; and students' attitudes might vary from being interested in sports and physical fitness to having already decided that physical activity is not for them. Middle and high school physical educators also work with students with a wide range of skills, physical fitness levels, and attitudes. In secondary subjects such as math, students are naturally grouped by skill (e.g., algebra, geometry, trigonometry, precalculus). However, many students have been playing organized sports for years and yet they are in the same physical education classes as those who have made the unfortunate decision that sport and physical activity are not for them. The poorly skilled may be disinterested; the athletic, fit youngsters may be bored. How do you design lessons that are interesting and enjoyable for both of these groups?

In addition, teaching physical education may not be the only responsibility of physical educators. Many lead rock climbing programs before school, organize juggling clubs or intramural sports at lunch, and coordinate after-school programs. Elementary physical education teachers are often asked for ideas to help classroom teachers provide activity breaks throughout the school day. A challenge faced particularly by secondary physical educators is the teacher–coach role conflict of teachers who are also assigned coaching responsibilities (Konukman et al., 2010). Although some elementary PE teachers coach, too, the challenge is deciding how much time to devote to both teaching and coaching.

This can be especially challenging when a teacher, who is really interested in developing a quality physical education program, is on a staff with one or more other teachers who are passionate about coaching and satisfied with rolling out the ball in physical education.

When a physical education teacher ends her day, she has typically interacted with several hundred students, several teachers and parents or guardians, and one or more principals, secretaries, custodians, and cooks—and she wonders why she is so tired. That's a challenging day.

Needless to say, few teachers complete their days under ideal circumstances. In elementary schools, some teachers' gyms become lunchrooms from 11:15 a.m. to 1:15 p.m. during cold and rainy weather, so PE is taught in halls, lobbies, and classrooms, and on stages. Teachers are often asked to teach a sport or activity in a gym that is way too small for the number of students in a class. Teaching golf, for example, on a field designed for football is less than ideal. So too is trying to teach soccer to a class of 30 in the space of a single soccer field.

Challenges also include how others view physical education. Some classroom teachers insist on bringing their classes to PE early and arrive late to pick them up. Others view PE as a time to help individual students catch up on math or reading; often, these are the students who enjoy physical education the most. Schedules are always a complex conundrum in elementary schools. The result is that a class of fifth-graders might be followed by kindergartners, followed by second-graders, and then by another fifth-grade class. Field trips and visiting speakers often present surprises to physical education teachers—especially when the principal and classroom teacher forget to notify them and they discover that the next class has just left on a bus to visit the entomology museum. Equipment budgets of $350 for the year represent yet another challenge to physical educators, who quickly learn the value of collecting soup labels and attending Parent-Teacher Organization (PTO) meetings at budget time.

Often, the elementary school physical educator is the only one at the school and thus does not have to coordinate with other physical educators. In contrast, secondary teachers typically have to work with one other teacher and sometimes four or five to share facilities and equipment and build schedules. Sharing gyms with another teacher presents interesting challenges—sometimes with noise, sometime with space, and sometimes with maintaining student attention. This can be especially challenging when teachers differ in such things as the purpose of the physical education program and instruction versus recreation.

These are but a few of the challenges and obstacles physical educators face. No doubt you can think of others. As virtually any physical education teacher will attest, these are real challenges. They weren't simply invented to catch your attention. Obviously, however, there are also rewards. If not, we wouldn't find many people willing to spend more than one or two years teaching physical education.

Benefits

Clearly, the primary benefit of teaching is not the pay, or the perks. We have yet to meet a physical education teacher with an expense account or company car. And summers, which appear on paper as two and a half months of rest and recuperation, are often spent taking courses required for continued certification—or working a second job. What, then, are the benefits?

One of the most obvious benefits of teaching physical education in an elementary school is simply the joy of being with children and youth—the contagious giggles, the naive curiosity, the honesty that makes you sometimes wish you hadn't asked, the exuberance and willingness to try, the hugs around the knees, the barely legible notes that mean *Thanks for paying attention to me*, the fact that the bad things that happened today will be forgotten by tomorrow, the refreshing lack of sophistication, the true need of so many of today's children to be with adults who can be trusted for their predictability and caring, the fun that children associate with physical activity and the brief respite from the classroom routine, the touch on the arm that says *I appreciate your caring*, and the opportunity to introduce children to the pleasures of moving. These small rewards occur frequently. In fact, as long as we remain sensitive to our students, few jobs are so gratifying.

A benefit that is more long term for K-12 teachers is the satisfaction of seeing youngsters grow and develop over several years. At the secondary level, many teachers and coaches also become important role models for their students and often serve as informal counselors as the teens strive to figure out who they are and how to negotiate all that is involved with growing up. Teachers who remain at a school for five or six years can be sobered when they observe their classes in May and realize that much of what the kids know or don't know about their bodies, their health, and the importance of physical activity is a direct result of the physical education program they provided.

Good teachers have a strong sense of expectation. They share a belief that, under the right circumstances, they can make a difference. In physical education they make this difference by introducing students to various forms of physical activity and helping them build a movement foundation that eventually leads to enjoyment, satisfaction, and participation in physical activity throughout a lifetime (SHAPE America, 2014). Many educators are convinced that the foundations of many skills are built or destroyed by the time a child leaves elementary school—in physical education, math, art, and reading.

In many ways physical educators with good programs do their part in making the world a better place to grow up in. When we help students lead their lives in productive ways, we can feel good about our work. Clearly, this is a benefit of teaching.

Some might label our comments thus far as optimistic. That's fine. We are optimists. In fact, for us, the terms *pessimism* and *teaching* are incongruous together. If we don't believe we can make a difference as teachers, then how can we accept the responsibility of working with children and adolescents?

Our combined 80-plus years of teaching experience tells us that good physical educators are optimists who believe fervently in the value of their work. They are also realists, however, recognizing the challenges and difficulties of the job. This book is written for just such teachers, whether you're just beginning your student teaching or are in your 30th year. This book is for those who believe in the importance of physical education and are willing to dedicate themselves professionally to providing high-quality programs for youngsters.

The Teacher Makes the Difference

Physical education teachers are really no different from teachers of any subject. They want their students to learn. They also want them to enjoy their classes.

Some physical education teachers emphasize learning motor skills and playing games and sports. Others emphasize the development of physical fitness. Still others place their

Hugs, Giggles, and Touches for the Elementary School Teacher

Pick one of your favorite elementary school classes, or observe a teacher with a favorite class. During the class, try to be keenly sensitive to all of the ways the children find to say that they like the teacher and the program. Be sensitive to the smiles, the touches, the nods, the ways they move close to the teacher, all of the ways they find to say *Watch me!* When the class is over, or as soon as you can, take a few minutes to bask in all of the warm feelings the children have shared.

major emphasis on the development of positive student attitudes toward themselves and physical activity. And of course, many teachers would list a blend of these purposes.

It's relatively easy to list goals for a program. It's relatively difficult, however, to accomplish these goals, especially when classes are large and meetings are limited to two or three days a week.

A few years ago, we began to understand that good teachers weren't necessarily so because of what they taught. Ten teachers could teach the same unit. Two or three might be highly successful (i.e., students report that they had enjoyed the unit, and a posttest demonstrates that, in fact, they had learned much of what had been taught). The posttest of students of two or three other teachers might reveal that they hadn't learned anything from the teacher, and they would say that they had disliked the unit. The students of the other four to six teachers might reveal mixed outcomes, with no apparent trend as a result of participating in the unit.

In the past 50 years or so, we have increased our understanding of how those two or three successful teachers worked with their students, so that the students learned from and enjoyed the unit. This book describes and analyzes many of the teaching approaches, behaviors, skills, and techniques (the pedagogical knowledge base) that successful teachers use to create effective lessons.

We don't fully understand the orchestrations of skills and attributes that combine to make teachers successful or effective, but we do know more than we did five decades ago. We also know that the use of teaching skills is situation specific and varies according to the content and the grade level.

Pedagogy Toolbox

One of the ways good teachers make a difference is by using the tools (skills, techniques, strategies, methods) that they have in their pedagogy toolboxes. Imagine workers who use a variety of tools in their trade, such as carpenters, plumbers, or car mechanics. If you looked into their toolboxes, you would find them chock full of specialized tools. Those who are good at their jobs not only have a wide variety of quality tools but also know how and when to use each one. Would you hire a carpenter whose toolbox has only a level and a pair of pliers? Or a plumber who grabs a hammer to fix a leaky faucet?

In the same way, we intend not only to fill your pedagogy toolbox with a variety of tools used by quality physical education teachers but also to show you how to use the tools well in a variety of teaching situations. Although you won't be exposed in this book to *all* the teaching tools used by good teachers, you will be introduced to many of the skills that good teachers possess. As you begin this book, you already have some tools in your pedagogy toolbox. By the time you finish it, we hope that you have more tools, as well as the knowledge of how and when to use them.

Working Definition of *Successful*

The purpose of this book is to define and describe the process of teaching used by successful physical educators. The emphasis on the word *successful* is an important one. This book is about more than simply keeping youngsters "busy, happy, and good" (Placek, 1984) two or three days a week to give classroom teachers planning periods or secondary students an activity break between "academic" subjects. *Successful* implies that students learn and develop positive attitudes, that teachers derive satisfaction from their jobs, and that physical education programs are consistent with the overall focus of a school.

Students' Goals

The first component of successful teaching, obviously, is the students. Successful physical education teachers and programs build a foundation for youth to become physically literate and active. Physically literate people have the "knowledge, skills and confidence to enjoy a lifetime of healthful physical activity" (SHAPE America, 2014; Whitehead, 2001, 2010). In 1995, the National Association for Sport and Physical Education (NASPE, 1995) developed the first national content standards for K-12 physical education programs that defined a physically educated person, which was reviewed by hundreds of physical educators during its development. Now, as the standards continue to be revised and updated, SHAPE America has provided a refined definition of a physically educated, or physically literate, person (see figure 1.1).

Teachers' Goals

For any program to succeed, the people responsible need to feel a sense of satisfaction and accomplishment, as suggested in the definition of someone who is physically literate. For teachers, this often results from acts of support and nurturing from administrators and parents or guardians. As in any profession, when teachers don't feel supported or cared about as professionals, it is too easy to give up and go through the motions. In physical education jargon, this often leads to rolling out the ball.

To continue to plan and develop innovative curriculums, teach actively and enthusiastically, and evaluate and assess hundreds of students a year throughout your career,

FIGURE 1.1 Characteristics of a Physically Literate Person

The goal of physical education is to develop physically literate individuals who have the knowledge, skills and confidence to enjoy a lifetime of healthful physical activity.

To pursue a lifetime of healthful physical activity, a physically literate individual:

- Has learned the skills necessary to participate in a variety of physical activities.
- Knows the implications and the benefits of involvement in various types of physical activities.
- Participates regularly in physical activity.
- Is physically fit.
- Values physical activity and its contributions to a healthful lifestyle.

Reprinted from SHAPE America 2014.

you must experience a sense of satisfaction (see chapter 14). Interestingly, this doesn't mean that the only way you can be happy is to have ideal conditions. In fact, it seems that part of the job description of any physical educator must be to battle continually for improved working conditions and an increased understanding of the important contribution physical activity makes to the health of all people—young and old. For example, many teachers seem to be constantly working toward one or more of the following:

- Convincing other teachers and administrators of the value of physical education so that classes are not considered breaks that can be canceled for field trips, plays, and special events
- Obtaining more and better equipment for classes
- Advocating for being included in interdisciplinary planning teams, rather than teaching while others meet for common planning
- Attaining realistic teaching loads (e.g., a maximum of eight classes a day in elementary school and six in secondary school along with realistic class sizes)
- Arranging teaching schedules that provide reasonable transitions between grades (e.g., not a fifth-grade class followed by a first-grade class followed by a third-grade class in elementary school, or a swimming class sandwiched between a soccer and fitness class in high school)

From Birth to Adulthood

From birth, we learn by touching, seeing, and exploring the world around us through physical movement. Young children squeal with enjoyment at the opportunity to run around a field and explore a new space. Middle school students, although self-conscious about their bodies and developing sense of self, require opportunities to test their limits and learn about themselves in social environments. High school students becoming young adults learn by making choices and experiencing the consequences of their choices. The goals of the child in elementary school are different from the goals of the middle school student, which also differ from those of the high school student. Although improved health through physical activity may be an important outcome for policy makers, don't forget that the pure enjoyment of movement is integral to the development of the individual. You must do what you can to provide movement experiences that help your students maintain that joy of movement throughout their lives. That is what being physically literate is really about!

- Lobbying for daily physical education
- Advocating for appropriate class sizes comparable to those in other subjects (e.g., 30 students)
- Making sure school personnel recognize the importance of and the time required to provide lessons that lead to students achieving physical education learning outcomes
- Securing facilities that are truly designed for physical education

Despite these battles, teachers who are constantly struggling to improve their programs often feel effective. They have developed the understanding that successful physical education involves more than simply teaching students well—it entails other responsibilities, too.

One responsibility you will have as a teacher that warrants some discussion here is helping others understand the difference between physical education and physical activity. Since Judy Placek (1984) penned the concept of busy-happy-good, physical education teachers around the world have used her phrase to explain that physical activity is only one important part of quality physical education. PE teachers today are asked to do more and more, including coordinating before-, during-, and after-school activity programs as well as providing other teachers with classroom activity breaks. These added pressures, similar to the teacher–coach conflict mentioned earlier in this chapter, may well lead to physical activity replacing physical education (i.e., teachers offer little or no instruction as recommended in the national standards but rather simply provide opportunities for youngsters to be physically active). We recognize that offering physical activity throughout the school day is important; however, quality physical education can have a much more powerful and sustained impact when students attain the skills, knowledge, and dispositions they need to become physically literate and active for life. Let's be sure that our students in PE are busy, happy, good . . . and learning!

So You Want to Teach Physical Education?

If you are thinking about teaching physical education as a career, ask yourself these four questions:

- Do you like physical activity?
- Do you like being around kids all day long?
- Do you need to make a lot of money?
- Are you willing to work in a profession that requires a career-long battle for recognition and support?

These might help you start thinking about the characteristics of someone who truly enjoys teaching physical education and finds it a satisfying career—and whether you have those characteristics.

The remaining 13 chapters in the book provide a plethora of research-based evidence, along with our years of experience, to guide you along your journey to becoming a successful physical education teacher. We hope you find these insights both practical and useful as you, in turn, guide youngsters in the process of becoming physically literate adults.

Summary

In this book, we hope to answer this question: *What do successful physical education teachers actually do when they teach?* The focus is on the skills and techniques good teachers use, not on the content of their lessons.

In recent years we have come to understand that there is no such thing as the perfect lesson that will succeed for every teacher. A good teacher can take virtually any content area and weave it into an interesting and worthwhile learning experience. Unfortunately, an ineffective teacher can take virtually any content, no matter how appealing it might seem, and present it in such a way that the students not only fail to learn anything but also fail to enjoy the experience.

This book describes and analyzes the pedagogy of physical education—the orchestration of techniques and skills teachers use to involve kids in physical activities that are interesting and worthwhile. It is designed for the teacher, or future teacher, whose goal is to help youngsters develop the skills, knowledge, and attitudes to eventually become physically educated adults who enjoy the benefits of physical activity for a lifetime.

Questions for Reflection

1. When you think about teaching physical education, what do you see as the biggest challenges? How do you think you will meet them as a teacher?

2. Chapter 1 describes a number of benefits of teaching physical education. Which of the benefits are the most motivating to you?

3. If we talked with students you teach (or plan to teach), what would you like them to say about you as a teacher? What kinds of things might you do to encourage youngsters to feel the way you would like them to feel about you and your program?

4. Why does this book make a distinction between the teaching process (pedagogy) and the content (what is taught)?

5. For five minutes, watch another teacher (or a video of yourself) teaching a lesson. What questions might be going through that teacher's (or your) mind while in the eye of the hurricane?

6. What is one major difference, besides the kids, between teaching in an elementary school and teaching in a middle or high school? Explain.

References

Borich, G.D. (2013). *Effective teaching methods: Research-based practice.* New York: Pearson Higher Education.

Brophy, J., & Good, T.L. (1986). Teacher behavior and student achievement. In C.M. Wittrock (Ed.), *Handbook of research on teaching* (3rd ed., pp. 328-375). New York: Macmillan.

Graham, G., Castenada, R., Hopple, C., Manross, M., & Sanders, S. (1992). Developmentally appropriate physical education practices for children: A position statement of the Council on Physical Education for Children (COPEC). Reston, VA: National Association for Sport and Physical Education.

Konukman, F., Agbuga, B., Erdogan, S., Zorba, E., Demirhan, G., & Yilmaz, I. (2010). Teacher-coach role conflict in school-based physical education in USA: A literature review and suggestions for the future. *Biomedical Human Kinetics, 2,* 19-24.

Locke, L.F. (1975, Spring). *The ecology of the gymnasium: What the tourist never sees.* Paper presented at the meeting of the Southern Association for Physical Education for College Women, Gatlinburg, TN.

Metzler, M.W. (2014). Teacher effectiveness research in physical education: The future isn't what it used to be. *Research Quarterly for Exercise & Sport, 85* (1), 14-19.

National Association for Sport and Physical Education (NASPE). (1995). *Moving into the future: National standards for physical education.* Reston, VA: Author.

Placek, J. (1984). A multicase study of teacher planning in physical education. *Journal of Teaching in Physical Education, 4,* 39-49.

Rink, J.E. (2003). Effective instruction in physical education. In S.J. Silverman & C.D. Enis (Eds.), *Student learning in physical education: Applying research to enhance instruction* (pp. 165-186). Champaign, IL: Human Kinetics.

Rink, J.E. (2013). Measuring teacher effectiveness in physical education. *Research Quarterly for Exercise and Sport, 84* (4), 407-418.

Schon, D.A. (1990). *Educating the reflective practitioner.* San Francisco: Jossey-Bass.

SHAPE America. (2014). *National standards & grade-level outcomes for K-12 physical education.* Champaign, IL: Human Kinetics.

Siedentop, D., & Tannehill, D. (2000). *Developing teaching skills in physical education* (4th ed.). Palo Alto, CA: Mayfield.

Silverman, S. (1991). Research on teaching in physical education. *Research Quarterly for Exercise and Sport, 62,* 352-367.

Stork, S., & Sanders, S. (1996). Developmentally appropriate physical education: A rating scale. *Journal of Physical Education, Recreation and Dance, 67* (6), 52-58.

Ward, P. (2013). The role of content knowledge in conceptions of teaching effectiveness in physical education. *Research Quarterly for Exercise & Sport, 84* (4), 431-440.

Whitehead, M. (2001). The concept of physical literacy. *European Journal of Physical Education, 6,* 127-138.

Whitehead, M. (Ed.). (2010). *Physical literacy: Throughout the lifecourse.* Routledge: England.

Creating a Positive Learning Environment

After reading this chapter, you should be able to do the following:

- Discuss the concept of teacher expectancy and its importance in creating a pleasant atmosphere in physical education.
- Explain teacher stereotypes of students and how to avoid them.
- Describe management protocols that teachers develop with classes.
- Relate the important difference between explaining and teaching management protocols.
- Describe the characteristics of teachers who create positive environments in physical education.

How do you prefer to teach? Are you loud and excitable, or do you prefer an atmosphere that is relatively quiet and calm? Do you signal your students to stop by blowing a whistle, hollering, giving a hand signal, or beating on a drum? Are you loud when you teach, or do you talk in a conversational tone? Do you play music during your classes? What are the characteristics of a pleasant physical education atmosphere that also encourages students to become involved in activity?

Obviously, there is no single definition of a pleasant atmosphere. We all have our preferred approaches to working with students in a physical education setting. The significance of these questions, however, is that they are decisions made by you, not your students. You choose the environmental characteristics over which you have control—and then you need to teach your classes to function within that environment.

The atmosphere you create is important. After all, this is your job! You spend many hours in school, and it makes sense to make the atmosphere as pleasant as possible within your limitations. A gymnasium or multipurpose room is not a luxury hotel. There are many things you can do, however, to build a pleasant, positive atmosphere. This chapter addresses ways to create a positive environment for lessons that both you and your students can enjoy—and that encourage your students to want to come to physical education class.

Why place the chapter on creating the learning environment so early in the book? Most books that address this topic place it at the end or near the middle, not at the beginning. We placed it here for three reasons.

The first reason is that, especially for beginning teachers, the question *Will I be able to control the students?* is very important. It's a genuine concern that deserves some attention. Beginning teachers have a genuine fear that students may run wild and never stop and listen—hardly a pleasant atmosphere in which to work every day. So why put off a discussion of how to achieve order in physical education classes, when it is foremost in the minds of many novice teachers?

Rachel's Fear

This excerpt is from Dolly Lambdin's dissertation, for which she interviewed elementary school teachers about their lives. Rachel describes a fear that most teachers have had at one time or another in their careers.

> I remember when we had double first grade classes. I sat down one time and I just looked at that long line of kids and I thought, if they got organized they could tie me up, take out all the equipment, have a wonderful time, because there were 60 of them. And there would not be anything I could do. (Lambdin, 1992, p. 13)

The second reason this chapter is at the beginning of the book is that successful teachers begin to develop an environment for learning at the beginning of school. In fact, they start the process on the first day of the school year (Carter & Doyle, 1989; Fink & Siedentop, 1989; Solmon, 2006). This is why it seemed logical, albeit unorthodox, to place this chapter near the start of the book—partly because it deals with frequently asked questions for which solutions require early and carefully planned and implemented strategies.

The third reason is the most important: If you cannot create a positive, productive learning environment, then most of what is written in the subsequent chapters of this book will be of little value. Students won't listen to you. They will bicker with one another and argue over equipment, who's in their group, who pushed whom in line, and whose turn it is. You will find yourself continually nagging students to listen, use appropriate language, and keep their hands to themselves. What could be a positive physical education experience for both you and your students will at best be unpleasant, and at worst, negative. The best-made plans rarely work as intended—and thus, too many physical education classes end up being frustrating and unpleasant for all involved.

Teacher Expectancy

It is up to you to design and then build the atmosphere for your classes. You need to decide, perhaps in conjunction with your students, how you want your classes to operate. Beginning teachers often find this attitude, known as teacher expectancy, difficult to develop (Martinek, 1983). Many believe that youngsters are a certain way and that they have to adjust to them—not true. Students can learn to stop, for example, when they see you raise your hand or when they hear a hand clap. Whistles can work in outdoor spaces, and blowing different patterns can mean different things (e.g., two blows means *Stop*, one long blow means *Bring it in*). You might choose to use a drum or play music depending on the environment. The type of signal doesn't really matter (as long as it can be heard or seen); what matters is that students learn to understand and follow your directions. You need to expect certain things (e.g., not to push and shove others, to listen when you are talking) and then insist that the students follow these rules in your class. Interestingly, it can be difficult to learn to expect students to operate within the framework that you want to establish for the gymnasium, field, or playground. Perhaps an example will illustrate this point.

In church we expect people to behave a certain way. There are times when it's unacceptable to speak out loud. Many churches also have dress codes. We teach our children these protocols for operating in church as soon as we can. Gradually, they learn to function in concert with the protocols of the church we attend. It doesn't happen simply because we tell them not to talk in church, for example. We have to work at it together—often over a period of weeks or even months.

In many ways the same is true in physical education classes. The protocols are obviously different, but the process of learning them takes time and practice. And just as parents and guardians insist that their children learn how to behave in church, you need to insist that students behave in physical education. The challenge, however, is to teach 25 or 35 students the protocols of behavior.

For most teachers, I suspect, this is one of the least enjoyable parts of teaching. There's not much satisfaction in teaching youngsters how to put away equipment or choose a partner. Consequently, many are tempted to devote less time to these protocols than might be necessary. Nevertheless, to be satisfied in your teaching, you must teach your students the customs of your gymnasium, playground, and field. When you do, your teaching life becomes far more enjoyable.

Music Creates a Mood

Many teachers use music with their classes to make it a more pleasant and enjoyable atmosphere. Some teachers select the music, while others allow their students to have input. Two of the more popular free music stations are Pandora and Spotify. Bluetooth speakers with a remote control device can be used inside or outside. Be careful to screen the music to make sure the lyrics are appropriate for school use. For many teachers music is an important, and enjoyable, part of creating a positive learning environment for their classes.

Teacher Stereotypes

Also extremely important to becoming a good teacher is avoiding stereotypes. This is every bit as difficult to do as creating teacher expectancy, often because stereotyping is more subtle and covert. As a teacher, you need to be aware of your personal stereotypes related to ethnic origins, socioeconomic status, gender, sexual orientation, developmental challenge, religion, ability, and physical appearance (Colvin, 1998; Davis & Dillon, 2010; Hutchinson, 1995; Lyter-Mickleberg & Conner-Kuntz, 1995; Solmon & Lee, 2008; Williamson, 1993).

Following are some of the most common stereotypes associated with physical activity:

- Boys are better throwers than girls.
- African Americans are fast runners.
- Girls like gymnastics, dance, and yoga.
- Boys like football.
- Developmentally disabled youngsters are poorly coordinated.
- Latinos are good soccer players.
- Boys don't mind being hollered at.
- Girls cry when you holler at them.
- Girls can't do regular push-ups.

These are just a few of many stereotypes. As a physical educator, you have to be especially sensitive to stereotypes because they can quickly become self-fulfilling prophecies for young people if you promote them as inevitable truths (Williamson, 1993). How can you avoid them?

An important first step is to become aware of your stereotypes. Do you agree with any of the listed statements? If so, you are stereotyping youngsters. Although any of these statements may be true for some, they are not true for all. For example, some girls throw better than some boys; some African Americans are slow runners; some developmentally disabled youngsters are excellent athletes. The important point is that you cannot accurately generalize about any race or gender or physical characteristic. Doing so makes it extremely difficult for youngsters who might not fit the stereotype to avoid the self-fulfilling prophecy. If, for example, gymnastics was offered only for girls, then a boy who had Olympic potential might never have the opportunity to uncover his talent.

In addition to your internal stereotypes, you also need to be sensitive to your behaviors. For example, do you interact differently with girls than with boys? Do you spend more time with attractive youngsters than with unattractive ones? Do you kid around more with athletes than with nonathletes? Do you provide more feedback to poorly skilled students (Solmon & Lee, 2008)? You can become aware of how you treat students and identify a hidden (unintended) curriculum by video recording a class and then watching the video with another teacher or a trusted friend and asking whether the person noticed any obvious differences in the ways you interacted with the youngsters.

Finally, it is important to avoid the trap of thinking, *These are just kids. They don't notice.* Oh, but they do! And the covert messages you send as a physical educator are exceedingly important to youngsters at such an impressionable age as they make decisions about the sports and physical activities they will do for the rest of their lives. Physical educators who send messages (usually inadvertently) that youngsters cannot do something because of race or gender or ability may cut them off from a sport or physical activity in which they may excel as adults. What if a physical educator had convinced Diana Taurasi, the three-time Olympic gold medalist and two-time WNBA championship–winning professional basketball player, that basketball was a boys' sport? What if a teacher was somehow able to convince Tiger Woods that golf was only for white kids? Physical education classes should be a positive place for learning about physical activities, and your attitudes—including both expectancy and stereotypes—are vitally important parts of creating this positive environment.

Creating an Emotionally Safe Environment

Teacher expectancy and teacher stereotypes clearly affect the way physical educators interact with youngsters. As you become sensitive to your own attitudes, you can do several things to create supportive and emotionally positive physical education classes. Consider the following guidelines (Helion, 1996):

1. **People are not for hurting.** This refers to physical harm but also to behaviors such as name calling, belittling, intimidating, and making fun of others.

2. **Never use sarcasm.** A comment from you such as "Nice throw" to a boy who throws the ball well over the head of his partner not only is painful to the boy who threw the ball but also signals to other youngsters that sarcasm is acceptable in your class.

3. **There are no stupid questions.** When you teach 8 to 10 classes a day, you often hear the same question in every class. It is easy to lose patience—but you need to remember that it is the first time this youngster has asked the question. You also need to develop a protocol that encourages students to ask questions, but also be careful that the question-and-answer session does not last so long that it takes away from activity time, which often happens with a class of young children who enjoy being recognized by the teacher.

4. **Physical education is for everyone.** Team games are often dominated by a few highly skilled youngsters. This does not constitute physical education for every student because the less skilled often become competent bystanders rather than active participants. Small-sided games with two or three players on a team are one way to heighten the chance that every student is an active participant (Graham et al., 1992; National Association for Sport and Physical Education, 2009).

5. **Walk your talk.** Children are keen observers. They learn from what they see you do—perhaps more than from what you say. Whether you want to be or not, you are a role model for youngsters.

Determining Management Protocols

Technically, the word *protocol* refers to established forms or courtesies that have been predetermined and used, for example, in official dealings among heads of state or in medical practices. Most physical education classes are far from ceremonial or official, however. Nevertheless, there should be predetermined ways for students to act in your classes. You should also establish courtesies you want them to extend to you and to one another. These protocols form the foundation for the routines you expect your students to follow to create a positive and productive learning environment. In addition to the classroom or school rules posted on the wall, you should have protocols that you teach and reinforce in your classes. These protocols should clearly define the observable behaviors you expect of all students. For example, you can have protocol expectations for the locker room; entering and leaving the playing area, gym, or outside space; starting and stopping on your signal; gathering up equipment when the stop signal is given; getting out equipment and putting it away; and selecting partners, teams, and groups.

 Establishing Protocols The web resource provides brief videos of several teachers working to establish protocols with their students. You will find these examples especially useful for understanding how successful teachers establish their protocols.

Entering and Leaving the Gym or Outdoor Space

In elementary schools, whenever possible, it's preferable to have classroom teachers bring the children to physical education. This allows you to teach longer classes; given the limited time, every minute is important. In the beginning of the year, however, you may want to go to the room and talk with the children about the protocols for entering and leaving the gym as well as the signals for stopping and starting. (Ideally, classroom teachers would be present on the first day of class when the protocols are explained to the children so that they understand the expectations for the youngsters.)

Most elementary school principals insist that children walk to and from physical education in quiet, orderly formations—typically in lines. If you are responsible for bringing the children from the classroom, practice the protocol for walking to and from physical education. Because children are often excited about PE classes and eager to begin, this can be somewhat problematic.

What seems to work best is to have children practice moving from the classroom to the playground in a quiet and orderly manner. In fact, this is an important part of the first day's lesson. Once children get to the playground, they are expected to do one of several things. Some teachers have them line up in squads; some have them sit quietly on a circle or line; some write instant activity (chapter 6) directions on a whiteboard or poster board telling the children what to do that day. Regardless of the way you begin the class, the routine needs to be practiced. In some cases (e.g., the children run noisily

through the hallways), the children may have to return to the classroom and practice the routine (protocol) again.

In middle and high schools, class often begins in the locker room. Ideally, students can move immediately to the gym or outdoor space after changing clothes and begin engaging in activity. Protocols for what to do when a locker combination is forgotten, when to leave the locker room, how to move to the gym (including the route), and what to do on arrival in the gym all need to be taught and reinforced. The important point for the students to realize is that this is a protocol. It's the routine used at their school for getting to and from the gym. It's not just a nice idea. It's a routine to be followed (even if it means returning to the locker room several times) every time they come to physical education class throughout the year.

How Children Define Walking

Children have interesting definitions of walking. For many, it means that as long as they don't bend their knees much, they can travel as fast as they can and it would still be considered walking. You have seen children do this—stiff upper bodies, heads erect, wildly swinging arms, rushing to be first. When reprimanded, they reply in unison, "We were walking!" Perhaps you shouldn't define the mode of traveling, but rather, the speed. One idea is to tell the students that if they get to the gym in 45 seconds or less, they will be given a speeding ticket. The penalty is to return to the classroom to try again.

Dressing Out for Physical Education

Requiring students to wear uniforms for physical education classes is certainly a controversial subject. There is agreement on one aspect of a uniform, however: shoes! Clearly some shoes are inappropriate—flip flops, leather-soled shoes, and high heels, to name a few. Some schools allow students to wear hiking shoes (boots) for PE. Most K-12 schools, however, require students to wear shoes designed specifically for running and playing sports.

There is less agreement on other parts of a uniform. Some secondary schools require all students to change into a physical education uniform (shorts, T-shirt) for physical education class. Other schools require students to change clothes for physical education but do not require a specific uniform. And of course, some schools have no dress requirement. Most agree, however, that it is a good idea to change clothes because hopefully students will perspire during many (ideally all) PE classes. No matter the policy, there is general agreement that whether a student dresses appropriately for physical education classes should *not* be a major consideration in grading for physical education.

Taking Attendance

Most middle and high schools require physical education teachers to take attendance. Although it is important that this be done accurately, the process should take as little time as possible to allow for more activity during the lesson. Probably the slowest, least efficient technique is calling the name of each student in the class. There are much faster ways that are also accurate. Here are a few suggestions:

- Paint numbers on the floor (or playground), and assign each student a number corresponding with your attendance book. At some point during the instant activity (see chapter 6), you can say "Numbers," which directs the students to quickly stand on their numbers so you can take attendance.

- Jeffrey Merzbacher, who teaches at Hawthorne Elementary School in San Diego, posted interesting alternatives to the use of numbers on the website PE Central. For variation, he sometimes uses letters, sometimes element symbols from the periodic tables, and sometimes keyboard symbols (e.g., # or & or %). He enjoys hearing from a student, for example, that hydrogen is missing today.

- Assign students to squads. The captain of the squad reports who is absent from the squad on that day. Of course, you should check to be certain the report is accurate.

- Use sign-in sheets as the students enter the gym or leave the locker room. A related technique is to make boards with tags for each student in the class. The students place their name tags in a box if they are present. The names left on the board are those of absent students.

- If you use warm-up stations, you can rotate to each station to take attendance as the students are warming up.

- Assign each student a numbered heart rate monitor or activity tracker stored in a hanging bag in the locker room. Each arriving student picks up a heart rate monitor or activity tracker and puts it on. You take attendance by observing which activity trackers or monitors remain in the bag.

- Ask the students to dribble balls with their hands (in the gym) or feet (on a field) around in a large circle (an alternative to just running laps) as you take attendance.

Starting and Stopping Signals

Once the students have entered the gym or outdoor space according to your protocol, you need to have a method to capture their attention. The type of signal you use doesn't really matter as long as the students can hear or see it. Inside, most teachers use their voices. Some, particularly elementary school teachers, use a hand clap or a drumbeat. Others use music with a remote control to stop and start songs. Some use a whistle, but, especially inside, many prefer to create a more pleasant, businesslike atmosphere as opposed to a loud and rowdy recess environment. The voice or hand clap seems to be preferred because it is less harsh and piercing than a whistle, and the students need to keep their talking at a level that permits them to hear the signal. Outside, depending on how large the teaching space is, you may want a whistle or some other method of capturing student attention. Different tunes or signals on the whistle can indicate different things. For example, blowing the whistle once could mean *Stop, look, and listen*; three whistle blows could mean *Come and stand by me*.

As with entering and leaving the gym, stops and starts need to be practiced. It's reasonable to expect all your students to be stopped two or three seconds after you give the signal. And you should give the signal only once, not four or five times.

Teaching Stopping and Starting in Elementary School

Several activities are excellent for helping elementary school children learn to listen while they move. Numbers is one such activity. Ask the children to walk, hop, or skip in a defined area. When you call out a number, they quickly form groups totaling that number. For example, four children group up when you say "Four." The key is to say, rather than shout, the number so that the children have to listen carefully. A variation of this game is called colors. Call out different colors marked on the floor or pavement. As quickly as they can, the children hop or skip to that color. Body parts is another version. When you call out various body parts, the children touch those parts to the ground or floor (e.g., hands and feet, seat, back, elbows, knees).

The starting signal most teachers use is *Go*. This is important because students, especially young children, typically don't want to stop and listen for long; once they think they understand your directions, they want to begin immediately. Often, however, you will have another item or two to add; thus, it's important for them to wait until you are finished talking before they start. As with the stop signal, this needs to be practiced. If some students start before the signal, call them back and reminded to wait for the *Go* signal. To keep their attention, some elementary teachers vary the word that means *go* to encourage children to listen carefully (e.g., *hopscotch, Friday, Xbox*).

Typically, the word *stop* or *freeze* signals the class to stop moving and be silent. For elementary classes, sometimes a drum is necessary, such as when they are dribbling balls and it is hard to hear over the noise made by the balls hitting the floor. You might want to use a whistle outside.

Once you have given the stop signal, insist that the students listen to you and to classmates who might be responding to you. This needs to be practiced. The best way to do this is to start over if you think the students are inattentive and to repeat your comments. Another tactic that helps students listen is to practice talking as briefly as possible without repeating your comments (see chapter 5). This takes time to learn, but it does help students listen more intently. When teachers fall into the trap of repeating comments two or three times, it's no wonder students don't bother to listen to every word. Our collective experience suggests that teachers probably talk far more than is necessary for classes to understand directions, especially when a demonstration accompanies the instructions.

What Do Students Hear?

A number of students in schools do not speak English as their native language. We are always fascinated to see how quickly these students are able to follow the teacher's directions even though they didn't understand precisely what the teacher said. We also see youngsters who talk the entire time the teacher is talking, yet can begin the task quickly. Obviously, they have learned to rely on observing their peers and not on listening to the teacher.

Equipment Protocols

Instructions are often related to the equipment used in a lesson. The three most common protocols to establish in relation to equipment are how to get it out, what to do with it when you are talking, and how to put it away.

Getting the Equipment

Students usually can't wait to get started, so all 25 want to rush up and get their equipment so they can begin. Two approaches are useful for distributing equipment quickly and efficiently. The quicker way is to spread the equipment throughout the area in small piles. This prevents the overcrowding that results when everyone in the class tries to get a ball from the same basket at the same time.

Another approach is to call on a few students at a time to get their equipment. Some elementary school teachers tap children on the shoulder as a signal to get their equipment. Another technique used in elementary schools is to call out birth months; color of shirts, hair, or eyes; or type of shoes to signal different groups to get their equipment. Secondary school teachers often have their classes organized in squads or some other grouping to distribute equipment efficiently.

Once classes have the equipment, they need to know what to do with it. Some teachers ask students to get their equipment and then hold on to it. Many find it more productive to provide a task for students to begin working on once they get their equipment (e.g., "After you get your hoop, find a self-space and warm up by jumping over your hoop," or "Once you've picked up your workout sheet and activity log, begin the activity"). It seems particularly difficult for students to stand still and hold a ball; it's as if they were given a chocolate ice cream cone and asked to hold on to it without taking a lick until everyone in the class has a cone.

I Want the Blue One
Distributing equipment is easier when the types and colors of equipment are either identical or very different. When all balls but two are yellow, some children will compete to get one of the two differently colored balls. The same is true for ropes, hoops, and so on. For this reason many teachers try to purchase equipment of either the same color or a variety of colors. At secondary schools there may be one or two balls of higher quality than the others. Just like younger children, the students know which ball they want and there will be a mad scramble to get it. To an adult this seems like a trivial matter, but it's not to children or adolescents.

Holding on to Equipment

The difficulty of holding a ball without playing with it is one reason to have a protocol for what to do with equipment after you give the stop signal. You might require students to place their balls immediately on the ground, or to hold them next to their belly buttons. If you fail to teach a protocol, however, you will likely find yourself constantly repeating, "Remember not to play with the ball when I'm talking."

Before-Class Preparation
Be prepared to get to school early and check your equipment, gym, and outdoor areas. Check your equipment, and pump balls up before the day starts. Walk your gym or outdoor space to pick up dog piles or broken glass, fill ankle-breaking gopher holes, and mop up sticky soda spills on the gym floor. Spending time before school each day can help maximize the time during class and avoid many distractions to the creation of an efficient and positive learning environment.

Putting Equipment Away

Students can't wait to get equipment, and once they get it, they don't want to put it away. This, too, needs to be practiced.

Some teachers use the same technique as for getting equipment—it's done in groups or individually. Others prefer to have students simultaneously replace the equipment where they got it. One of the greatest temptations, of course, is to throw a ball from 30 feet (9 m) away and try to land it in the equipment cart. This is why it is important to teach the technique of placing, not throwing, equipment. One technique you can use is to ask one or two students to show the remainder of the class how the equipment is to be placed, not thrown, when putting it away. As with the other protocols discussed in this section, you need to teach this protocol—and have students practice it until they learn it—at the beginning of the school year.

Practice! Practice! Practice!

Protocols need to be practiced over and over to get them to stick. Practice might look like this: You want the students to learn and practice the protocol for stopping and starting on your signal, and for placing the equipment on the ground in front of them on the stop signal. You give the stop command. If the entire class stops with the equipment on the ground in less than 10 seconds, you move on to another task or activity. If it takes more than 10 seconds, you practice again. Gradually, you can reduce the amount of time it takes to stop and place the equipment on the ground to 7 seconds, then 5 seconds, and so on.

Protocols for Selecting Partners, Teams, and Groups

Throughout the year you will often be asking students to work with partners or in groups. This is an especially important time to be careful not to damage youngsters' self-concept. In the old days, teachers used to assign captains to pick teams. Today, far too many adults have suffered through the emotional pain of being picked last class after class and who continue to be against physical education, largely because of the embarrassment of repeatedly being chosen last (NASPE, 2009).

Fortunately, we know better today. One technique that many teachers use is simply to ask students to find a partner or form a group of five, for example. The advantage of this approach is that it is relatively quick and students tend to select partners or groups of about the same ability level. The game of numbers can also be used to form groups quickly throughout the year. Call out a number and, as quickly as possible, students gather into groups with that number of students. (As the game progresses and you call out various numbers, it is fun to call out "One" and watch them scramble to find others until they realize that for this number they don't need to find a partner or a group.) The number you call identifies the number of students you would like in a group. So, if your task needs them in groups of three, you would call out "Three," and they would be ready to go once you explain the task. Whenever you group by numbers, you represent the lost and found area. Youngsters who don't have partners or groups should quickly come to you for help. At times you will want to form groups or teams yourself to accomplish a specific purpose. Ideally, this is done ahead of the class so it doesn't use up a lot of valuable class time.

Boys Do This; Girls Do That

Some teachers use gender as a way to group students—the boys here, the girls there. This tends to perpetuate the boy–girl stereotypes emphasizing differences rather than similarities. It also seems to discourage the idea of boys and girls cooperating and working together, especially in the upper grades. For this reason many teachers discourage grouping students by sex. It is interesting that fifth-grade boys and girls, for example, will work together on a project in the classroom but expect not to work together on the playground. We hope that, in a few years, grouping by gender will be as rare as captains picking teams.

There are many ways to organize classes into groups. Most important is that students learn how to do this quickly and without hurting the others' feelings. Secondary school students may moan or roll their eyes when partnered with someone they don't like. This may be one of the trickiest expectations to teach, but if you have a clear picture of how you expect students to treat one another, you will be able to hold them accountable to those expectations. Role-playing the right and wrong ways to treat others at the beginning of the year can be the first step to explaining and holding students accountable to your expectations. Many teachers do not allow students to refuse a classmate who asks to be their partner or in their group.

As with every protocol, however, there are exceptions. Some students, for whatever reason, are very difficult to work with as partners or in groups. With these youngsters, exceptions need to be made if, for example, they continually ask the same person to be their partner. This is the art of teaching: How do we take care of a youngster's feelings and remain fair to all involved?

Grouping Strategies

- Teacher-selected groups: Organize groups before class, print them out, and post them on the wall.
- Jigsaw: For example, if you need five groups, have students self-select into groups of five. The youngsters in each group then number off from 1 to 5 and regroup by the new number.
- Deck of cards: Hand out playing cards to students as they enter the gym. You can quickly use color, suit, or number (e.g., odd/even or groups of numbers such as 1-3, 4-6, 7-9, and 10-K), to organize into the number or size of groups needed (Lambdin, 1989).
- Birth month: Group students by the month of their birthday; for example, January to March birthdays in one group, April to June in another, and so on. Groups will likely be uneven, so just move students as necessary from larger groups to smaller ones after the students group themselves.
- Cross your arms: Have all students fold their arms across their chest. Create three groups by organizing if right hand, left hand, or no hands are visible. Move individuals to even up the groups if necessary.
- Youth interlock fingers: Find the closest partner that has the opposite thumb on top as you. Split the class in two by grouping right thumb on top together and left thumb on top together.

Other Protocols

It goes without saying that there are other protocols that we haven't discussed—as well as variations in implementing the ones we have (Bell, 1998; Solmon, 2006; Todorovich

& Curtner-Smith, 1998). Some other important protocols to consider include what students do

- during a fire drill or a tornado drill;
- when an accident or injury occurs during class;
- about drinking water during physical education class;
- when they need to go to the bathroom during class;
- when they bring valuables to class, such as jewelry or money; and
- regarding the use of cell phones, headphones, and music players.

Good teachers prepare for situations in advance. For example, the worst time to teach students how to behave when a student is injured and bleeding is when an accident has occurred (Almquist, 2001). If the protocol is taught and practiced ahead of time, students will understand how to summon assistance and what the teacher needs to do. But, as with any of the protocols mentioned, these situations will need to be practiced so that the students remember them and use them appropriately.

Decision to Practice Protocols

One of the most important decisions you will make, once you have thought through your protocols, is the decision to spend time practicing them. This is especially difficult in physical education because the time is so limited, yet this is exactly why the protocols need to be rehearsed—to save time. When protocols aren't learned, an inordinate amount of time is wasted over the course of a year.

Many teachers ask, "How long do I practice protocols?" One answer is "As long as it takes." Early in the school year or semester, you may focus the first three or four lessons on protocols. Classes comprised of students you taught in previous years will require less time to learn, or remember, the protocols.

A second answer to how long protocols should be practiced is "Always." Most crucial is that protocols be consistently followed and reinforced. Remember that they are designed so students know what to expect, which leads to a comfortable learning environment. When protocols are applied inconsistently, students struggle to know what to expect and teachers struggle to maintain a healthy environment conducive to learning. Chapter 7 describes positive pinpointing, an effective technique for reinforcing protocols.

The research on teaching physical education is very clear on the topic of protocols. Unfortunately, students in physical education classes spend more time listening, managing, and waiting than they do in purposeful physical activity (Sallis, Carlson, & Mignano, 2012). In fact, students commonly spend less than a third of class time being physically active. When your students learn the behavior protocols at the beginning, you can devote more time to the content of physical education the rest of the year—instead of nagging them about listening, getting out equipment, and so on.

Teaching Behavior Protocols

Deciding on the management protocols to use in your classes is relatively easy. The challenging part is teaching those protocols until students know them and they become a part of every class you teach over the entire year.

As with any teaching process, no single approach works for all teachers. However, teachers who create pleasant atmospheres seem to display certain attributes as they work on building their class environments. They are firm but warm while also being critically demanding. They also post their rules for classes to see and often discuss them so that students feel a certain degree of ownership.

Firm but Warm

At one time we believed that successful teachers threatened students: that is, that they scared them into being good. Today we know better (Bulger, Mohr, & Walls, 2002; Downing, Keating, & Bennett, 2005; Doyle, 1986; Fernandez-Balboa, 1990; Kounin, 1970). Successful teachers exhibit a certain degree of firmness: they mean what they say. At the same time, however, they are warm and caring toward the students. They don't want to frighten them, but they want them to know they mean business. Students quickly learn to discern whether teachers mean what they say. Good teachers mean what they say, and they exhibit it by not allowing their students to get away with not following the protocols. They don't get excited or hysterical or threaten, however. In calm, reassuring, firm ways, they simply and consistently communicate the message that things are going to be done a certain way and that not much else is going to happen until the protocols are learned. This is one of those skills used by effective teachers that is difficult to put into words. However, if you watched 10 teachers, you would quickly identify those who are firm but warm.

Critically Demanding

If we could write this section in flashing neon lights, we would, because this is an especially important teaching skill that makes a huge difference in the learning environment.

In addition to being firm but warm, effective teachers also are critically demanding. You can quickly recognize this quality when you see it. Teachers who are critically demanding have a built-in expectation that students follow the protocols, and they *insist* that they do. For example, they know how they want their students to enter the gym. When students enter that way, the lesson proceeds as planned. When they don't, these teachers don't accept their behavior. They insist (demand) that they go back and enter the gym the way they had practiced earlier.

This is especially difficult because, typically, you will want to get on with the lesson you have planned. It's hard to spend time having students go back and reenter the gym.

In the long run, however, you will spend less time on these distracting events than if you hadn't spent the time reinforcing your expectations at the beginning of the year. One advantage for your students is that they know exactly what to expect. You can be consistent day after day because you know what is reasonable for your students and you expect that behavior of them.

One of the easiest ways to understand the quality of being critically demanding is to think back to when you were in high school. Did you have a curfew? What happened if you were late? If your parents or guardians were critically demanding, they followed through on the consequences you had discussed before (e.g., being grounded for a week or denied television). If your parents or guardians were not critically demanding, however, they likely let things slide and you knew that they really didn't mean what they said.

Rules—Clear, Positive, Posted

Posted rules also help with consistency. Rules are essentially brief reminders of the behavior protocols. Most teachers list five or six rules, state them in positive ways, and post them prominently (figure 2.1). Simply writing and posting them, however, is no guarantee they will be followed. They also must be practiced.

Physical Education Rules

Physical education rules might look like those in figure 2.1. One reason for posting rules, in addition to serving as reminders, is for the benefit of students new to the school. Posted rules allow you to briefly review the behavior protocols with new students. You may also video record classes in which you explained the behavior protocols and include student demonstrations. The video can then be made available to new students so that they can see exactly what is expected of them in physical education class.

Behavior videos are a good idea in places where teachers are often threatened with malpractice lawsuits. In this case, every new student should be required to view the video before participating in physical education. In extreme instances, teachers may quiz students (in writing or orally) or ask them to sign a copy of the rules, indicating that they have viewed the video. We also suggest that this behavior video be placed on the physical education section of the school website.

Locker Room Rules

Secondary programs frequently require students to change clothes in a locker room. You may need rules and protocols specific to the locker room. Here are some examples:

- Take pride in our school and keep the locker room CLEAN!
- Leave food, candy, gum, drinks, and cell phones in your locker or other space outside the gym or PE area.
- Act appropriately (keep your hands to yourself, no bad language).
- Be in the locker room when the bell rings.
- Enter and exit the locker room from the appropriate hallway.
- Dress at your locker.
- Be responsible for locking up all belongings and valuables.

Although these suggestions might seem extreme, teachers who have been involved in malpractice lawsuits will quickly recognize the benefit to posting such rules. This is especially important in schools with high rates of student turnover.

Figure 2.1 Example of posted rules.

Some teachers send letters home to parents and guardians at the beginning of the school year outlining policies on dress for physical education (especially footwear), medical notes, and what the students will be learning in the coming year. These letters typically provide information about contacting the teacher if questions arise about classes, policies, or other issues (Hopple, 1998).

Developing Ownership

Rules (behavior protocols) are followed more closely when students, and parents and guardians for that matter, understand why they are necessary, and also when students have a sense of ownership of them. For this reason many teachers discuss rules with students to help them understand their importance. A video of students not following the rules can illustrate what happens when this occurs. (You will have no problem recruiting a class to help you make a video demonstrating all of the ways *not* to behave in the gym!) The video then becomes an excellent resource for involving students in discussions about why management protocols are important to have and follow.

In addition to sharing the rules with your students, provide the principal and classroom teachers with a copy of the rules. This is especially important if your school does not have a unified discipline plan (e.g., assertive discipline; see chapter 10). It might also be worthwhile to share the rules with parents and guardians, perhaps on the school website, especially if you plan to send notes home about students who do not follow the established behavior protocols. This will depend, however, on such factors as the philosophy of the school and the policies of the principal and the board of education.

The next chapters address many of the teaching skills effective physical educators use. The bottom line, however, is that if students do not practice the behavior protocols, as stated in the posted rules, until they become an understood and accepted way of doing business, then many of the pedagogical skills discussed later will have limited effect. Although it's not a lot of fun for you or your students to practice the behavior protocols that are critical to the development of a positive (enjoyable, fun, interesting) learning environment, it's absolutely necessary. If you want to enjoy teaching, spend time practicing the protocols. If you want to spend time nagging youngsters, skip the protocols and start trying to teach.

Summary

This chapter emphasizes and provides a number of tips on how successful teachers create learning environments that are pleasant, positive, and encouraging for youngsters. The critical point is that teachers who fail to establish a positive learning environment with their classes find teaching less enjoyable and satisfying than those who do.

The chapter begins by discussing the expectations teachers have about their students and also emphasizes becoming aware of stereotypes teachers possess, either knowingly or unknowingly. The next section focuses on establishing routines and rules about how classes, and students, are expected to act in physical education class. These are called protocols and include entering and leaving the gym or outdoor space; dressing out; taking attendance; stop and start signals; getting out and putting away equipment; selecting partners, teams, and groups; and emergency protocols.

The next section focuses on the importance of actually teaching and practicing the protocols. The literature suggests that teachers who develop positive learning environments are often firm but warm and critically demanding; they also have clear, positive rules that are posted for their classes to see. The chapter concludes with ideas for how teachers can develop student ownership in the rules so that they understand and follow them.

Questions for Reflection

1. Think of yourself teaching a physical education class. Briefly describe five characteristics of a pleasant teaching environment that are important to you. Can you explain why?

2. Why is teacher expectancy such an important aspect of establishing a pleasant learning environment?

3. When you think of yourself teaching, which of the protocols is the easiest to develop? Which is the hardest? Do you know why?

4. Why is a distinction made between explaining the management protocols and teaching them?

5. You are no doubt aware of teachers who, intentionally or unintentionally, stereotype students. What are two examples of teachers stereotyping their students from your experiences?

6. Reflect on teachers you have had in the past. Recall the teachers you had who were firm but warm or who were critically demanding. Do you think these are natural attributes, or do you think they can be learned?

References

Almquist, S. (2001). The emergency plan. *Strategies, 14* (5), 30-32.

Bell, K. (1998). In the big inning. *Teaching Elementary Physical Education, 9* (4), 12-13.

Bulger, S.M., Mohr, D.J., & Walls, R.T. (2002). Stack the deck in favor of your students by using the four aces of effective teaching. *Journal of Effective Teaching, 5* (2). Retrieved from http://uncw.edu/cte/et/articles/bulger/.

Carter, K., & Doyle, W. (1989). Classroom research as a resource for the graduate preparation of teachers. In E. Woolfolk (Ed.), *Research perspectives on the graduate preparation of teachers* (pp. 51-58). Englewood Cliffs, NJ: Prentice Hall.

Colvin, A.V. (1998). Learning is not a spectator sport: Strategies for teacher-student interaction. *Journal of Physical Education, Recreation and Dance, 69* (2), 61-63.

Davis, T., & Dillon, S. (2010). *Physical educators' adapted physical education desk reference.* Blacksburg, VA: PE Central.

Downing, J., Keating, T., & Bennett, C. (2005). Effective reinforcement techniques in elementary physical education: The key to behavior management. *Physical Educator, 62* (3), 114-122.

Doyle, W. (1986). Classroom organization and management. In M.C. Wittrock (Ed.), *Handbook of research on teaching* (3rd ed., pp. 392-431). New York: Macmillan.

Fernandez-Balboa, J.-M. (1990). Helping novice teachers handle discipline problems. *Journal of Physical Education, Recreation and Dance, 67* (2), 50-54.

Fink, J., & Siedentop, D. (1989). The development of routines, rules, and expectations at the start of the school year. The Effective Elementary Specialist Study [Monograph]. *Journal of Teaching in Physical Education, 8* (3), 198-212.

Graham, G., Casteneda, R., Hopple, C., Manross, M., & Sanders, S. (1992). Developmentally appropriate physical education for children: A position statement of the Council on Physical Education for Children (COPEC). Reston, VA: National Association for Sport and Physical Education.

Helion, J.G. (1996). If we build it, they will come: Creating an emotionally safe physical education environment. *Journal of Physical Education, Recreation and Dance, 67* (6), 40-44.

Hopple, C.H. (1998). Happy new year! *Teaching Elementary Physical Education, 9* (4), 4-7.

Hutchinson, G.E. (1995). Gender-fair teaching in physical education. *Journal of Physical Education, Recreation and Dance, 66* (1), 42-47.

Kounin, J.S. (1970). *Discipline and group management in classrooms.* New York: Holt, Rinehart and Winston.

Lambdin, D. (1989). Shuffling the deck: A flexible system of classroom organization. *Journal of Physical Education, Recreation and Dance, 60* (3), 25-28.

Lambdin, D. (1992). *The interaction of elementary school teachers' lives and cares: An interview study of physical education specialists, other specialists and classroom teachers.* Unpublished doctoral dissertation, University of Massachusetts.

Lyter-Mickleberg, P., & Conner-Kuntz, F. (1995). How to stop stereotyping students. *Strategies, 8* (6), 6-21.

Martinek, T. (1983). Creating Golem and Goleta effects during physical education instruction: A social psychological perspective. In T. Templin and J. Olson (Eds.), *Teaching in physical education* (pp. 59-70). Champaign, IL: Human Kinetics.

National Association for Sport and Physical Education (NASPE). (2009). *Appropriate instructional practice guidelines, K-12: A side-by-side comparison.* Retrieved from www.shapeamerica.org/standards/guidelines/upload/Appropriate-Instructional-Practices-Grid.pdf

Sallis, J.F., Carlson, J.A., & Mignano, A.M. (2012). Promoting youth physical activity through physical education and after-school programs. *Adolescent Medicine: State of the Art Reviews, 23* (3), 493-510.

Solmon, M.A. (2006). Creating a motivational climate to foster engagement in physical education. *Journal of Physical Education, Recreation and Dance, 77* (8), 15-22.

Solmon, M.A., & Lee, A.M. (2008). Research on social issues in elementary school physical education. *Elementary School Journal, 108* (3), 229-239.

Todorovich, J., & Curtner-Smith, M. (1998). Creating a positive learning environment in middle school physical education. *Teaching Elementary Physical Education, 9* (4), 10-11.

Williamson, K.E. (1993). Is your inequity showing? *Journal of Physical Education, Recreation and Dance, 4* (8), 15-23.

Long-Term Planning

After reading this chapter, you should be able to do the following:

- Analyze the important link between planning and teaching that leads students to adopt a physically active lifestyle.
- Describe the tendencies to avoid extensive planning and ways to avoid these tendencies.
- Discuss the challenges of long-term planning and having limited time in which to teach.
- Justify reasons for eliminating some sports and physical activities from the curriculum and including others.
- Explain why planning a scope and sequence is so important in physical education.
- Describe how and why long-term and daily planning are connected.

In chapter 1 we described teaching as an orchestration of teaching skills selected from the pedagogy toolbox of good teachers. Chapter 2 described critical teaching skills that teachers use to create positive learning environments (i.e., environments that encourage learning). Once you have created a positive learning environment, and only then, can you address the obvious next question (discussed in this and the next two chapters): Learn what? Chapters 3 through 5 divide planning into a three-part process: long-term planning, writing the lesson plan, and teaching from the lesson plan. This chapter focuses on multiyear, yearly, and unit planning. Chapter 4 discusses daily lesson planning, and chapter 5 discusses changing lesson plans during lessons to adapt to different classes and students.

One of the interesting challenges physical education teachers face is the lack of time to do all that they would like to do for their students. Elementary school teachers who see their students only once or twice a week, middle school teachers who see them one semester a year, and high school teachers who see them one year out of four face a real dilemma: what can they teach in such a small amount of time? This assumes, of course, that their goal is to teach students important concepts, skills, and strategies.

Programs that consist of simply introducing some fun games, neat stunts, and a few dances or sports that students enjoy require little planning. It is simply a matter of choosing activities with little thought to progression and sequencing. Planning for this type of teaching can be done relatively quickly at the beginning of the year.

When you truly focus on what and whether students are learning, planning is more involved. You must carefully select and sequence lesson content considering long-term goals based on recognized standards and student outcomes. Then you must design each lesson to maximize student learning based on your observations and reflections from previous lessons (i.e., what each student in each class needs). Without careful and thoughtful planning, however, lessons often become haphazard and random with virtually no educational benefit.

The authors of this book believe that physical education programs should be designed so that students learn fundamental motor and sport skills and concepts that become the foundation for a lifetime of enjoyable participation in physical activity and sport (SHAPE America, 2014). We believe that physical education can, and should, be far more than just keeping youngsters physically active for the majority of a lesson. We also believe that playing games with no instruction or practice related to the skills and strategies to play them well is not in the best interest of the students we teach. Therefore, our goal is to guide youngsters in the process of becoming physically literate as outlined in the national standards document (figure 3.1).

To develop a program that truly leads to physical literacy (becoming physically active for a lifetime), planning is an essential part of your teaching process. What can you teach in your lessons and units, from year to year, that will lead your students to adopt physically active lifestyles?

Planning is to teaching as writing music is to a symphonic performance. It's analogous to the notes, the scales, the written plan that the musicians follow. Without the written music, a symphony orchestra would be reduced to nothing more than discordant noise with no connection or purpose. Without a plan that focuses on what students are expected to learn (not just do) in that lesson, you are simply keeping youngsters "busy, happy, and good" (Placek, 1984). Good teachers develop goals and objectives, plan lessons to accomplish those goals, and then assess to determine whether the goals and objectives are being met (chapter 13). This is referred to as instructional alignment (Petersen & Cruz,

National Standards for K-12 Physical Education

THE GOAL

The goal of physical education is to develop physically literate individuals who have the knowledge, skills and confidence to enjoy a lifetime of healthful physical activity.

To pursue a lifetime of healthful physical activity, a **physically literate individual**:

- Has learned the skills necessary to participate in a variety of physical activities.
- Knows the implications and the benefits of involvement in various types of physical activities.
- Participates regularly in physical activity.
- Is physically fit.
- Values physical activity and its contributions to a healthful lifestyle.

THE STANDARDS

Standard 1. The physically literate individual demonstrates competency in a variety of motor skills and movement patterns.

Standard 2. The physically literate individual applies knowledge of concepts, principles, strategies and tactics related to movement and performance.

Standard 3. The physically literate individual demonstrates the knowledge and skills to achieve and maintain a health-enhancing level of physical activity and fitness.

Standard 4. The physically literate individual exhibits responsible personal and social behavior that respects self and others.

Standard 5. The physically literate individual recognizes the value of physical activity for health, enjoyment, challenge, self-expression and/or social interaction.

Source: *National Standards & Grade-Level Outcomes for K-12 Physical Education* (SHAPE America & Human Kinetics, 2014). Visit www.shapeamerica.org/standards/pe for more information.

THIS WAY!

The Road to a Lifetime of Physical Activity

ELEMENTARY SCHOOL
Foundational skills, knowledge & values

MIDDLE SCHOOL
Application of skills, knowledge & values

HIGH SCHOOL
Lifetime-activities skills, knowledge & values

COLLEGE/CAREER-READY
Physically active lifestyle

SHAPE America
SOCIETY OF HEALTH AND PHYSICAL EDUCATORS
health. moves. minds.

| 1900 Association Drive • Reston, VA 20191-1598 • 703-476-3400 • 800-213-7193 **www.shapeamerica.org**

Figure 3.1   National Standards for K-12 Physical Education.

2004), which is also called backward design (Wiggins & McTighe, 2005), or designing down and teaching up—that is, determining the goals and then teaching to accomplish them. The U.S. national standards are an excellent place to start the planning process to determine the content that experts recommend students learn in K-12 physical education.

I Think I'll Skip These Chapters

When we envision you reading this book, we wonder if you will be tempted to skip the three planning chapters and get to "the good stuff." If you do, we hope you will return to these chapters at some point. They provide not only realistic and candid thoughts on the importance of planning but also ways planning can be done in the real world of teaching.

Need for Planning

In theory, teachers spend an hour or two each day at their desks planning. In fact, teachers plan in the shower, on the drive to work, at meetings, and as they are falling asleep at night—as well as at their desks (Graham et al., 1993; Hall & Smith, 2006; Placek, 1984).

Few question the importance of planning (Byra & Coulon, 1994; Coulon & Reif, 1994; Hall & Smith, 2006; Hastie & Vlaisavljevic, 1999). The question is "How much planning is necessary?" You know that in the beginning of your career, you need to spend a lot more time planning than you do after you have gained experience. This is no different from taking a trip for the first time. You likely start with Google or MapQuest to select your route based on the time you have; check the weather forecast; check landmarks, gas stations, and restaurants along the way; and consider the needs of your passengers. After you have made a trip several times, often choosing different routes, you can spend far less time planning your route.

The amount of planning necessary is also related to the type of program and content you decide to provide (Moore, Johnson, & Thornton, 2013). Teachers who roll out the ball probably spend 5 to 10 minutes a week thinking about what they will do (Placek, 1984). In contrast, teachers who have truly educational programs spend considerable time reviewing student outcomes, considering lesson ideas from a variety of online and print resources, and then designing lessons that fulfill the needs of their students, as detailed in the next chapter. Our assumption is that your goal is to become a subject matter expert and develop a high level of teaching expertise (Hastie & Vlaisavljevic, 1999) and that you are a teacher who sincerely wants to develop the best physical education program that will lead your students to becoming physically literate. This requires extensive planning. You need to plan so that you meet the national and state physical education standards, can deal with limited teaching time per grade, consider the context of your school and classes in lesson and unit selections, and increase your content knowledge to enrich your program.

Meeting the Content Standards and Guidelines

Planning is of utmost importance in creating a physical education program that meets the U.S. national (and state) standards and grade-level outcomes, as identified by SHAPE America (2014).

- **Elementary school outcomes (K-5).** By the end of grade 5, the learner will demonstrate competence in fundamental motor skills and selected combinations of skills; use basic movement concepts in dance, gymnastics, and small-sided practice tasks; identify basic health-related fitness concepts; exhibit acceptance of self and others in physical activities; and identify the benefits of a physically active lifestyle (p. 26).

- **Middle school outcomes (6-8).** By the end of grade 8, the learner will apply tactics and strategies to modify game play; demonstrate fundamental motor skills in a variety of contexts; design and implement a health-enhancing fitness program; participate in self-selected physical activity; cooperate with and encourage classmates; accept individual differences and demonstrate inclusive behaviors; and engage in physical activity for enjoyment and self-expression (p. 42).

- **High school outcomes (9-12).** By the end of high school, the learner will be college or career ready as demonstrated by the ability to plan and implement different types of personal fitness programs; demonstrate competency in two or more lifetime activities; describe key concepts associated with successful participation in physical activity; model responsible behavior while engaged in physical activity; and engage in physical activities that meet the need for self-expression, challenge, social interaction, and enjoyment (p. 56).

Many districts rely on these standards and outcomes to develop their K-12 school or district curriculum scopes. Essentially, the curriculum scope answers the question "What are we going to teach (or not teach) and when (what grade levels)?" The scope of the curriculums that schools and districts develop is strongly influenced by four factors: the amount of time allocated for physical education; the context of the school; the background and expertise of the teachers; and the support of fellow teachers, administrators, and parents and guardians.

Codes for National Standards and Grade-Level Outcomes

In 2014 the Society for Health and Physical Educators, known as SHAPE America, revised the U.S. national standards and also developed grade-level outcomes for elementary, middle, and high school students. Throughout this book you will find references to the five standards and also to grade-level outcomes. The grade-level outcomes are referenced by a code consisting of numbers and letters that refer to one of the five standards, the grade level (K-12), and the number of the outcome related to that grade level and outcome. For example, the code S1.M5.8 refers to standard 1, middle school outcome 5, eighth grade, under the category games and sport, invasion games—"Throws a lead pass to a moving partner off a dribble or pass" (SHAPE America, 2014). When you have a chance to review the national standards and grade-level outcomes, the explanations for the codes will become clearer (www.shapeamerica.org/standards/pe/).

Limited Teaching Time

The minimal amount of time allotted for physical education in many schools is one of the major reasons planning is so crucial. The school year in most states in the United States is 180 days. Ideally, students have instructional physical education every day of the school year from grades K through 12. Realistically, however, many schools have physical education taught by a qualified and licensed physical education teacher far fewer days. Assuming that students attend physical education in elementary school two days a week, that amounts to 72 days a year. A quick glance at table 3.1 reveals the number of

TABLE 3.1   **Number of Outcomes for Grades 2, 5, 7, and 9 Related to Each of the Five National Standards**

National standards	Grade 2	Grade 5	Grade 7	Grade 9
1. Motor skills and movement patterns	23	32	24	3
2. Concepts, principles, strategies, and tactics	3	8	13	4
3. Health enhancing (fitness)	5	7	18	14
4. Responsible personal and social behavior	7	7	7	4
5. Value of physical activity	3	4	6	3
	41	**58**	**68**	**28**

outcomes students are expected to learn at the end of certain grades. Students do not have much time to reach the outcomes described in the national standards if they have physical education only twice a week. For example, in grade 2 one of the grade-level outcomes is for youngsters to be able to hand dribble a ball in general space without losing control (S1.E17.2b; SHAPE America, 2014). If you have worked with seven-year-olds, you understand that this manipulative skill is not learned in one or two 30-minute lessons. Children require a lot more time, and practice, than that to achieve that outcome. Even if hand dribbling is taught in grades 1 and 2, less than 60 minutes a year is not enough time to learn to dribble a ball. So, what is a teacher (or district) to do?

When physical education time is limited, a teacher or district has two choices. One is to simply expose students to the content suggested in the grade-level outcomes. The second choice, a much harder one, is to decide which outcomes to focus on in one year. This means that some of the outcomes will receive much less attention and time than others. Obviously, this requires that the teacher or district make some difficult choices when planning the curricular scope for the program (Erwin & Castelli, 2008; Graber & Locke, 2007; SHAPE America, 2014).

Contextual Factors in the Learning Environment

In addition to making use of limited time for physical education, you also need to plan carefully because of the contextual factors that influence your lessons (Moore, Johnson, & Thornton, 2013). Class sizes, equipment, and facilities all dictate what can be taught. So does the climate. Teachers in Florida and southern California can teach outside comfortably much of the year; in Anchorage the tennis courts used in warm weather become ice hockey rinks in cold weather.

Even though experts recommend that physical education class sizes not exceed that of any other classroom, classes of 50 or 60 in PE are still all too common. Planning for this many students in one class is a challenge and requires additional thought and preparation. Facilities also differ from school to school. Many elementary teachers use cafeterias and multipurpose rooms during the winter months and on rainy days. Secondary teachers often need to squeeze two or three classes into one gym during inclement weather. Equipment for physical education also varies. Although equipment has improved since the days when a teacher started the program with three red rubber playground balls that wouldn't hold air past lunch and two dozen wooden bats and softballs, many programs still lack adequate equipment to teach a variety of sports and activities.

Lastly, keep in mind that one of your most important tasks when planning is learning the backgrounds of your students. Not all students, or classes for that matter, are identical. One fifth-grade class is different from another. Schools are different also. Contextual factors change in classes, and in schools, according to the communities in which the students live, opportunities and barriers they have outside the school environment, and their cultural backgrounds. Should the skills of basketball be taught in an inner city, where many students play basketball continually at recess, after school, and on weekends? Should the skills of soccer be taught in a suburban school where most of the youngsters have opportunities to join a soccer team when they're five years old?

These contextual factors require that you plan carefully and adjust your lessons according to your environment. Fortunately, these limitations shouldn't prevent you from developing a quality physical education program, but doing so does require creative and thoughtful planning (SHAPE America, 2014).

Pedagogical Content Knowledge

Your personal experiences and background also influence your planning. If you don't know something very well (e.g., dance or rhythms), you will need to spend a lot more time planning and developing the expertise to teach that activity well.

Teacher expertise is often referred to as pedagogical content knowledge (PCK) (Ayvazo & Ward, 2011; McCaughtry & Rovegno, 2003). PCK includes knowing about teaching in general (pedagogical knowledge), knowing about the content in general (content knowledge), and knowing about students and how they learn, and then combining the three kinds of knowing into an integrated whole (McCaughtry & Rovegno, 2003). We all recognize expert professionals when we see them at work: She could teach a broomstick to polka! This book focuses on the first of the three characteristics of PCK, pedagogical knowledge. It explains and provides examples of some of the pedagogical tools expert teachers use so that you can include them in your pedagogy toolbox.

Some teachers enrich their content backgrounds through reading or using the Internet (see chapter 14). Others attend conferences and workshops. Some ask other teachers for help. In recent years teachers have started to exchange videos of successful lessons. Some districts organize monthly sharing meetings that focus on a topic of interest to the teachers in the district.

The elementary school physical education teacher, for example, is expected to be an expert in virtually every subject taught in physical education—similar to what is expected

of the classroom teacher. This means that they often need to find ways to learn about new activities or ones that were neglected in their teacher preparation programs so that they can offer students a complete and well-rounded program (SHAPE America, 2014). This is also a part of planning.

Secondary teachers often find themselves needing to learn about new sports, physical activities, or techniques that would benefit their students. In recent years high schools have added activities such as inline skating, yoga, climbing, Pilates, and spinning to their programs when one or more of their teachers made the effort to learn about these activities that are so popular with teens. In some instances school districts require teachers to acquire certifications before they are allowed to teach certain subjects (e.g., archery, scuba diving).

Overall School Goals

An important responsibility of any teacher is finding ways to contribute to the overall goals of the school. Your primary purpose as a physical educator is to develop and implement a program that guides youngsters in the process of becoming physically active for a lifetime as outlined in the national standards and grade-level outcomes (SHAPE America, 2014). Additionally, you can contribute to attaining a number of holistic child development school goals, depending on your state, district, or school.

Another reason physical education teachers need to plan is that, in many cases, they assume the role of school leader and expert in physical activity in contributing to the overall goals of the school. Many schools have comprehensive school physical activity programs (CSPAP) that include quality physical education, classroom movement, physical activity opportunities before and after school, staff wellness and involvement programs, and community engagement. Physical educators are often asked to provide guidance in physical activity promotion throughout the school environment (see the Physical Activity Leader [PAL] Learning System professional development resource in the Let's Move! Active Schools initiative at www.shapeamerica.org/prodev/workshops/lmas) or to coordinate before-, during-, and after-school physical activity and intramural sport programs.

The best way to get buy-in from the principal, classroom teachers, and parents and guardians to create active environments is to educate them on the value of physical education. Start with sharing the physical education program's yearly plan, scope and sequence, and intended student outcomes. Invite them to visit the physical education class, collaborate on cross-disciplinary learning activities, and take part in paper-and-pencil assessments in the classroom. Additionally, you can provide brief descriptions of activity breaks teachers can use during or between classroom lessons.

You may be asked to integrate the Common Core State Standards (CCSS) that some states in the United States have adopted. In integrating the CCSS, you might address reading or math standards because they can use movement skills such as dribbling and running to solve problems. A high school student may develop a personal fitness plan to meet the CCSS of "writing in technical subjects" (www.corestandards.org).

Similarly, some schools are focusing on STEM (science, technology, engineering, and math) education to encourage students to focus on these areas of expertise and to ignite a desire to become proficient in these fields. Some states or school districts across the United States now recognize STEM schools at the elementary and secondary levels and encourage all teachers to incorporate integrated content across the STEM subjects. Examples include elementary students learning about the solar system as they perform manipulative skills (e.g., kicking, dribbling) through a solar system pathway and answer questions related to the planets. Secondary students might use activity tracker bands to track daily physical activity, read and interpret graphs generated, and set and track goals.

The goals of quality physical education programs are compatible with the overall goals of good schools. Your primary responsibilities as a physical educator are to provide a quality program and help students learn, feel positive about themselves, and work cooperatively with others toward common purposes. When you plan a physical education program that is aligned with national and state standards and meets the overall goals of your school, it will be viewed as successful.

Because conditions and situations are so unique, teachers' planning needs differ. Planning is necessary, but it's not necessarily the most enjoyable part of teaching. Consequently, many teachers tend to avoid it.

TECH TIPS Planning With Others

Social media can be a great way to make connections, post ideas, and gather new ideas. Setting up a professional Twitter account is easy and allows you to connect with other teachers worldwide. You might even find someone far away who is willing to start a Google Doc to develop a yearly plan together.

Tendencies to Avoid Planning

Because the content of physical education is so enjoyable to many students, it's relatively easy to avoid a lot of planning. Every PE teacher has a bag of tricks to pick from to provide 30 minutes of enjoyment. Because of this, it is tempting to avoid careful planning.

Another reason teachers avoid planning is that although there is a general consensus that the purpose of physical education is to develop physically literate people, there is no universally agreed-upon approach to accomplish this aim. Some teachers focus on physical fitness; others emphasize motor skill learning. Some focus on cognitive understanding, others teach lead-up games and sports, and others emphasize cooperating with others. There is no single recognized goal. In contrast, math and reading teachers seem to agree on a generally accepted and recognized purpose for their programs. The National Standards for K-12 Physical Education (SHAPE America, 2014) provide an excellent starting point for physical education teachers and program coordinators to reach a consensus on the most important goals of physical education for the youngsters in their schools or districts.

Another reason some physical education teachers avoid planning has to do with the perceived value of physical education in their schools. When a content area such as physical education, art, or music is undervalued, teachers have difficulty remaining convinced that their work is important (Graham et al., 2002). When this is the case, it's harder to put the time and energy into planning a truly educational program.

Many administrators and parents and guardians do not understand the value of a quality physical education program. As long as students appear happy and there are no serious injuries or parent or guardian complaints, they are satisfied with the program. Thus, little accountability is placed on physical education teachers. This is in marked contrast to reading and mathematics, for example, in which students are continually tested and evaluated. As physical education becomes more valued by school districts and administrators, and student learning in physical education class is assessed and reported to parents and guardians, teachers are being held more accountable for delivering quality curriculums. The result is that the rewards of good planning become even more evident.

Planning Formats and Components

If we had written this book 20 years ago, we would have suggested a single format for planning. Today, teachers have many ways of organizing and planning the content. No single approach to planning can be expected to succeed for every teacher. Both research (Byra & Coulon, 1994; Graham et al., 1993; Hall & Smith, 2006; Housner & Griffey, 1985; Placek, 1984) and our own collective teaching experiences of more than 50 years tell us that we also plan differently as we gain experience. This section divides planning into two sections: program outcomes and yearly planning. Daily planning is covered in detail in chapter 4.

Program Outcomes

As stated earlier in this chapter, our goal is to guide our students in the process of becoming physically literate (SHAPE America, 2014). This process begins during the earliest years. What do you want your first-graders to know (be able to do) in five years when they move on to middle school? What skills and knowledge do you expect your middle school students to have acquired by the time they begin high school? These are hard questions, but obviously they are both valuable and necessary to answer if you truly want to make a difference in the lives of your students.

How Long Will It Take to Learn?

Following is a list of five skills and concepts that students at various grade levels are expected to achieve in physical education, as reflected in the U.S. national standards (SHAPE America, 2014). Estimate how many lessons (or minutes, if you prefer) you think it will take for students to reach these goal. Compare your notes with those of other teachers; expect to find differences in both your estimates of time and your description of when a skill or concept has been learned (i.e., your operational definition of when students have truly acquired a skill or concept). If you are a beginning teacher, try to compare notes with an experienced teacher. How many lessons (minutes) are required to meet the following goals?

- Second-graders can demonstrate balance on different bases of support, combining levels and shapes (S1.E7.2a).
- Third-graders can catch a gently tossed hand-size ball from a partner, demonstrating four of the five critical elements of a mature pattern (S1.E16.3).
- Fifth-graders can give corrective feedback respectfully to peers (S4.E3.5).
- Seventh-graders can foot dribble and pass in a variety of practice tasks (S1. M9.7).
- Tenth-graders can create a practice plan to improve performance for a self-selected skill (e.g., putting in golf, a tennis serve) (S3.H6.L1).

Obviously, a physical education program that uses the grade-level outcomes outlined in the national standards to create a K-12 curriculum would need to decide what gets taught and when. Tables 3.2 and 3.3 provide two examples of curriculum scopes (for an elementary school and a middle school, respectively) that are consistent with the national standards and grade-level outcomes (SHAPE America, 2014). Both take into account factors previously discussed, including limited time and contextual variables. These scopes and sequences would vary from district to district. Our goal in providing these examples is to give you a place to start thinking about the content of a physical education program, when it is taught, and for how long. These are not intended to be used as written here. Rather, our goal is to encourage you to think about what you believe should be taught in elementary, middle, and high school physical education programs.

Table 3.2 is adapted from the book *Children Moving* (Graham, Holt/Hale, & Parker, 2012). It provides an example of how a school or district might focus on movement concepts and skill themes throughout the school year. In the primary grades (K-2), more lessons are devoted to establishing a learning environment and teaching movement concepts and traveling skills. In the intermediate grades (3 through 5), emphasis is more on skill themes that involve manipulating a ball or other object (e.g., throwing, catching, and batting) and then applying these skills in game contexts. This scope provides a guide to the amount of time to devote to the various topics throughout the year. The next step is transferring these topics to a yearly calendar to clarify what you want to teach and when. The final step is developing lesson plans for each of these topics, as described in chapter 4.

Table 3.3 is a middle school physical education scope that was created by teachers in a rural, mountainous area of the United States. The teachers wanted their curriculum scope to include content related to their local environment, culture, and families. To make sure they addressed the national and state standards and outcomes, they had to delete some

TABLE 3.2 Sample Curriculum Scope for Primary and Intermediate Grades for a Two-Days-a-Week Program (72 lessons a year)

Concepts, themes, lesson topics	Primary grades— weeks per year	Intermediate grades— weeks per year
Establishing a learning environment	3	2
Space awareness	6	2
Effort	4	4
Relationships	4	3
Traveling	5	3
Chasing, fleeing, dodging	3	3
Jumping and landing	4	4
Rolling	5	5
Balancing	4	3
Transferring weight	4	5
Kicking and punting	5	5
Throwing and catching	5	6
Volleying	2	4
Dribbling	2	3
Striking with rackets	3	5
Striking with hockey sticks	1	2
Striking with golf clubs	1	2
Striking with bats	2	2
Physical fitness and wellness	6	6
Field day and other events	3	3
	72	**72**

Adapted, by permission, from G. Graham, S. Holt/Hale, and M. Parker, 2012, *Children moving: A reflective approach to teaching physical education,* 9th ed. (New York: McGraw-Hill), 30. © The McGraw-Hill Companies.

TABLE 3.3 **One School District's 6-8 Middle School Curriculum Scope (18 weeks a year)**

Unit	Grade 6	Grade 7	Grade 8
Archery	2	2	2
Cycling	2	2	2
Disc golf	2	2	2
Fitness	2	2	2
Hockey	0	0	2
Rock climbing	2	2	2
Rhythms and dance	1	1	1
Slacklining	1	1	1
Soccer	2	2	0
Tennis	0	2	2
Volleyball	2	0	2
Softball and Wiffle ball	2	2	0
Total weeks per year	**18**	**18**	**18**

popular team sports that they might have otherwise taught. For example, they did not include basketball, reasoning that the kids who enjoyed basketball already played it a lot on their own. Others who had already been exposed to the sport did not enjoy it. So, given the limited time to teach each of the units, they decided to leave basketball and a few other commonly played sports to intramurals and outside-of-school opportunities that were available to the kids in their community.

Note that the elementary scope in table 3.2 lists skill themes and the middle school scope uses more traditional units. As students become more skillful, activities planned in the skill theme of dribbling with the feet may be very similar to those seen in a soccer unit. Likewise, if middle school students are not as skillful in dribbling with the feet, the learning tasks planned in a soccer unit may very well resemble the learning tasks planned for the skill theme of dribbling with the feet.

The natural progression of skill learning moves gradually from isolated skill practice to dynamic game play; it's not an on/off switch. For example, dribbling a ball with the feet in self-space leads to dribbling in shared space (noncompetitive). Steps after that are to add progressively more dynamic and eventually unpredictable variables to the environment to bridge the gap from static skill practice to dynamic game play (Palmer & Hildebrand, 2005). Tasks progress to cooperative dribbling and passing, dribbling with the feet against defenders who have to keep one foot on a spot, defenders who can move within a specific area but cannot cross lines on the gym floor, and so on. All of this leads to using the skill of dribbling with the feet in game play. Once again, the shift from isolated skill practice to dynamic game play is progressive rather than a distinct shift and takes months if not years (Palmer & Hildebrand, 2005).

Ideally, a school district plans the curricular scope and sequence from K-12 so that elementary school physical education links with the middle school curriculum that then progresses into the high school curriculum, as suggested in the national standards and outcomes. Unfortunately, this seems to be rare in physical education. The elementary school program may or may not dovetail with the middle school program. This explains, at least in part, why middle and high school teachers often wonder aloud, "What do they

teach in the elementary school?" An exchange day, in which teachers move up or down to different schools for a day, can help answer such questions. "I didn't realize . . ." and "No wonder . . ." preface many of the comments teachers make after an exchange day.

Because the content of physical education is somewhat less understood than many of the other content areas taught in the schools, communication between grade levels is especially important. It makes little sense, for example, for an elementary specialist to teach the rules for playing various sports when the students will spend several days learning them again in sixth or seventh grade. It also doesn't make much sense for students to be taught how to grip a bat or throw a ball in 10th grade when they learned to do so in fourth grade. Ideally, a school district has a K-12 curricular scope and sequence that is followed by the staff.

When Should _____ Be Taught?

With several other physical educators (ideally, elementary through secondary teachers), discuss these questions:

- At what level (elementary, middle, or high school) should the rules for team sports be taught?
- What basic motor skills can children be expected to learn by the time they leave elementary school?
- At what level should a major emphasis be placed on learning the important concepts of physical fitness?
- Should folk and square dance be taught at the elementary, middle, or high school level? Should the same dances be taught, or different ones?
- Basketball dribbling lessons, at all levels, often begin with the basic cues about using the finger pads, looking over the ball, and so forth. By what grade should children have learned these refinements so it is no longer necessary to start with them?

Obviously, as the discussion progresses, you will think of many more questions that will help to make the connections among elementary, middle school, and high school program outcomes. During a group discussion, you may want to refer to the national standards and grade-level outcomes (SHAPE America, 2014), as well as tables 3.2 and 3.3 to guide your discussions.

Planning for the Year

It's hard to know what you can accomplish in five or six years. It's somewhat easier to figure out what you can achieve in a single year. Some teachers accomplish this task using a calendar. They list the days and weeks of the school year and then write in the topics for various days. Some teachers believe that students learn best when a series of lessons on the same topic are combined into units (e.g., striking with paddles or rackets; table 3.2). Others believe that topics should be distributed throughout the year and organize their years around themes (e.g., balancing, kicking, striking; table 3.2) (Graham, Holt/Hale, & Parker, 2012).

In either case, you need to make realistic assessments of what your students can learn in a semester or year. These assessments will serve as a guide for the year's lessons. Without such assessments, you may be tempted to plan the year more by how you feel on a given day than by a systematic plan that leads in a desired direction.

The physical education teacher who doesn't stick to a plan for the year is no different from the history teacher who announces one day in April, "We need to cover the second half of the book in the final six weeks of the year." Time spent on unrelated topics or unfocused discussions in the beginning of the year detracts from the overall direction.

What we have written up to this point might suggest that good teachers stick to a plan regardless of their students' progress. This is not true. If students aren't grasping an important concept, skill, or strategy, good teachers spend more time on it than they allotted on their yearly calendars. They readjust while remaining sensitive to the overall plan for the year, however, and attempt to stay on schedule if possible. In fact, some teachers even post the calendar for the year with the units and themes listed so that students have an idea of what they will be learning and when. This has the added benefit of avoiding the ever-present question students of virtually every teacher ask: "What are we going to do today?"

There is no single right answer to the question of how to sequence content for the year. Content can be massed (sequential lessons and tasks all focused on the same skill) or distributed (lessons focused on one skill or topic distributed throughout the instructional period, a semester or year). Distributing practice allows you to review important ideas to promote retention and understanding. When this isn't done, students seem to forget key concepts from one year to the next. For example, when they are reminded three or

WELL, WE SPENT 30 WEEKS ON GAMES, SO NOW WE'LL HAVE TO TRY AND SQUEEZE DANCE AND GYMNASTICS INTO THE LAST TWO WEEKS OF THE YEAR.

four times a year, several months apart, to turn their sides toward the target when striking with a racket, the potential for remembering that important cue is far higher than if they heard it for one week in October and then not again until the next fall (Graham, Holt/Hale, & Parker, 2012).

Research has shown that distributing practice in tasks (e.g., the golf putt) leads to improved retention of concepts (Wright, Sekiya, & Rhee, 2014). On the other hand, learners who are more skilled often benefit from a focused massed practice approach. This traditionally looks like units of instruction in secondary programs (e.g., a volleyball unit). Secondary school teachers have to decide how long to devote to specific sports and physical activities. Should units be two or three weeks long? Six weeks long? An entire semester? Is physical fitness a semester-long class, or should fitness be emphasized in every lesson? Table 3.3 shows how one district answered these questions.

The yearly plan must be realistic to be of any value. We have seen lists of motor skills that students were going to learn (not simply do) in a twice-a-week program. These lists must have been written to appease a superintendent or coordinator or state department because they were virtually impossible to accomplish—even for a super teacher. There was just not enough time in the year for the teacher to do anything but expose students

Using Technology in Physical Education

Teachers are using more and more technology applications as part of their physical education programs. Our technology integration experts, Matthew Pomeroy and Misti Wajciechowski, remind us of some considerations to remember to help integrate technology successfully into your physical education program:

- Do not use technology in physical education classes for the sake of using technology—use it to enhance the learning experience (i.e., make content more rich and exciting, formatively assess each student quickly and more frequently, generate higher-quality and more specific feedback, create experiences in summative assessment, allow for greater individuality and student-centered learning opportunities).
- Use technology to help you, the teacher (i.e., get more information about your students that you can store and access after the lesson, gain a better understanding of each student's knowledge level, make better adjustments for upcoming lesson content).
- Using technology during a lesson with a less-than-optimal learning environment, such as too many students or limited space, can provided alternatives that enhance learning and understanding of material while still getting high levels of physical activity rather than sitting or standing while waiting their turn to be active.
- The use of technology for student-centered learning opportunities actually leads to less lecturing or teacher demonstration time and more time to be actively engaged in the content while creating differentiated learning opportunities.
- If using smart devices, make sure that all students have access to one. If students are being permitted to use their own devices, and all students do not have one, then design activities that can be done as a group or in pairs.
- When used creatively, technology will enhance the level of physical activity, not inhibit it as some might think. Middle and high school students are particularly motivated by technology integration in physical education classes.

Look for more technology tips from Misti and Matt throughout this book.

to these skills because there were so many. In that sense the yearly plan is similar to an unrealistic budget or diet plan—easy to write, but quite hard to stick to.

SHAPE America's national standards and grade-level outcomes (2014) recommend what students should be learning in K-12 physical education. In a sense it is an ideal, and few schools allot the time for students to learn all of the outcomes outlined in this document. Realistically, then, you need to decide which outcomes your students can learn—and when to teach them. Once you have made these difficult decisions, the next step is developing lesson plans for each of the topics that will lead to the accomplishment of these outcomes. Chapter 4 examines the lesson planning process.

TECH TIPS Organize Your Planning

> One challenge as a teacher is having the time to plan your entire year, by grade level, while coordinating with all of the other school activities. Use a website such as Portaportal or even Pinterest to keep your entire unit resources in one space for access wherever you are!

Summary

Planning is an essential skill if you want a purposeful program that contributes to the physical literacy of your students. It begins with what appear to be two relatively simple questions: What am I going to teach in my program? and When am I going to teach it?

Five factors (meeting the standards, limited time, contextual factors, pedagogical content knowledge, and overall school goals) are critical parts of long-term physical education planning. Each influences what is taught in a program (curriculum scope) and when (curriculum sequence).

The U.S. national standards and grade-level outcomes (SHAPE America, 2014) should inform the creation of curricular scopes and sequences in grades K-12. Several tables provide examples related to the depth of the grade-level outcomes (table 3.1) and also examples of scopes and sequences for an elementary school (table 3.2) and a middle school (table 3.3).

As a physical educator, you also need to consider how to sequence your content (massed versus distributed). Long-term planning is crucial for leading your students along the road to physical literacy.

Questions for Reflection

1. What are the consequences of not planning? Can you think of any examples from your past that might have been a consequence of either limited or superior planning?

2. Why do you think teachers tend to avoid planning? Do you think it has any connection to the universal distaste for homework?

3. Think about your school or a school you attended. What contextual factors would a teacher have to consider in planning at that school? (For example, my [GG] elementary school had no grass, only blacktop.)

4. All teachers, beginning through advanced, have a tendency to describe their goals and objectives in general or overly optimistic terms. Why do you think they do?

5. Table 3.1 lists the number of grade-level outcomes for grades 2, 5, 7, and 9 based on the national standards. Which of the five standards (figure 3.1) do you believe

should receive the most emphasis in a physical education program? Which should receive the least?

6. Table 3.2 provides a sample elementary school curriculum scope for primary and intermediate grades. Revise the table based on your beliefs. Add new topics. Delete others. Then provide a rationale for the changes you made.

7. Table 3.3 provides an example of a middle school curriculum scope. Revise the table based on your beliefs. Add new topics. Delete others. Then provide a rationale for the changes you made.

References

Ayvazo, S., & Ward, P. (2011). Pedagogical content knowledge of experienced teachers in physical education: Functional analysis of adaptations. *Research Quarterly for Exercise and Sport, 82* (4), 675-684.

Byra, M., & Coulon, S.C. (1994). The effect of planning on the instructional behaviors of preservice teachers. *Journal of Teaching in Physical Education, 13*, 123-139.

Coulon, S.C., & Reif, G. (1994). The effect of physical education curriculum development on the instructional behaviors of classroom teachers. *The Physical Educator,* (Early Winter), 179-187.

Erwin, H.E., & Castelli, D.M. (2008). National physical education standards: A summary of student performance and its correlates. *Research Quarterly for Exercise and Sport, 79* (4), 495-505.

Graber, K.C., & Locke, L.F. (2007). Chapter 7: Are the national standards achievable?—Conclusions and recommendations. [Article]. *Journal of Teaching in Physical Education, 26* (4), 416-424.

Graham, G., Holt/Hale, S., & Parker, M. (2012). *Children moving* (9th ed.). New York: McGraw Hill.

Graham, G., Hopple, C., Manross, M., & Sitzman, T. (1993). Novice and expert children's physical education teachers: Insights into their situational decision-making. *Journal of Teaching in Physical Education, 12*, 197-217.

Graham, G., Wilkins, J.M., Westfall, S., Parker, S., Fraser, R., & Tembo, M. (2002). The effects of high-stakes testing on elementary school art, music and physical education. *Journal of Physical Education, Recreation and Dance, 73* (8), 51-54.

Hall, T.J., & Smith, M.A. (2006). Teacher planning, instruction and reflection: What we know about teacher cognitive processes. *Quest, 58* (4), 424-442.

Hastie, P.A., & Vlaisavljevic, N.C. (1999). The relationship between subject-matter expertise and accountability in instructional tasks. *Journal of Teaching in Physical Education, 19*, 22-33.

Housner, L., & Griffey, D. (1985). Teacher cognition: Differences in planning and interactive decision making between experienced and inexperienced teachers. *Research Quarterly for Exercise and Sport, 56*, 45-53.

McCaughtry, N., & Rovegno, I. (2003). Development of pedagogical content knowledge: Moving from blaming students to predicting skillfulness, recognizing motor development, and understanding emotion. *Journal of Teaching in Physical Education, 22*, 355-368.

Moore, E., Johnson, C., & Thornton, M. (2013). Planning effective outdoor lessons for physical education. *Journal of Physical Education, Recreation & Dance, 84* (5), 11-13.

Palmer, S.E., & Hildebrand, K. (2005). Designing appropriate learning tasks. *Journal of Physical Education, Recreation and Dance, 76* (2), 48-55.

Petersen, S., & Cruz, L. (2004, May/June). What did we learn today? The importance of instructional alignment. *Strategies*, 33-36.

Placek, J. (1984). A multicase study of teacher planning in physical education. *Journal of Teaching in Physical Education, 4*, 39-49.

SHAPE America. (2014). *National standards & grade-level outcomes for K-12 physical education.* Champaign, IL: Human Kinetics.

Wiggins, G.P., & McTighe, J. (2005). *Understanding by design* (2nd ed.). Alexandria, VA: Association for Supervision and Curriculum Development.

Wright, D.L., Sekiya, H., & Rhee, J. (2014). Organization of practice. In A.G. Papaioannou & D. Hackfort (Eds.), *Routledge companion to sport and exercise psychology: Global perspectives and fundamental concepts* (pp. 289-307). New York: Routledge/Taylor & Francis Group.

Writing the Lesson Plan

After reading this chapter, you should be able to do the following:

- Explain the concept of task progression.
- Describe how tasks are designed for higher- and lower-skilled learners.
- Explain the use of cues (critical elements) and why they are necessary for effective teaching.
- Discuss challenges and how to use them to heighten student interest in a task.
- Describe the components of a daily lesson plan.

Now that you have decided what you want to teach and when (the curriculum scope and sequence described in chapter 3), the next step is to develop your lesson plans. This is the second of the three planning chapters. Chapter 5 addresses teaching from the written lesson plan. The focus of this chapter is the process of writing daily lessons that help students achieve the grade-level outcomes referred to in chapter 3 (SHAPE America, 2014).

Writing the Daily Lesson Plan

As with yearly planning, there is no single correct way to plan individual lessons. Some beginning teachers, for example, spend many hours writing detailed plans. They consult notes and texts and reflect on their own experiences to develop interesting lessons guided by national, state, or district outcomes. Some lesson ideas can be found in books and articles. Other sources are on the Internet.

As you will see in this chapter and the next, effective lesson planning involves more than simply listing a bunch of games or activities. Effective lesson plans vary based on grade levels, classes, and students. Because elementary school physical education specialists typically teach 7 to 11 classes a day, they often group the classes (e.g., first and second, third and fourth). Some plan for each grade level; others use different clusters. Secondary teachers who teach six periods of ninth-grade classes need only one lesson plan. Those who teach different grade levels create several lesson plans each day (e.g., yoga for first period, team handball for second period).

Where's the Perfect Resource?

I (GG) remember how I planned my lessons during my first years of teaching. I would get to school early, start the coffee, and then go to my desk. I always wanted to find the perfect plans for the day in a single book. Before long, however, I had six or seven books spread over my desk as I tried to discover the best way to accomplish my objectives for that day. No single book seemed to have all the ideas I wanted for a single lesson—even ones I had coauthored!

The resources listed at the end of the chapter will help you plan for, and teach, student-centered lessons.

Experienced teachers who have developed a schema for their content typically type or write less than beginning teachers do because their planning takes the form of mental processing (Byra & Coulon, 1994; Graham et al., 1992; Hall & Smith, 2006). Nevertheless, because of their years of experience and insights, effective teachers seem to have an acute sense of the purpose of the lesson and its place within the yearly scope. The purpose of the lesson is also clear to the students and the occasional observer.

Lesson Purpose: Learnable Pieces

As with program planning and yearly planning, one of your challenges in lesson planning is determining what students can realistically learn within the time allotted (Graber & Locke, 2007). What is a realistic learnable piece for your lesson? You might, for example, list the purpose of a lesson for second-graders as "Striking an object upward with a paddle using consecutive hits" (S1.E24.2) or one for middle school students as "Consistently making a jump shot in basketball" (S1.M2.7) (SHAPE America, 2014). If you were asked whether students could realistically learn these skills in 25 minutes, you would quickly realize that it takes a lot more practice time to learn to strike a ball with a paddle or make a jump shot consistently. In contrast, standing with the side toward the target, rather than facing the target, or following through in a basketball shot are cues students can grasp in a single lesson.

Interestingly, when you designate an achievable objective for a 20- or 30-minute lesson as a learnable piece ("side to the target"), you teach differently than you would if your objective were simply unrealistic. You would probably improvise more to develop experiences (pedagogical content knowledge) that really help students learn to stand with their sides toward the target. When the objective is unrealistic, lessons seem to consist of simply presenting a series of activities without modification or adaptation (Griffin, Chandler, & Sariscany, 1993).

When writing objectives (i.e., realistically defining a learnable piece for that time period), it is helpful to be as specific as possible. Otherwise, your objectives will be general and hard to evaluate. For example, the statement "The students will learn to volley a ball" is not only general but unrealistic for one 30-minute lesson. "The students will learn to bend their knees as they receive and volley a ball," in contrast, is a specific direction or focus for you and, as you will see in subsequent chapters, becomes the focus of the entire lesson. Specificity is important in thinking about the purpose for the lesson. Here are some helpful questions to ask when writing objectives:

- Is this truly a learnable piece for the 30-minutes lesson—that is, will the majority of the students be able to understand, and demonstrate, the objective at the end of the lesson? In the next lesson? In six months?

- Can I actually see whether I have accomplished these goals when I observe my students?

- Could someone else see whether I have accomplished these objectives?

- Do my objectives let me know how successful my program has been?

- Am I thinking about my objectives when I am actually teaching, or are the objectives just statements on paper?

- Does an assessment (check for understanding; see chapter 7) verify that the students have grasped the concepts or critical components that are the learnable pieces for the lesson (see chapter 13)?

TECH TIPS Voice to Text App

Do you sometimes have your greatest lesson ideas while driving to work? Use Dragon Dictation (a free app) to translate your voice into text. You can e-mail yourself your notes and be ready for class!

Developing the Content

Developing lesson content in a daily lesson plan is far more than simply planning a few activities while sitting at a desk or driving to work. Content development refers to the dynamic process of designing or choosing a developmental progression of activities so that youngsters achieve the objectives (learnable pieces) you developed. This is called backward design, or instructional alignment, and it refers to matching intended outcomes (lesson objectives) with the teaching process and assessment (Davidovitch, 2013; Peterson & Cruz, 2004; Siedentop & Tannehill, 2000). You make your decisions as you observe your students, reflect on your plan, and ask yourself, What will most benefit the class I am teaching at 10:15 on Tuesday morning?

To be a successful teacher, give your students instruction and practice opportunities that provide the following:

- Learning that is faster than trial and error
- A developmental progression of content that sequentially leads to improvement
- A functional understanding of the correct ways to perform skills so that they don't spend time in later years unlearning bad habits formed through trial and error without instruction or feedback
- Instruction in a variety of skills rather than just a few that students might select, only to wish in later years that they had been introduced much earlier to racket sports, for example (SHAPE America, 2014)

In chapter 3 we discussed the long-term planning process. This chapter focuses on developing the content (Rink, 2013) for lessons by selecting tasks (activities, drills) that are organized in a logical progression and instructionally aligned with your long-term plan (chapter 3). The tasks you choose must lead to improvement, be challenging, and pique students' interest so that they will be motivated to practice them.

TECH TIPS Using Evernote

An app called Evernote can be used to write most lessons across all platforms. You can access each lesson on your phone while teaching and even embed pictures and videos into your lessons. After the lesson you can embed audio clips to use to reflect on the lesson. Evernote lessons can easily be shared with other physical educators or substitute teachers, or even students, if necessary. Planning your lessons using Evernote in combination with Google Drive apps such as Google Docs, Google Presentation, and Google Drawings gives you even more options and accessibility.

Major Parts of a Lesson Plan

The major part of the lesson plan are as follows:

- *Tasks* (drills or activities) organized in a logical progression
- *Cues* (critical elements) that provide information about how to perform a task efficiently and effectively
- *Challenges* to motivate students to keep performing the task so that they can improve

We recommend that you overplan by developing an extensive grid of tasks, cues, and challenges. Fifteen task progressions is a good place to start. One of the worst feelings in the world is having 10 minutes left in the class after progressing through all of your tasks, cues, and challenges. So plan extensively. This will help you learn the content you are going to teach and also save a lot of time as you develop and teach lessons for different grades and abilities.

Tasks

After determining an objective, the next step in creating the lesson plan is developing a progression of tasks (also referred to as drills or activities) that will help students accomplish the objective (learnable piece) for that lesson. A learning task progression is a logical, developmentally appropriate sequence of tasks that leads to skill development, physical fitness improvement, or concept understanding. For example, an initial task might be to toss a volleyball up in the air, forearm pass it into the air to yourself, and then catch it. Subsequent tasks that focus on the forearm pass would gradually increase in difficulty stemming from the initial task. Multiple learning tasks can be used within a single lesson. Shifting the focus to serving a volleyball would reflect a new task from the forearm pass progression.

Where should you start with task development? The good news is that for many activities you will be teaching, you already have a pretty good idea of task progression based on your personal experiences and your teacher education program. A number of good references also provide suggestions for where to start. The grade-level outcomes of the U.S. national standards (SHAPE America, 2014) are one of the most logical places to begin.

An example of task progression, adapted from the text *Children Moving* (Graham, Holt/Hale, & Parker, 2012), is shown in figure 4.1. Here you will see a progression for dribbling with the hands based not on grade levels but on skill levels. Resources such as this are good places to begin developing your task progressions.

The sequence of tasks should be planned to enable the highest- and lowest-skilled student in every class to succeed and learn. It is rather easy to understand this concept. Changing tasks, however, so that they match the ability of the youngsters and, just as important, provide them with useful practice opportunities in a logical progression is more difficult and is detailed in chapter 5.

It's easy to find or invent stuff that students will enjoy. Unfortunately, all too often these experiences are a dead end because they don't lead to improved motor performance (the objective for many lessons). If you just want to keep students happy, fun activities are appropriate. Schools don't hire professionals, however, solely to keep youngsters entertained.

 Task Progression The web resource includes brief video segments that show teachers developing a progression of tasks with their students. The video segments are edited from 30- to 50-minute lessons so you can see how these teachers present a series of tasks to the students (that is, it is not the entire lesson).

Learning to develop good lesson plans (subject matter expertise) and pedagogical content knowledge takes time and practice. In one study (McCaughtry & Rovegno, 2003), novice physical educators were blaming the children for being off task until they gained the insight that good task progression and analysis requires a thorough and detailed understanding of children's motor skill development. One student said this about the children: "I thought they (the children) weren't trying. Now I realize that I was the one not paying enough attention. We (other novice teachers) were too stuck on seeing them as a problem to be able to break (the tasks) down and pay attention to what they were doing wrong" (McCaughtry & Rovegno, 2003, p. 364).

FIGURE 4.1 Developmental Progression of Tasks for the Skill Theme of Dribbling

Precontrol Level
- Striking a ball down and catching it
- Striking down (dribbling) continuously with both hands
- Dribbling with one hand

Control Level
- Dribbling at different heights
- Dribbling continuously while switching hands
- Dribbling with the body in different positions
- Dribbling in different places around the body while stationary
- Dribbling and traveling

Utilization Level
- Dribbling and changing speed of travel
- Dribbling while changing directions (i.e., forward, backward, sideways)
- Dribbling in different pathways
- Dribbling around stationary obstacles
- Dribbling against an opponent: one on one

Proficiency Level
- Starting and stopping; changing directions quickly while dribbling
- Dribbling against opponents (e.g., 3 versus 1)
- Playing Dribble Tag
- Passing with a partner while traveling
- Dribbling and passing in game situations
- Dribble Keep-Away
- Dribbling and shooting at a target
- Using Harlem Globetrotters' dribbling and passing routines
- Playing small sided basketball games

Adapted, by permission, from G. Graham, S. Holt/Hale, and M. Parker, 2012, *Children moving: A reflective approach to teaching physical education*, 9th ed. (New York, NY: McGraw-Hill), 524. © The McGraw-Hill Companies.

Even with the best resources, you will no doubt want to make some tasks easier or harder to match the skills and abilities of your students. This allows you, whether acting as teacher or coach, to sequence tasks in a logical progression. If you don't understand the content, your progression might be uneven (e.g., the change in difficulty from one task to the next is too large) or unproductive (e.g., the tasks don't lead to skill improvement) (Hastie & Vlaisavljevic, 1999; Quinn & Carr, 2006; Stodden et al., 2008; Tjeerdsma, 1997). In general, six factors are typically modified to change the difficulty of a task: the nature of the movement (static versus dynamic), the number of movements, the number of students, the equipment, the space, and defenders. Not all of these factors can be applied to every skill.

Be Careful With the Internet

As you know, the Internet is jammed with information about every topic imaginable. Some of the information is excellent. Some of it, however, is written by people with little or no expertise—but who believe they are experts. The bottom line is that just because something is on the Internet does not guarantee that it is accurate or worthwhile or even safe. So be smart and be certain that the information you use is written by those who are qualified and knowledgeable—and that it connects to the scope and sequence described in chapter 3. Be an informed consumer!

Nature of the Movement (Static Versus Dynamic)

One way tasks are made harder is by changing a movement from static (one movement done in self-space) to dynamic (combining two or more movements and often changing space), or vice versa. Running and throwing a ball is harder than simply throwing from a standing position; rolling after a jump is harder than rolling from a standing position; and dribbling a ball while traveling is harder than doing so while remaining in one place.

Number of Movements

The number of movements in a task also contributes to its difficulty. Jumping and then making a shape in the air is harder than simply making a shape on the floor. It's more difficult to jump and then catch or throw a ball than to catch or throw from a stationary position. Rolling at different speeds and in varying directions increases the challenge of rolling.

Number of Students

A third factor influencing task difficulty is the number of students. Moving in relation to a partner or in a group is typically harder than moving alone. This is especially true with synchronized movements, in which youngsters must match the movements of their partners. In the upper grades, the task of moving in relation to four or five others in a game or dance is complex. It takes a lot of time and practice to reach a recognizable relationship with others that can be maintained as the speed and the spaces change. In the same vein, games with two are typically easier to organize and implement than games with six or eight. In addition to the challenge of moving in relation to others, students

NOW FIND A PARTNER AND TRY TO KICK THE BALL SO IT GOES DIRECTLY TO YOUR PARTNER.

also learn about cooperating with others to achieve a common goal (chapter 12) (SHAPE America, 2014).

Equipment

Modifying equipment is another way to change the difficulty of a task. In the past few years, sporting goods companies have made tremendous progress in the design of equipment for children. Foam balls, paddles, and hockey sticks are a few examples. Smaller, lighter, more colorful balls that don't hurt when they hit are another. Basketball goals and nets that can be easily adjusted for height are great teacher aids, as are plastic bats and Wiffle balls. In fact, adult equipment is becoming increasingly rare in elementary schools. If this trend continues, wooden bats, softballs (which aren't soft), and official size and weight basketballs, volleyballs, footballs, and soccer balls in elementary schools might someday be as rare as inkwells are now.

Successful teachers also use modified equipment at the middle and high school levels. Foam balls, for example, are used with youngsters who have yet to develop catching skills. Shorter rackets may be used when teaching tennis for students who have never attempted to hit a ball with a racket.

Space

The size and shape of the learning space can also significantly change the difficulty or even focus instruction on a learnable piece. For example, when teaching throwing and catching in a dynamic environment, a 2 (offense) versus 1 (defense) learning task is common. Quite often students continue to run straight down the field for a long pass. Changing the shape of the field to a triangle with the thrower at the base of the triangle will encourage students to make shorter passes that have a higher success rate. Larger areas are more difficult to defend, but they make offensive instruction easier. If the lesson focuses on defending, using smaller spaces can provide greater success. Cones and spots are wonderful tools for adjusting the size and shape of the task space throughout a lesson.

Defenders

A sixth factor that affects many game task progressions is the challenge of eluding opponents. Attempting to dribble, catch, or kick a ball when guarded is far more difficult than attempting to do so unhindered. Our sense is that this principle of progression has been violated more than any of the others by physical education teachers in the past. Youngsters were placed in game settings long before they were ready to play against an opponent. Poorly skilled students quickly concluded that they were no good because they could not elude a defender—and this still happens in elementary, middle, and high school physical education classes. These youngsters often then resort to the role of competent bystander (Tousignant & Siedentop, 1983). They are found as far from the action as possible, allowing others to take their turns in games such as soccer and basketball.

One way you can help poorly skilled students succeed is to introduce defenders into games gradually. For example, after students have become reasonably competent at dribbling a ball while traveling, you can have only one or two attempt to steal the ball from the entire class. As all the students become more adept at dribbling against opposition, you can increase the number of stealers to four or five.

Another example of an uneven-sided game is four students trying to maneuver a ball into a goal against one defender (4v1) in soccer or lacrosse. As the skill of working in this dynamic setting increases, the game might be changed to 3v2. The advantage of uneven sides is that the student who is unaccustomed to playing in games with defenders has the chance to ease gradually into this setting without being overwhelmed. This is also why small-sided games, with two or three on a side, are generally recommended for children in elementary schools (Graham et al., 1992; National Association for Sport and Physical Education, 2009).

As stated earlier, the progression of tasks you use to develop the content is crucial to help students improve their skills in the limited time allotted for physical education (Masser, 1987). Students don't learn to throw or jump or balance or move rhythmically in an hour or two—it takes a lot of practice. And they need to have some success to want to continue to practice. Here's an insight gained by a novice teacher in the study by McCaughtry and Rovegno (2003): "You have to find things that can be successful because no one wants to do things they aren't good at. You don't want to swing at a ball all day if you're not going to hit it. They (children) want some success, and that is what we (teachers) should gear ourselves toward" (p. 362).

So how do the tasks (drills and activities) appear in a written lesson plan? Table 4.1 provides an example of a task progression for primary grade classes for dribbling with the hands. In the next two sections, cues and challenges are added to the lesson plan so you can see how to develop a plan logically.

How Many Tries?

We often wonder how many tries a student who is a true beginner at a skill needs to become proficient. Think of a professional baseball pitcher or a dancer. How many times did that person throw a ball or leap before becoming truly proficient? The number is staggering— certainly well into five figures, probably six for most athletes.

TABLE 4.1 Primary Grade Task Progression for Dribbling With the Hands

Hand dribbling task progression
• Standing on a carpet square, bounce the ball to the ground and catch it. • Bounce twice before catching.
• Bounce the ball continuously with two hands; stay on your carpet square. • Bounce with one hand; then use the other hand. • Bounce at a high or low level.
• Stand on a carpet square and dribble the ball. • Dribble high and low. • Switch hands.
• Walk around your carpet square and dribble your ball. • Speed up; then slow down. • Switch hands.
• Walk in general space and dribble the ball. • Dribble at high and low levels. • Jog (speed up). • Skip, gallop, or slide. • When the drum beats, stop traveling but continue dribbling. • Walk in curvy, straight, and zigzag pathways.
• Dribble following a partner around in general space. Every 40 dribbles, switch to a new leader. • Dribble at different speeds and in different pathways.

Cues (Critical Elements)

Learning requires that students adopt the most efficient ways to perform motor skills: the proper form, technique, or strategy. These are often called cues or critical elements (SHAPE America, 2014) and are typically written in the lesson plan as objectives. Obviously, a task (game or drill) can be appropriate for the skill level of the students, but that doesn't necessarily mean that students are performing it correctly. Cues help students learn a skill quickly and correctly so that they can avoid developing bad habits (Masser, 1993; Pellet & Harrison, 1995). The cues form the basis for teacher feedback (chapter 9). Just as a good coach is constantly giving players feedback, you can tell your student how they can improve by using the cues in your lesson plan that you have developed in conjunction with the learning tasks.

Clearly, one of the teaching skills demonstrated by quality instructors of any sport or physical activity is providing the right cue at the right time. Good teachers and coaches provide vivid mind pictures that focus learners on the cues that improve performance (Buchanan & Briggs, 1998). They also provide practice opportunities that encourage their students or players to focus on those cues.

Someone with a minimal background in physical education often uses the cue "Keep your eye on the ball" for many skills—catching, batting, kicking, punting, hitting a tennis ball. Occasionally this is the right cue. More often, however, it is inappropriate—the student is missing the ball not because of where the eyes are focused. You can provide appropriate cues that enable your students to concentrate on an aspect of the movement that leads to an efficient motor pattern for that skill.

 Using Cues   The web resource includes a video that shows several teachers explaining and demonstrating the use of cues with their students.

As with the process of developing tasks in a logical progression, you need to understand the critical elements of a movement and their sequence of development in youngsters to know which cues to focus on and when. The cues used for beginners will not be very helpful for advanced students, and vice versa. Figure 4.2 shows cues that might be helpful for beginners and more advanced students. As a physical educator, you face the challenge of understanding many skills for many activities as you introduce the cues for a variety of motor skills (SHAPE America, 2014). In contrast, high school track coaches need only know the cues appropriate for advanced performers of a single sport.

Magic Cue

A popular misconception about teaching physical activity is that there is a magic cue. If you can just find that cue, the learner will instantly improve and become proficient. Golfers are notorious for trying to discover the magic cue. In reality, we know that the cue might be appropriate but that one single trial is not enough to make a cue a habit. It won't automatically help the first time it is explained and demonstrated. When I (GG) was learning to downhill ski, for example, the cue that initially helped me the most was to keep my weight forward. But the first time I heard that cue and concentrated on it, I didn't magically ski the hill without falling. Fortunately, my instructor kept repeating it, and eventually I incorporated the cue into my motor pattern and began to fall less and less (Schmidt & Wrisberg, 2008).

Because you likely know skills so well and because time is so short, you may be tempted to overload your students with more information than they can remember or use (see chapter 7). In the past, physical educators explained and demonstrated five or six cues at the beginning of the lesson—and expected their classes to remember all of them! Today, we know that it is more effective to focus on one cue at a time (e.g., tucking the chin to the chest during a forward roll; Schmidt & Wrisberg, 2008). Instruction includes a brief explanation and demonstration, and then feedback (chapter 9) focuses on this cue. When you use this format, you and your students are thinking about the same cue ("Tuck the chin to the chest"). When you present several cues at the same time, your students might think about one cue while you are thinking about another, thereby making your feedback incongruent (chapter 9).

FIGURE 4.2 Throwing Cues for Beginners and More Advanced Students

Beginner Cues for the Overhand Throw (S1.E14.2, S1.E14.3)

- Side to the target
- Step with the opposite foot
- Arm way back
- Rotate hip as you throw
- Follow through toward target

Intermediate and Advanced Cues for the Overhand Throw (in baseball) (S1.M2.6)*

- Whip the ball through, snap your wrist
- Long step toward the target
- Make an L shape with your throwing arm
- Wrist to opposite knee

Advanced Cues for the Overhand Throw (in baseball) During Game Play (S1.M2.7, S1.M2.8)

- Quick hop, side to target, when catching or collecting the ball and preparing to throw
- Throw to the correct base to keep runners from advancing
- Throw to get the lead runner out

*Based on Fronske 2012.

A question we are often asked is "How do you know which cue to focus on?" The simple answer is that we observe our students (chapter 5)! The challenge of developing a good lesson plan is selecting one cue that will be most beneficial and then focusing on that cue until the students correctly use it before moving to another one. The grade-level outcomes developed as part of the U.S. national standards often refer to several critical elements for a single skill. For example, five cues (critical elements) comprise a mature pattern for striking with a golf club or bat ("grip, stance, body orientation, swing plane and follow through" [S1.E25.4]; SHAPE America, 2014). Through observation you can determine the critical elements (cues) that are most effective with the task progression that you developed. If you observe, for example, that virtually all of the students are gripping the bat correctly in a lesson designed to teach batting, it makes no sense to teach them how to grip the bat.

As you develop your written lesson plan grid, place the cues in the same row as the task so that you can easily provide the cue that will help students better perform the task. Table 4.2 is an example of matching the cues with the tasks outlined in the task progression (figure 4.1). We recommend placing only one cue in the same row as a task to remind yourself to focus on the cue that is most critical for performance. This will also remind you to focus on one cue at a time as detailed in chapter 9. In this example, the cue "Use your finger pads" is the critical element that guides children away from slapping at the ball with their palms as they learn to dribble with their hands.

At times, however, the task is appropriate, but the one cue listed on the plan for that task is not. In this case, list multiple potential cues for each task so that you can select the most appropriate one, just as you would choose the most appropriate task. For each

TABLE 4.2 Primary Grade Task Progression and Cues for Dribbling With the Hands

Task progression	Cues
• Standing on a carpet square, bounce the ball to the ground and catch it. • Bounce twice before catching.	Use your finger pads, not your palms.
• Bounce the ball continuously with two hands; stay on your carpet square. • Bounce with one hand; then use the other hand. • Bounce at a high or low level.	Use your finger pads.
• Stand on a carpet square and dribble the ball. • Dribble high and low. • Switch hands.	Use your finger pads.
• Walk around your carpet square and dribble your ball. • Speed up; then slow down. • Switch hands.	Use your finger pads.
• Walk in general space and dribble the ball. • Dribble at high and low levels. • Jog (speed up). • Skip, gallop, or slide. • When the drum beats, stop traveling but continue dribbling. • Walk in curvy, straight, and zigzag pathways.	Look over the ball.
• Dribble following a partner around in general space. Every 40 dribbles, switch to a new leader. • Dribble at different speeds and in different pathways.	Look over the ball.

task, you can have multiple cues from which to choose based on your content knowledge and student observations.

Coaches of athletes at all levels, from beginners through professionals, continually refer to the fundamentals. The cues (critical elements) are the fundamentals! And youngsters need to practice and practice them to develop an enjoyment of sports. Thousands of adults throw and step with the same hand and foot (no opposition), for example, even though many of them were in physical education classes. They were reminded to step with the opposite foot, but they weren't reminded often enough to have learned it. One or two lessons focused only on this cue are sufficient for most youngsters to learn the concept, assuming, of course, that the skill is revisited throughout the years.

Typically, students can describe a cue before they can actually do it. First they understand it. Then they begin to incorporate it into the schema of that movement. Eventually, after a lot of practice, the skill becomes automatic.

One way to understand the importance of cues and of teaching them one at a time is to think of learning to drive a car that has a stick, rather than an automatic, shift. When you start, you understand that to shift without grinding gears you have to step on the clutch. You understand it. You can't do it, however. After many attempts at shifting, the process becomes internalized, and you no longer have to think about stepping on the clutch as you shift. At that point in learning to drive, however, the proper way to step on the clutch is the cue you need. Until you learn this, it doesn't make much sense for your instructor to tell you how to drive in snow or enter a freeway at high speeds. You belong in the parking lot, not on the freeway.

The same principle applies to learning other motor skills. The right cue at the right time is crucial for enhanced and enjoyable learning. When you present one or two cues many times throughout a class while focusing on proper technique, it is obvious to an observer which cues you are emphasizing—and most important, it is clear to your students. During closure (chapter 7), they can recall the cues because they have heard and observed them throughout the lesson.

You may want to emphasize several cues in a single lesson depending on the students and how quickly they grasp the concept and can incorporate it into their motor patterns. Most of the time, however, you should emphasize cues one at a time for the reasons we have explained.

Challenges

Students don't learn cues just because you have explained and demonstrated them. They require practice. Lots and lots of practice. Students, however, don't necessarily see the value in continuing to practice a skill. The connection between practicing and learning is neither understood nor valued by most youngsters. The dilemma is how to maintain their interest in a task so that they continue to focus on the cue until they have internalized it. Challenges, also called applications (Rink, 1994), are designed to maintain students' interest in continuing to practice a task without making the task more difficult for those who are not yet ready.

Challenges also have the advantage of placing a task in a context in which the skill is used. For example, when students are ready to practice dribbling and keeping the ball away from defenders, they should practice that skill well before they are playing an official game of basketball. You might design a game in which all students except two are dribbling basketballs in general space. The two without basketballs attempt to steal the ball from the dribblers. Gradually, as the students become more adept dribblers, you can increase the number of stealers. The cue (learnable piece or critical element) you might focus on in this example is "Keep your body between the ball and the stealer."

 Presenting Challenges The web resource includes a video that shows several teachers providing challenges to their students in actual lessons.

An example from math might illustrate how to use challenges. When teaching a simple math strategy, such as how to carry a number in long division, good instructors use their pedagogical content knowledge to devise a variety of ways to keep students involved with the concept until they have learned it and can apply it to other problems. Ineffective teachers cover the process, but not until the students have internalized it; consequently, the students have difficulties later when they are expected to use the concept to solve problems.

The process works the same in physical education. When youngsters can't volley a ball thrown gently to them or strike a ball accurately with the hand, it makes little sense to require them to play an official game of volleyball. Students who have yet to learn the prerequisite skills should continue to practice those skills; those who have the necessary skills are ready to begin using these skills in games (chapter 8).

Teacher, You Just Left Me Behind . . . Again

One of the criticisms of education (not only physical education) is that students who don't learn as quickly as others are left behind. Tumbling comes immediately to mind. Teachers often start, for example, with a log roll, then progress to a forward roll, a backward roll, a cartwheel, headstand, handstand, and so forth. Many students, however, need to stay at the backward roll. They haven't learned it yet, but the teacher keeps introducing new skills. The process of challenging students, as described in this chapter, provides a way to maintain the interest of those who have learned the backward roll while still working with those who are slower to grasp the cues. Here are some examples:

- "Some of you might want to try two backward rolls in a row."
- "Can you and your partner start and stop your backward rolling at the same time?"
- "If this is easy for you, you might want to combine a forward roll and a backward roll."

Providing challenges is a technique for maintaining the interest of the students *without changing the task*. As with task development, you can challenge your students in a number of ways. As you read through these seven techniques, you will see that some work better with elementary school children; others, with middle schoolers or high schoolers. All are designed to make the practice of motor skills more fun and also interesting.

Repetitions

One of the simplest ways to challenge your students, without making the task harder, is to provide self-tests that encourage them to meet a goal you suggest. In the following examples, students are already doing the task (e.g., jumping over a hoop, attempting to catch a ball, dribbling a ball). They continue the task, but you challenge them to meet a standard or goal.

- "Can you jump over the hoop and land without falling three times in a row?"
- "How many times can you catch the ball on a fly?"
- "See if you can beat your old record."
- "Bounce the ball for each letter of your first name (or the name of the school, the capital of your state or province, the president of the United States)."

Cognitive Challenges

Cognitive challenges are another way to interest your students in continuing to practice a task. These challenges reinforce what they are learning in the classroom while making the task more enjoyable and fun.

- "This time, strike the ball with your paddle as many times as the answer to this problem—10 divided by 2."
- Students dribble to pieces of papers taped to the wall (or floor) and answer the question on the paper, such as "What is the capital of Virginia?"
- Students jump over vocabulary words (taped to the floor) they are studying in class and say the words out loud while in the air.
- Set up an obstacle course in the gym. Each time students complete part of the obstacle course (e.g., skip along a bench, crawl through a hoop backward without knocking it down), they take a word from one of the buckets on the obstacle course. Challenge them to make a complete sentence with the words they find.

Needless to say, classroom teachers and principals are delighted when physical educators reinforce concepts being taught in the classroom.

Timing

Another self-testing technique is competing against the clock. Here are examples:

- Students attempt to jump and land in a balanced position. Challenge them by asking, "Can you hold the balance for at least five seconds?"
- Students are throwing and catching, or kicking or striking a ball with a paddle to a partner. Challenge them to keep the ball going for 30 seconds.

- Students are jumping rope, and you challenge them to jump continuously for 10 seconds, 15 seconds, and so on.

Keeping Score

Some skills (movements) lend themselves to keeping score. When students are playing a game with defenders (e.g., 2v2), you can challenge them to figure out a way to keep score. This will motivate some to practice longer. Sometimes scores can be cooperative (how long can one pair keep a ball going?). Although it is not always feasible, scoring seems to work best when students are given a choice (e.g., to keep score only if they want to; chapter 8).

Typically, more skillful youngsters are interested in competing; they find this challenging because they have mastered the skill in static environments and are now applying it in more dynamic game environments. They truly enjoy and benefit from opportunities to use their skills in competition.

Replays

Replays, a fifth way to challenge students, are used more in gymnastics and dance settings. You might ask your students, "Can you repeat the movement exactly so that both tries appear identical?" This is a true challenge, especially if they are trying to repeat a sequence of several movements. It's even harder when the sequence is performed with a partner. To heighten the challenge, you might say, "Imagine that I recorded your sequence. Let's see if you can do it again exactly as I recorded it."

Recording or Performing for Others

In the preceding section, the video was imaginary. When video recording is available, however, encouraging youngsters to work on their sequences or dances to improve them to performance quality for recording can be highly motivating. Students of all ages enjoy seeing themselves on video. The possibility of being recorded often provides an incentive to continue working on a project they might otherwise abandon for lack of interest. Obviously, you want them to continue improving the quality of their movements.

Another technique similar to pinpointing (discussed in chapter 7) is to ask students to show others in the class how they are performing a task. This challenge should motivate them to continue practicing so that they show others their best performances. You can present this technique several ways, such as the following:

- "All those on this side of the gym will do their sequences three times. After that we will switch, and that half of the class can sit down and become spectators."
- "Which group would like to demonstrate a game for the rest of the class?"
- "I am looking for routines that clearly show the speeds and levels that can be shown to the class at the end of the lesson."
- "Steve and Jenny have found a different way to make their balance. Let's see how they solved the problem."

Challenges for Young Children

Young children have limited movement vocabularies. Thus, challenging them by having them combine two skills often doesn't work. Given the limited vocabulary and short attention spans of four- and five-year-olds, a minor change in a task (it is embellished more than changed) is often enough. The following examples, although minor, interest young children because they are developmentally appropriate. For them, minor changes are new challenges.

- "Now find a different carpet square to balance on." (The balance might be the same, but now it is on a blue rather than a brown carpet square.)
- "After you throw five times, find a different-colored beanbag to throw." (The throw is the same except that it is now done with a yellow instead of a red beanbag.)
- "Now see if you can walk on a blue line without falling off." (They are challenged to find the color blue although they are still focusing on balancing on a line.)
- "Make a different shape with your rope. Then try to jump over the rope and land without falling." (The focus is still on jumping and landing; only the shape of the rope is different.)
- "Now turn and skip the other way around the hoop." (The task has been changed from a clockwise to a counterclockwise skip.)

In each of these examples, the challenge remains the same. The children, however, are motivated by the opportunity to try the task in what is (for them) a new setting.

Like tasks and the cues, challenges are a significant part of the lesson plan. Because challenges should not be new tasks, but rather a way to motivate students to keep practicing the same task, they are listed in the same row as the task and cues in a written lesson plan grid. Table 4.3 includes the challenges along with the tasks and cues described in tables 4.1 and 4.2.

TABLE 4.3 Primary Grade Task Progression, Cues, and Challenges for Dribbling With the Hands

Task progression	Cues	Challenges
• Standing on a carpet square, bounce the ball to the ground and catch it. • Bounce twice before catching.	Use your finger pads, not your palms.	Each time you bounce and catch, turn and face a new wall and try again.
• Bounce the ball continuously with two hands; stay on your carpet square. • Bounce with one hand; then use the other hand. • Bounce at a high or low level.	Use your finger pads.	As you dribble, chant a song or rhyme quietly to yourself (e.g., five little monkeys).
• Stand on a carpet square and dribble the ball. • Dribble high and low. • Switch hands.	Use your finger pads.	Say a letter of the alphabet every dribble. How far in the alphabet can you get?
• Walk around your carpet square and dribble your ball. • Speed up; then slow down. • Switch hands.	Use your finger pads.	Every time around the carpet without losing the ball, give yourself 2 points. How many points can you get?

> continued

TABLE 4.3 > *continued*

Task progression	Cues	Challenges
• Walk in general space and dribble the ball. • Dribble at high and low levels. • Jog (speed up). • Skip, gallop, or slide. • When the drum beats, stop traveling but continue dribbling. • Walk in curvy, straight, and zigzag pathways.	Look over the ball.	When I hold up my fingers, tell me how many. When you pass someone, say his or her name.
• Dribble following a partner around in general space. Every 40 dribbles, switch to a new leader. • Dribble at different speeds and in different pathways.	Look over the ball.	Can you keep up with your partner? Can you match what your partner does the whole time?

Look at the challenges in this lesson plan grid in figure 4.3. If you have asked your students to dribble around their carpet squares using two hands, it wouldn't make sense to challenge them to see how many fingers you are holding in the air. Once they can walk and dribble in general space, however, that would be an appropriate challenge. This is why the tasks, cues, and challenges are aligned in the same row—to provide a fundamentally sound content develop progression. It is the exceptional teacher who can develop the content without thoughtful and extensive preparation. For most of us, the authors included, good lessons require a lot of careful planning.

Lesson Components

Now that we have finished describing the major parts of a lesson plan, we thought it would be useful to include an example of an entire lesson plan. This example (figure 4.3) includes the lesson topic and objective, an instant activity (detailed in chapter 6), and a set induction (also detailed in chapter 6). It also includes a fourth column that describes things such as the equipment needed for a task, formations, and groupings (especially useful for beginning teachers). This example concludes with a closure (detailed in chapter 7) and adaptations for students with special needs.

In addition to one or two objectives, most lesson plans include the following:

- A format for indicating the topic of the lesson, the grade level, the date, and other information helpful for keeping track of which class has been taught which lesson. This is especially important if you teach 20 or more classes in the same week—especially if you teach at more than one elementary school.

- An introduction to the lesson that is quickly organized and stimulating. This instant activity may or may not be related to the remainder of the lesson (chapter 6).

- A brief introduction to the purpose of the lesson to provoke interest. This is often called a set induction or anticipatory set. This portion of the lesson frequently relates to previous lessons (chapters 6 and 9 provide additional information about this component).

- Organization and transition ideas. One reason for listing a number of tasks is to ensure that a lesson flows smoothly from one task to the next in a logical and orderly progression. When a sequence of tasks isn't done ahead of time, there is a tendency in the beginning to skip around and lose sight of the lesson objective. Listing equipment or drawing or describing how the task is organized can help you transition quickly from one task to another.

- Finally, a closure is often included as a way of slowing down the end of the lesson and reminding students of the important features (chapter 13). Often, this is in the form of a question or two related to the objectives of the lesson. You may also want to use this time to assign PE homework.

In some of your lesson plans, you might want to include an assessment, as detailed in chapter 13, and also modifications for youngsters with special needs (e.g., hearing impairments, use of a wheelchair).

I Remember

I (GG) remember watching a student teacher whose lesson was focused on jumping and landing. She decided to use hoops for the children to jump over. About halfway through the lesson, some of the children began picking up their hoops and tried to use them as hula hoops. Others quickly followed. The lesson ended with the teacher trying to show the children how to hula-hoop—hardly the focus she had started with 20 minutes before.

Some teachers use planning books, others use three-ring binders, and many use computers or mobile devices to keep track of their lesson plans. In time, teachers typically write less as they develop the schemata of various sequences of lessons. This economy comes from teaching 10 or 20 classes a week on the same topic. This isn't meant to suggest, however, that experienced teachers don't plan. They do. But the format they use is different from that of beginning teachers.

In addition to the content development part of the lesson, teachers include other information that they find useful for individual lessons and from year to year. Figure 4.3 includes some of these items.

Adapting Lessons for Students With Special Needs

It is important to plan for students with special needs who may require individual attention outside of the regular individualized instruction for the class. The lesson plan in figure 4.3 addresses a student with a hearing impairment.

The first step in working with students with special needs is to identify tasks that are appropriate and accessible. Make sure to consider how those tasks are organized, and be sure that the student can transition between tasks. Consider how you might make the tasks easier or harder and the time needed to perform them, as well as any need for assistance, additional equipment, and boundaries. Finally, identify ways to include the student in the regular class, as appropriate, rather than having him or her work independently.

If you are unsure of how to adapt your lessons to accommodate all students in your classes, a certified adapted physical educator in your district may be able to help. If such a professional is not available, attending a student's individualized education plan

FIGURE 4.3   Sample Lesson Plan

Instructor: Ms. Smith

Lesson focus: Dribbling with hands

Situation: Primary grades

Equipment: Carpet squares and basketballs (enough so every student has one)

Objective: Use the finger pads to dribble a ball (S1.E17.K, 1, 2a, 2b)

Instant activity (energizer): Builders and bulldozers

Set induction: Demonstrate slapping a ball with your palm and losing control. Ask students whether they have ever lost control of a ball when dribbling. In today's lesson, you are going to teach them one of the tricks used by great basketball players to dribble without losing control.

Task progression	Cues	Challenges	Organization/transition
Standing on a carpet square, bounce the ball to the ground and catch it. Bounce twice before catching.	Use your finger pads, not your palms.	Each time you bounce and catch, turn and face a new wall and try again.	One carpet square (spread throughout general space) and one ball for every student
Bounce the ball continuously with two hands; stay on your carpet square. Bounce with one hand; then use the other hand. Bounce at a high or low level.	Use your finger pads.	As you dribble, chant a song or rhyme quietly to yourself (e.g., five little monkeys).	One carpet square (spread throughout general space) and one ball for every student
Stand on a carpet square and dribble the ball. Dribble high and low. Switch hands.	Use your finger pads.	Say a letter of the alphabet every dribble. How far in the alphabet can you get?	One carpet square (spread throughout general space) and one ball for every student
Walk around your carpet square and dribble your ball. Speed up; then slow down. Switch hands.	Use your finger pads.	Every time around the carpet without losing the ball, give yourself 2 points. How many points can you get?	One carpet square (spread throughout general space) and one ball for every student
Walk in general space and dribble the ball. Dribble at high and low levels. Jog (speed up). Skip, gallop, or slide. When the drum beats, stop traveling but continue dribbling. Walk curvy, straight, and zigzag pathways.	Look over the ball.	When I hold up my fingers, tell me how many. When you pass someone, say his or her name.	One ball for every student
Dribble following a partner around in general space. Every 40 dribbles, switch to a new leader. Dribble at different speeds and in different pathways.	Look over the ball.	Can you keep up with your partner? Can you match what your partner does the whole time?	Partners (closest person; assign any extras to create groups of three), each student with a ball

Closure: Hold both hands over your head. Point to the part of the hand that we don't want to use when trying to dribble a ball. Now point to the part of the hand we want to use.

Additional modifications for special needs (hearing impairment): Give the student's aide a written lesson plan before class, have the aide demonstrate each task or challenge, and give appropriate instruction or cues in the student's self-space before the start signal.

(IEP) meetings can help you become more aware of inclusion strategies and get help in developing goals that fit your curriculum as well as the unique needs of the student. Also, seeking professional development opportunities in your district or online can help you better understand the Adapted Physical Education National Standards (APENS) and ensure that all students are included in your PE curriculum. You can find helpful information about adapted physical education online at various websites, including PE Central (www.pecentral.org).

Teaching With a Purpose

Keep in mind that just because a teaching idea or activity comes from a reputable journal, website, or professional meeting, or that people rave about it, doesn't mean that it is appropriate for your program or in physical education. Although fun is important, do not choose activities just because they are fun. What may appear fun may not lead to physical literacy. We hope this book, along with SHAPE America's appropriate practices document that describes both appropriate and inappropriate practices in physical education (SHAPE America, 2009) and the national standards and grade-level outcomes (SHAPE America, 2014), will make you an informed consumer. Our hope is that the activities you choose meet state and national standards and are connected from lesson to lesson, theme to theme, and year to year. When you find activities you are interested in including in your curriculum, ask yourself these questions:

- Where does it align with my state or national standards?
- Where does it fit in my yearly plan and scope and sequence?
- What skill(s) will be enhanced or practiced?
- Does it meet appropriate practices (i.e., all students are involved)?
- Is this a productive use of time for my students?

The bottom line is that the content you choose should lead to student learning.

Really a Good Game?

Recently, I (GG) saw a game described on Facebook as really fun. It looked like a human version of the board game Hungry Hippos: four students were actively trying to gobble up, or collect, balls using buckets while their teammates looked on and supposedly cheered. Only four students were active at a time—the rest were waiting! The comments from people on Facebook, many of whom were self-proclaimed physical education teachers, implied that the game was used in PE and was a big hit with the students. Although the game may have been exciting for some, I don't consider this a good game. How the game could contribute to kids becoming skillful was my first question, and I certainly wondered about the high amount of waiting time. It bothers me that teachers were raving about this game when all I could think was that it should be added to the hall of shame list (Williams, 1992, 1994, 1996, 2015). Needless to say I didn't hit "like" on Facebook. In fact, I wished I could find the unlike button. I can't help but wonder whether the teachers who liked this game focus on student learning or just roll out the ball with whatever fun game keeps their kids busy, happy, and good (Placek, 1983). I also wondered whether they were keeping up-to-date as professionals.

Summary

Initially, writing lesson plans takes time and can be complicated. Over time, however, as you work with lesson plans using a content development format (comprising tasks, cues, and challenges), you will find that planning not only takes less time but also creates lessons that are both logical and useful to students. Planning is a dynamic process that changes from class to class. A more static or linear lesson plan includes a warm-up (calisthenics and running laps), a drill or two, and a game. Although this format has been used for years, it has not resulted in physical education that leads to student learning and enjoyment. This static format assumes that all classes are identical. If you are a physical education student, think about your classmates. Do you all have the same skill levels and interests? Would an identical lesson plan work for everyone in your class? This is the reason we are sharing a dynamic planning format that accounts for differences.

Once you have developed a curriculum scope and sequence (chapter 3), the next step is to develop lesson plans that achieve the objectives implied in the grade-level outcomes (SHAPE America, 2014). In the format we suggest, the lesson plan uses a grid format consisting of columns and rows. The first column is a progression of tasks (activities, drills) appropriate for the skill level of the students (table 4.1). The second column consists of cues (critical elements) that help students perform the skills properly (table 4.2). The third column contains challenges to motivate students to continue practicing the tasks (table 4.3). The tasks, cues, and challenge are aligned in rows to complement one another and to ensure that you use them appropriately. Figure 4.3 shows a lesson plan with all of the components.

Questions for Reflection

1. In contrast to developing content to help students learn, some teachers simply teach fun activities with little thought about progression or cues. Their goal appears to be to keep them busy, happy, and good but not necessarily learning. Why do you think that is so?

2. Develop a progression of 10 tasks (drills, activities) that will lead to a fifth-grade outcome as described in the grade-level outcomes (SHAPE America, 2014). Provide the code for that grade-level outcome.

3. Pick a skill you know well. List three cues that might be used for beginners and three cues that might be used for advanced performers.

4. Assume that you are teaching a middle or high school class. Pick a subject that is typically taught in these programs. Create three challenges that you think would motivate your students.

5. Using the column and row format described in this chapter, develop your own lesson plan for a skill, concept, or strategy that you know well. Start with one or two lesson objectives (learnable pieces), and then list seven tasks, cues, and challenges.

Resources

Active Academics (www.activeacademics.org)

Colvin, A., Markos, N., & Walker, P. (2016). *Teaching fundamental motor skills* (3rd ed.). Champaign, IL: Human Kinetics.

Fronske, H.A., & Heath, E.M. (2015). *Teaching cues for sport skills for secondary school students* (6th ed.). San Francisco: Pearson Benjamin Cummings.

Graham, G., Holt/Hale, S., & Parker, M. (2012). *Children moving* (9th ed.). New York: McGraw-Hill.

PE Central (www.pecentral.org)

Rovegno, I., & Bandhauer, D. (2012). *Elementary physical education: Curriculum and instruction.* Burlington, VT: Jones and Bartlett Learning.

Young, D. (2011). Moving to success: K-5 curriculum. www.movingtosuccess.com

References

Buchanan, A., & Briggs, J. (1998). Making cues meaningful: A guide for creating your own. *Teaching Elementary Physical Education, 9* (3), 16-18.

Byra, M., & Coulon, S.C. (1994). The effect of planning on the instructional behaviors of preservice teachers. *Journal of Teaching in Physical Education, 13*, 123-139.

Davidovitch, N. (2013). Learning-centered teaching and backward course design—From transferring knowledge to teaching skills. *Journal of International Education Research, 9* (4), 329-338.

Fronske, H.A. (2012). *Teaching cues for sport skills for secondary school students* (5th ed.). San Francisco: Pearson Benjamin Cummings.

Graber, K.C., & Locke, L.F. (2007). Chapter 7: Are the national standards achievable?—Conclusions and recommendations. *Journal of Teaching in Physical Education, 26* (4), 416-424.

Graham, G., Castenada, R., Hopple, C., Manross, M., & Sanders, S. (1992). Developmentally appropriate physical education for children: A position statement of the Council on Physical Education for Children (COPEC). Reston, VA: National Association for Sport and Physical Education.

Graham, G., Holt/Hale, S., & Parker, M. (2012). *Children moving* (9th ed.). New York, NY: McGraw-Hill.

Griffin, L.L., Chandler, T.J.L., & Sariscany, M.J. (1993). What does "fun" mean in physical education? *Journal of Physical Education, Recreation and Dance, 64* (9), 63-66.

Hall, T.J., & Smith, M.A. (2006). Teacher planning, instruction and reflection: What we know about teacher cognitive processes. *Quest, 58* (4), 424-442.

Hastie, P.A., & Vlaisavljevic, N.C. (1999). The relationship between subject-matter expertise and accountability in instructional tasks. *Journal of Teaching in Physical Education, 19*, 22-33.

Masser, L. (1987). The effect of a refinement on student achievement in a fundamental motor skill in grades K through 6. *Journal of Teaching in Physical Education, 6*, 174-182.

Masser, L. (1993). Critical cues help first-grade students' achievement in handstands and forward rolls. *Journal of Teaching in Physical Education, 12* (3), 301-312.

McCaughtry, N., & Rovegno, I. (2003). Development of pedagogical content knowledge: Moving from blaming students to predicting skillfulness, recognizing motor development, and understanding emotion. *Journal of Teaching in Physical Education, 22*, 355-368.

National Association for Sport and Physical Education (NASPE). (2009). *Appropriate instructional practice guidelines, K-12: A side-by-side comparison.* Retrieved from www.shapeamerica.org/standards/guidelines/upload/Appropriate-Instructional-Practices-Grid.pdf

Pellet, T.L., & Harrison, J.M. (1995). The influence of refinement on female junior high school students' volleyball practice success and achievement. *Journal of Teaching in Physical Education, 15* (1), 41-52.

Peterson, S., & Cruz, L. (2004, May/June). What did we learn today? The importance of instructional alignment. *Strategies,* 33-36.

Placek, J.H. (1983). Conceptions of success in teaching: Busy, happy and good? In T. Templin & J. Olson (Dir.), *Teaching in physical education* (pp. 46-56). Champaign, IL: Human Kinetics.

Quinn, R., & Carr, D. (2006). Developmentally appropriate soccer activities for elementary school children. *Journal of Physical Education, Recreation and Dance, 77* (5), 13-17.

Rink, J.E. (1994). Task presentation in pedagogy. *Quest, 46*, 270-280.

Rink, J. (2013). *Teaching physical education for learning* (7th ed.). New York: McGraw-Hill.

Schmidt, R.A., & Wrisberg, C.A. (2008). *Motor learning and performance* (4th ed.). Champaign, IL: Human Kinetics.

SHAPE America. (2009). Appropriate instructional practice guidelines, K-12. www.shapeamerica.org/standards/guidelines/apppracticedoc.cfm

SHAPE America. (2014). *National standards & grade-level outcomes for K-12 physical education.* Champaign, IL: Human Kinetics.

Siedentop, D., & Tannehill, D. (2000). *Developing teaching skills in physical education* (3rd ed.). New York: McGraw-Hill.

Stodden, D.F., Goodway, J.D., Langendorfer, S.J., Roberton, M.A., Rudisill, M.E., Garcia, C., & Garcia, L.E. (2008). A developmental perspective on the role of motor skill competence in physical activity: An emergent relationship. *Quest, 60*, 290-306.

Tjeerdsma, B.L. (1997). A comparison of teacher and student perspectives of tasks and feedback. *Journal of Teaching in Physical Education, 16* (4), 388-400.

Tousignant, M., & Siedentop, D. (1983). A qualitative analysis of task structure in required secondary physical education classes. *Journal of Teaching in Physical Education, 3* (1), 47-57.

Williams, N. (1992). The physical education hall of shame. *Journal of Physical Education, Recreation and Dance, 63* (6), 57-60.

Williams, N. (1994). The physical education hall of shame, part II. *Journal of Physical Education, Recreation and Dance, 65* (2), 17-20.

Williams, N. (1996). The physical education hall of shame, part III. *Journal of Physical Education, Recreation and Dance, 67* (8), 45-48.

Williams, N. (2015). The physical education hall of shame, part IV: More inappropriate games, activities, and practices. *Journal of Physical Education, Recreation and Dance, 86* (1), 36-39.

Teaching From the Lesson Plan

"While teaching a unit on kicking, the students were learning how to kick using the part of their foot with the shoelaces. One student was wearing shoes with Velcro straps. He looked at me and said "I don't think I can play this game because I don't have any shoelaces.""

Harrison Sundgren,
Castle Rock, Colorado

Reprinted with permission from PE Central (www.pecentral.org).

After reading this chapter, you should be able to do the following:

- Provide personal examples of subject-centered and student-centered physical education teaching.
- Describe four techniques that enhance observation when teaching classes.
- Explain the importance of teaching only one cue (critical element) at a time.
- Discuss four key content development (progression) techniques that are critical to successful teaching, starting with safety.
- Describe three content development patterns.

77

So now that you have written a logical progression of tasks, cues, and challenges as explained in chapter 4, the next step is to teach from your plan. This involves constantly observing and evaluating the students to determine their progress, and then, based on your observations, determining the logical next step using your lesson plan (Hall & Smith, 2006). This practice of obtaining the information needed to adjust your teaching while you are teaching is known as formative assessment.

Observe your class and make a decision about what to do next. This probably sounds simple; it's not! Here's an example to make our point. Imagine that you see a young child tying her shoe. You might be tempted to help her, but what if she already knows how to tie her shoe? Would you teach her? Of course not. The same is true in physical education. Successful physical educators observe their classes and, based on their observations, decide what to teach and when (student-centered teaching). Ineffective physical educators, in contrast, teach their students things they may or may not need to learn—and then wonder why their students appear frustrated, disinterested, or bored (subject-centered teaching).

Student Centered Versus Subject Centered

One of the premises of this book is that quality physical education teachers design their programs specifically for the students they are teaching: Their programs are student centered. This means that each lesson is designed for a particular class of students. Lessons aren't rigid and unchanging; they're dynamic and interactive (Davidovitch, 2013; Hautala, 1989). For example, no single lesson on the overhand throw or batting a ball will work for every second- and third-grade class in a school. Moreover, no single lesson on playing defense will work with every seventh-grade class you teach. Because the skills of one class differ from those of another, you need to vary the way you develop your lesson content. Some classes progress more rapidly than others do. Some classes have had different opportunities than others have had. In short, your program should be student centered—that is, the tasks and activities, and the time you spend on them, should be based on your observations of your students.

Subject-centered teaching is the opposite of student-centered teaching. In a subject-centered class, the same lesson may be taught in the same way to all second- through fifth-grade classes. The assumption in a subject-centered curriculum is that students have the same abilities and can thus be expected to learn at similar rates. In these classes, teacher observation and analysis are not important because decisions on which activities to teach and how long to teach them are made before the beginning of a lesson and remain unchanged throughout—regardless of the success or failure of the students.

Two examples of subject-centered activities should help make the distinction between student- and subject-centered physical education clear. The first is from a kindergarten class. The children were partnered up. One in each pair was given a ball. The child with the ball was asked to dribble the ball and catch the partner who was running away—but who didn't have a ball to dribble. The task was interesting. Unfortunately, it was far too hard for virtually every child in the class. They were unable to maintain control of the ball while dribbling and standing still, let alone while running after a partner.

After attempting the task and failing, the children quickly made two adjustments so that they could succeed. Some who were supposed to be dribbling simply tucked the ball under an arm and raced to catch the fleeing partner. Others simply abandoned the ball and chased the partner around the gym. If the purpose of the lesson was to help the children improve their dribbling skills, the activity was ineffective—the children were simply not dribbling. The teacher, however, didn't seem to see (observe) the children, because the activity continued for several minutes with no change made to the task.

Requiring students to play by official, or adult, rules is another example of a subject-centered activity. Let's use volleyball as an example (we could just as easily use basketball, soccer, softball, or flag football). Following is what we often see when we observe a class of secondary students playing by official volleyball rules:

- Some students are afraid of the ball and move quickly away from it to allow the more skilled students to hit it.
- Some students never hit a successful serve.
- There is a lot of chasing after the ball and waiting because of the lack of successful rallies.

Volleyball is a great game—but only when players have developed sufficient skills to play it. The subject-centered teacher might require a class to play volleyball (official rules) for several days or even weeks in a row, often in a tournament format. The student-centered teacher, in contrast, would observe the students, analyze their ability, and then change the game to match their skill level. (Chapter 8 on motivating students provides some great examples of how to adapt content to make it student centered.)

Fortunately, we see student-centered volleyball in many schools today—lowered nets, softer and lighter balls, students serving as close to the net as necessary to get the ball over, letting the ball bounce, and opportunities to practice in small groups or play small-sided games over a rope tied to chairs or a line on the floor (Graham, Holt/Hale, & Parker, 2012). Teachers who make these changes have based their lessons on observations of the skill levels and characteristics of their students.

One Ball for an Entire Class?

One of the easiest ways to determine whether teachers are subject or student centered is to observe several lessons in a row at the same grade level. For instance, if all lessons taught to a sixth-grade class are virtually identical, the teacher is likely subject centered. If lessons vary (e.g., tasks are modified, different cues are used), then the teacher is probably student centered. Another way to assess whether a teacher is student centered or subject centered is to note the number of balls used in a game. If only one ball is used, does that assume that every student has the abilities required to play the game well and enjoyably? What if virtually all games played during a year involve only one ball?

Clearly, student-centered physical educators observe and analyze their students and classes and make adjustments to their lessons accordingly. Chapter 4 outlined a content development planning format that makes it easy to change lessons from one class to the next. Before you can teach from your written plan, however, you need to observe your classes to determine the appropriate tasks, cues, or challenges. Because observation and analysis are such important parts of becoming a student-centered teacher, the first part of this chapter is devoted to observation techniques. The second part describes patterns student-centered teachers use to develop the content (tasks, cues, and challenges) based on their observations.

Observation Techniques

Physical education teachers are continually required to observe 25 or more students simultaneously. Good teachers use a number of tricks (observation techniques) to help them analyze the appropriateness of the tasks, cues, and challenges (chapter 4) for their students (back to the wall, scanning, visitor observation, and one component at a time). These techniques will help you decide when and what type of feedback and cues will be most helpful (chapter 9). Simply knowing these observation techniques, however, is not enough. As with all of the skills described in this book, you need to practice them.

Back to the Wall

One of the most obvious observation techniques is to stand with your back to the wall or to the outside of the boundaries. This allows you to see most of what your students are doing. In contrast, if you are in the middle of the action, at any given time half of your students are out of sight (Arbogast & Chandler, 2005). Is the teacher in the cartoon demonstrating back-to-the-wall technique?

Scanning

Good teachers have developed the habit of constantly sweeping the teaching area with their eyes, even when they are providing feedback to a student, so that they are always aware of what their students are doing. In the beginning it is a good idea to consciously scan a class. You may find it easier to scan from side to side, taking 8 to 10 seconds to find out what the students are doing. With practice, this becomes automatic. You must always be vigilant, watching all of the students in your class.

Visitor Observation

A helpful technique is to ask yourself as you scan, What would a visitor think if she walked into my class right now? Think of the principal of your school, one of your university professors, a member of the board of education, or a parent or guardian as you scan. This can help you place observation in perspective and avoid the tunnel vision that mesmerizes teachers so that they see only one or two children and fail to see that many of the others have drifted off task.

We have seen basketball dribbling lessons in which the teacher focused on a poorly skilled student, only to look up several moments later to discover that several in the class had turned the dribbling lesson into a shooting and slam dunk contest. Thinking about visitors' observation can help you remember the importance of constantly being aware of every student in the class.

TECH TIPS Using Video in Your Lessons

Video clips can be very helpful during lessons. You can use video projects that your students created in the previous years or videos you create to demonstrate exceptional practice. Video clips can be shown in many ways, including connecting your computer to a TV or your phone to a streaming device such as Apple TV or Chromecast. Another option is using a computer linked to a projector.

One Component at a Time

Observing a movement to detect errors and provide constructive suggestions is not an easy teaching skill to acquire (Coker, 1998). Some would argue that it is one of the most difficult. One technique that can help you become a better observer is to select only one cue (critical element) at a time to observe. Rather than attempting to watch a learner perform and pick out all errors, select an important cue from the cue column of your lesson plan grid to observe from your lesson plan as detailed in chapter 4. Assign a task, and then watch to see whether the students incorporate the cue into their movement patterns. If they use the cue correctly, then focus your observation on a different cue (critical element). Why focus on something the student already knows? If you observe that many of the youngsters would benefit from focusing on a given cue, emphasize it and provide specific, congruent feedback (chapter 9) related to their use of that critical element.

For example, in a kicking lesson for first-graders, you might focus on using the inside of the foot rather than the toe (S1.E21.2; SHAPE America, 2014). In a lesson focusing on striking with hockey sticks for fourth-graders, you might focus on having the students keep the ball close as they dribble it around the field (S1.E25.4; Graham, Holt/Hale, & Parker, 2012; SHAPE America, 2014). Focus on only these components during observation until you are satisfied that your students understand them and are incorporating them into their movements; then move on to another critical element.

What Works for Beginners Works for Experienced Teachers!

When I (GG) watch beginning teachers, one of the things I realize is how difficult it is for the novice to see all that is going on in a physical education class. For this reason I recommended that they observe only one component at a time. Soon after, I observed only one component at a time in my own teaching. What a difference it made—and I wasn't a novice! It's not only easier but also more effective, and both the teacher and the student are much clearer about exactly what is being taught in that part of the lesson.

Four Key Content Development Questions

As we have already said many times, teaching is so complex that it isn't possible to focus on one teaching skill at a time—pedagogical skills are interwoven. The teaching skills of observation and analysis are no different. You must constantly watch students and ask questions. Figure 5.1 presents observation questions that should continually be on teachers' minds. The questions are listed in order of priority.

Are Students Working Safely?

As a teacher, you must constantly ask yourself whether your students are working safely (chapters 2 and 10). Obviously, the content of some lessons (e.g., gymnastics) will require that you ask this question more frequently. With so many students in a class, however, there is a constant need to observe for safety. It is a question that should never leave your mind.

Are Students On Task?

Teachers who spend time at the beginning of the year developing management protocols (chapters 2 and 10) probably need to ask this question less than others do. Some classes also stay on task better than others do. Nevertheless, this is a question that you should ask a number of times during every lesson. Experienced teachers ask this question subconsciously because they have developed a teaching sense that lets them know when something is awry almost as soon as it occurs, even when they are not directly observing students in that area.

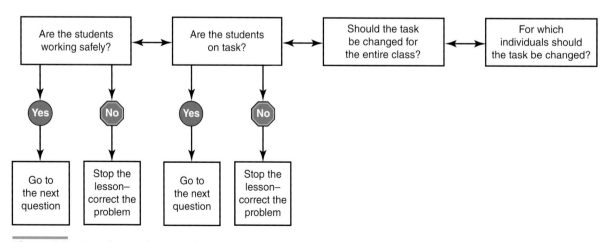

Figure 5.1   Key observation questions.

Adapted, by permission, from G. Graham, S. Holt/Hale, and M. Parker, 2012, *Children moving: A reflective approach to teaching physical education,* 9th ed. (New York, NY: McGraw-Hill), 121. © The McGraw-Hill Companies.

Is the Task Appropriate?

Another question, typically asked after the first two, relates directly to content development: Is the task or activity appropriate? Can students work at an 80 percent success rate so that they continue to be motivated to practice (chapter 8)? Does the entire class need a cue, or can you work with students individually to provide feedback? Teachers in student-centered programs of physical education ask this question constantly. Because each lesson varies from class to class, you need to continually observe to see whether the task is appropriate and helpful, using your written lesson plan as a guide (chapter 4).

How Are Students Using the Critical Element?

In the hypothetical observation schema in figure 5.1, once you have determined that the students are safe and on task and that the task is appropriate, the next question concerns the use of the critical element you are teaching. Initially, you might observe the entire class and then focus on individuals. For example, if the entire class is hitting tennis balls, you might observe to see whether they are turning their sides as they hit forehands and backhands. If they are, then you would decide not to focus on moving their feet to turn their sides to the target. You would choose another critical element (cue) from your lesson plan grid such as following through to the target.

Observing Individuals

In addition to observing the entire class to make decisions about the appropriateness of an activity, you must also observe individuals to determine how you can help them perform skills more efficiently. Done well, this is a lot harder than it sounds.

It's not enough simply to understand and analyze a movement. You must also make decisions about which cues and feedback the students will benefit from the most. The thoughts of Harvey Penick, a master golf teacher, are helpful for placing this discussion in perspective: "There are six different ways to make a [golf] grip weaker or stronger. You can raise or lower the hands. You can change the ball position, close or open the clubface, or adjust the hands on the club. There's no right answer for everyone" (Wade, 1989, p. 144). Once you have chosen the content of your feedback, Mr. Penick offers this sage advice: "You have to make corrections in your game a little bit at a time. It's like medicine: A few aspirin will probably cure what ails you, but the whole bottle might just kill you" (p. 144).

As we ponder Mr. Penick's comments, we can't help but wonder what he would suggest to physical education teachers who are responsible for teaching 25 to 30 students in a single class. We don't know. We do think he would agree that analyzing movement is a difficult task even under ideal circumstances. Clearly, the ability to provide feedback (chapter 9) and develop a logical progression of experiences based on observation is important. It allows you to provide the shortcuts and the proper foundations for productive practice that can lead to the eventual enjoyment of physical activity in adulthood.

Observing Classes for Content Development

We hope that, after reading the first part of this chapter, you are convinced that observation is a critical part of teaching. We also hope that you understand how challenging the practice of observation is to acquire. Although you may plan multiple tasks for any given class or grade level, you must select only those that the students need, rather than every learning task on your lesson plan. Presenting every task on your lesson plan grid (chapter 4), regardless of student needs or interests, is an example of subject-centered teaching.

A dynamic approach to content development based on student abilities and interests is to start with one of the tasks on your lesson plan (it may not be the first one) and then adjust its degree of difficulty as needed. The lesson plan grid in figure 4.3 in chapter 4 includes a progression of dribbling tasks and adaptations. You might have the students in one second-grade class dribble around their poly spots while those in another class start by dribbling around the gym or playground. Why? Because you know your students (from observation) and can adapt your lessons based on their abilities.

The next part of teaching from your lesson plan grid is to decide which task, cue, or challenge will work best with a given class. We know that it would be a lot easier to just go row by row from your lesson plan grid—task, cue, challenge, and then the next row. We also know, as do you, that this is not good teaching. So how do teachers develop the content from their lesson plans?

To provide productive practice, you have essentially three choices based on your observations (formative assessment) of the students in your class:

- Change a learning task (drill or activity) to make it easier or harder.
- Focus on how to do the task by providing cues that will make the students more efficient movers.
- Provide a challenge to give students an opportunity to test their abilities and motivate them to continue working on the task.

These three choices are challenging because classes vary, as do students' ability levels within a class (Graham et al., 1992). It would be much easier if all classes and students were identical! Then you could use a clock to determine when to change from one task to another rather than observing the students to assess how well they are grasping what you are teaching. However, clocks are poor judges of how long youngsters need to practice a given skill and which skill they need to practice next. Providing experiences that are developmentally appropriate requires that you constantly observe the students and make decisions about how to develop the content so that the progression of tasks is appropriate.

A number of content development patterns evolve as teachers work with different classes. A brief description of these patterns might help you better understand how teachers vary tasks, cues, and challenges. To aid understanding, these patterns can be graphed with a tool as shown in figure 5.2. The vertical axis contains tasks, cues, and challenges. The horizontal axis simply numbers each task, cue, or challenge to clarify the pattern of use. You can use this tool to identify your own content development pattern with the help of an observer (or you can make your own observations if you record one of your lessons and watch it). Each time you stop the entire class, the observer writes down what you say (summarizes the key points) and codes it later as a task, cue, or challenge. Later you can analyze the form completed by the observer to interpret your pattern of content development for that lesson.

All-Task Pattern

When initially working with classes, teachers often switch from one task to another very quickly. This occurs as the teacher attempts to discover the skill level of the students in that class (figure 5.3). This pattern is also observed frequently with beginning teachers who have yet to use challenges to keep students working at the same drill. Instead, they

FIGURE 5.2 Assessing Your Pattern of Content Development

Teacher's name _____ Observer _____

Class taught _____ Date _____

Lesson focus _____

Directions: Write down the statements the teacher makes to the entire class (not to groups or individuals) about motor skills (not about behavior or management). At times you may need to abbreviate, but try to capture the teacher's meaning. When the lesson is over, classify each statement as a task, cue, or challenge. Then graph the statements in the order in which they occurred. You may need to use the back of the sheet to record all of the statements.

1. _____

2. _____

3. _____

4. _____

5. _____

6. _____

7. _____

8. _____

9. _____

10. _____

(continue on back)

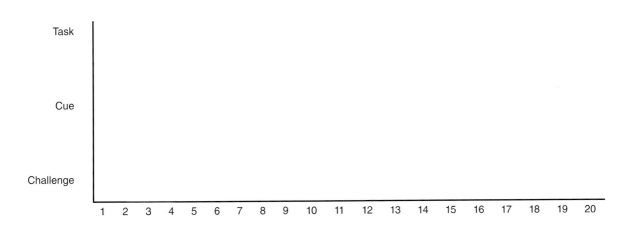

FIGURE 5.3   All-Task Pattern of Content Development

Teacher's name Ron   Observer Julie

Class taught Mrs. Speck's second grade   Date December 5

Lesson focus Dribbling with hands

Directions: Write down the statements the teacher makes to the entire class (not to groups or individuals) about motor skills (not about behavior or management). At times you may need to abbreviate, but try to capture the teacher's meaning. When the lesson is over, classify each statement as a task, cue, or challenge. Then graph the statements in the order in which they occurred. You may need to use the back of the sheet to record all of the statements.

1. Bounce the ball with two hands; stay on your carpet square.

2. Bounce the ball with one hand; stay on your carpet square.

3. Bounce the ball at a low level only; stay on your carpet square.

4. Bounce the ball with your other hand; stay on your carpet square.

5. Walk around your carpet square and dribble the ball.

6. Walk in general space and dribble the ball.

7. Walk in general space and dribble the ball at a low level.

8. Jog and dribble in general space.

9. Skip and dribble in general space.

10. When the drum beats, stop traveling but continue dribbling.

(continue on back)

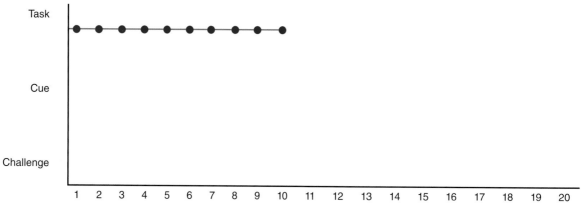

make the task harder when they think students are becoming bored, rather than providing them with a challenge while keeping the task the same.

Task-Cue-Task-Cue Pattern

Another common content development pattern is a repetition of task, cue, task, cue, and so on (figure 5.4). In this instance you might be reviewing previously taught tasks. If a lesson is not a review, however, and if the cue is different each time, this suggests that students might not be actually learning (understanding) the cues because they are not spending enough time to grasp the cues so that they remember them in the future. This is probably what happened for many adults today who failed to grasp the concept of opposition when throwing. In short, the teachers weren't observing their students' progress and devoting the time needed for their classes to internalize the concept of opposition.

Task-Cue-Cue-Challenge Pattern

The pattern of starting a task, followed by instruction and demonstration of the same cue several times, followed by a challenge (figure 5.5) suggests that a teacher is truly developing the content so that students can learn it (i.e., emphasizing the quality of the movement and keeping them on the same task because it is appropriate for their ability level). This pattern is often observed in experienced teachers who are familiar with the process of content development and who strive to help their students learn critical skill components (Masser, 1987).

Interpreting Content Development Patterns

You can observe and analyze a pattern of content development rather easily to determine how you are developing the content in a class. The patterns, however, provide information only about the number of tasks, cues, and challenges and their sequence. That's helpful to know.

It's at least as important, however, to make a judgment about the quality of the tasks, cues, and challenges. Simply using a particular content development pattern doesn't determine the quality of the lesson. The pattern always needs to be interpreted within the context of the lesson, considering such factors as students' skill level and experience, the number of times you have taught the skill previously, and the progression in which you presented the tasks.

In addition, you can judge the quality of tasks, cues, and challenges in terms of their appropriateness and effectiveness. Did the pattern work with that class? Why? Why not? How might you improve it? These decisions are based on the way the students are moving, as determined through observation. Let's assume that you record a lesson and then review it that evening at home. You might ask yourself these questions:

- Did the class understand and use the cues emphasized during the lesson? Were they actually moving quickly to the ball (a cue for that lesson)? If I ask them in two weeks (or six months), will they remember the cue?

- Was the cue appropriate? Was it the one they really needed at that point in their skill development?

- Was the progression of tasks too hard? Too easy? (Look at the success rate of the students and also make a judgment about their interest in the tasks.)

FIGURE 5.4 Task-Cue-Task-Cue Pattern of Content Development

Teacher's name __Kakki__   Observer __Marilyn__

Class taught __Ms. Bray's second grade__   Date __December 5__

Lesson focus __Dribbling with hands__

Directions: Write down the statements the teacher makes to the entire class (not to groups or individuals) about motor skills (not about behavior or management). At times you may need to abbreviate, but try to capture the teacher's meaning. When the lesson is over, classify each statement as a task, cue, or challenge. Then graph the statements in the order in which they occurred. You may need to use the back of the sheet to record all of the statements.

1. Walk around your carpet square and dribble your ball.

2. Use your finger pads, not your palms.

3. Walk in general space and dribble the ball.

4. Look over the ball.

5. Walk in general space and dribble the ball at a low level.

6. Look over the ball.

7. Jog and dribble in general space.

8. Try to push the ball ahead of you.

9. Skip and dribble in general space.

10. Try to push the ball ahead of you.

(continue on back)

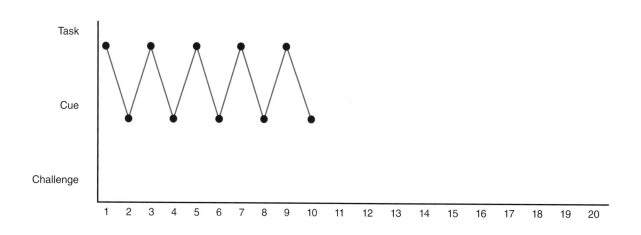

FIGURE 5.5 Task-Cue-Cue-Challenge Pattern of Content Development

Teacher's name __Steve__   Observer __Vickie__

Class taught __Ms. Sanders' 2nd grade__   Date __December 5__

Lesson focus __Dribbling with hands__

Directions: Write down the statements the teacher makes to the entire class (not to groups or individuals) about motor skills (not about behavior or management). At times you may need to abbreviate, but try to capture the teacher's meaning. When the lesson is over, classify each statement as a task, cue, or challenge. Then graph the statements in the order in which they occurred. You may need to use the back of the sheet to record all of the statements.

1. Walk in *general space* and dribble the ball.

2. Use your finger pads, not your palms.

3. Look over the ball.

4. When I hold up my fingers, tell me how many.

5. Jog and dribble in general space.

6. Look over the ball.

7. Try to push the ball ahead of you.

8. When you pass someone, call out his or her name.

9. Skip and dribble in general space.

10. Look over the ball.

(continue on back)

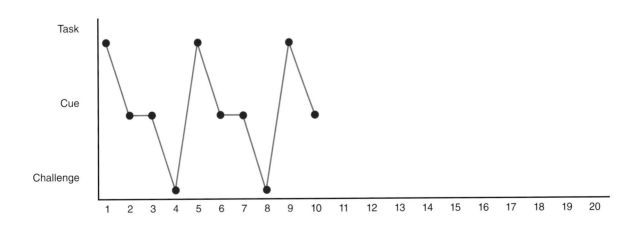

- Were tasks changed unnecessarily or too quickly? (This could happen if you had taught the same skill to five or six classes in a row and were tired of it, but the students were not.)
- Did the challenges motivate the students to practice longer?
- Were the tasks appropriate for accomplishing the objective for the lesson? Did they provide plenty of appropriate practice?

When you view a video in the relative solitude of your office or home, you can see many more things than you can during the turmoil of teaching. This is the time to truly evaluate the quality of your content development.

At the secondary level especially, teachers often focus on a cue or two in a lesson and then place the students in a game that requires them to use the cue during the game. For example, the teacher might be emphasizing keeping the body between the ball and a defender in a basketball or soccer setting. Then the students are divided into small-sided games (4v4). Once the small-sided games commence, the teacher continues to reinforce the cue of keeping the body between the ball and the defender. This also becomes the basis for feedback (chapter 9). All too often, however, once the games begin, teachers never mention the cue again. How effective is that?

Fun

Before we conclude these three chapters on planning, it seems important to discuss fun as a purpose for physical education lessons. Clearly, no one is against youngsters having fun in any class—math, science, or physical education (Griffin, Chandler, & Sariscany, 1993). When you can make learning enjoyable, it seems better for both you and your students. Because of the nature of the content we teach, it is not terribly difficult to make physical education fun—at least for many students in a class. Problems occur when fun becomes the sole purpose of physical education (Griffin, Chandler, & Sariscany, 1993).

If physical education class is nothing more than a time to have fun or a break from the classroom, it becomes increasingly difficult to justify its inclusion in a school curriculum. This is especially true as pressure increases for youngsters to pass standards in subjects such as reading, social studies, and science. Few question the value and importance of physical education as expressed in the national standards (SHAPE America, 2014). Fun, however, is not a standard! It is a by-product of an effective, developmentally appropriate program. When physical educators are forced to defend the existence of a physical education program to a school board, fun is never used as the sole reason for not eliminating or reducing physical education. Increasingly, administrators and parents and guardians want to be convinced that youngsters are learning in school—no matter what the subject. Physical education has valid and important goals for youngsters (SHAPE America, 2014). When these goals are achieved in enjoyable ways, few would suggest eliminating a program. When a program's goal is all fun, with no obvious learning taking place, most would suggest that physical education can be replaced by recess or play after school.

Unfortunately, many consider art, music, and physical education to be curricular frills—thus, it is increasingly important to make teachers accountable for what youngsters are learning in these subjects (chapter 13). In contrast, subjects such as reading and math are considered core subjects that every student needs to learn. Thus, teachers who create fun reading or math classes that result in little or no student learning are also apt to find themselves under scrutiny from parents, guardians, and principals. School is meant to be enjoyable, but learning is expected and standards are to be met, and teachers are increasingly being held accountable for doing so.

The bottom line in teaching physical education is that students should be *learning*! As a result of the time they spend in physical education, it is reasonable to expect a permanent change of behavior—that is, they should become better runners, throwers, catchers, jumpers, balancers, batters, and so on. Historically in physical education, the content, and the way it was delivered (pedagogy), has not led to children becoming skilled movers. This may be because not much time appears to have been directed to skill learning (McKenzie et al., 2006). The traditional model of doing calisthenics, running a lap, doing a drill or two, and playing a game has resulted in failure for too many. If you need proof, just observe a high school or college physical education class in which students need to throw and catch a ball. You will see far too many of the students, most of whom had elementary school physical education, who are unable to throw or catch a ball in game situations.

Summary

Subject-centered physical education differs markedly from student-centered physical education, which relies heavily on observation techniques, including back to the wall, scanning, visitor observation, and one component at a time. To develop the content in written lesson plans, you must always observe for safety first. Your next tasks are to see whether the students are on task, whether the task is appropriate for the skill level of the students (too hard, too easy), and how individual students are doing.

These four observation techniques and four guiding questions determine whether a different task, cue, or challenge would be appropriate. Student-centered teachers employ a variety of content development patterns as they teach their lessons. Three patterns are all-task, task-cue-task-cue, and task-cue-cue-challenge; a grid can be used to analyze them. Determining the quality of content development patterns is also important.

Fun is important in any learning situation. However, fun without learning does not result in a quality educational program.

Questions for Reflection

1. In some ways observing a class of students can be compared to watching a team sport—it's difficult to see everything that is happening. Describe the strategies you might use to observe a team sport and then compare them to observing a physical education class.

2. Provide two examples of subject-centered teaching from your experience. They don't have to be from physical education.

3. Give an example of subject-centered teaching in a sport such as soccer, hockey, or softball. Describe three changes you could make to make the lesson more student centered.

4. The chapter describes four observation techniques. Which one do you think is the easiest to use? The hardest? Why?

5. Observing one cue (critical element) at a time seems obvious. Why do you think teachers tend to try to observe many components simultaneously?

6. The chapter also describes four key observation questions. Which one of those do you think is the easiest to use? The hardest? Why?

7. The chapter describes several content development patterns. Use a blank form from the web resource to make up your own content development pattern, and describe a situation in which it might be helpful.

8. Think of the sports or activities you know best and those you know least about. Do you think your observation skills might be different during these sports or activities? How do you plan to observe in areas with which you are unfamiliar?

References

Arbogast, G., & Chandler, J.P. (2005). Class management behaviors of effective physical educators. *Strategies, 19* (1), 7-11.

Coker, C.A. (1998). Observation strategies for skill analysis. *Strategies, 11* (4), 17-19.

Davidovitch, N. (2013). Learning-centered teaching and backward course design—From transferring knowledge to teaching skills. *Journal of International Education Research, 9* (4), 329-338.

Graham, G., Castenada, R., Hopple, C., Manross, M., & Sanders, S. (1992). Developmentally appropriate physical education for children: A position statement of the Council on Physical Education for Children (COPEC). Reston, VA: National Association for Sport and Physical Education.

Graham, G., Holt/Hale, S., & Parker, M. (2012). *Children moving* (9th ed.). New York, NY: McGraw-Hill.

Griffin, L.L., Chandler, T.J.L., & Sariscany, M.J. (1993). What does "fun" mean in physical education? *Journal of Physical Education, Recreation and Dance, 64* (9), 63-66.

Hall, T.J., & Smith, M.A. (2006). Teacher planning, instruction and reflection: What we know about teacher cognitive processes. *Quest, 58* (4), 424-442.

Hautala, R.M. (1989). The tape recorder teacher. *Journal of Physical Education, Recreation and Dance, 60* (2), 25-28.

Masser, L. (1987). The effect of a refinement on student achievement in a fundamental motor skill in grades K through 6. *Journal of Teaching in Physical Education, 6,* 174-182.

McKenzie, T.L., Catellier, D.J., Conway, T., Lytle, L.A., Grieser, M., Webber, L.A., Pratt, C.A., & Elder, J.P. (2006). Girls' activity levels and lesson contexts in middle school PE: TAAG baseline. *Medicine & Science in Sports & Exercise, 38* (7), 1229-1235.

SHAPE America. (2014). *National standards & grade-level outcomes for K-12 physical education.* Champaign, IL: Human Kinetics.

Wade, D. (1989, July). An interview with Harvey Penick—golf teacher for Tom Kite and Ben Crenshaw. *Golf Digest,* 144-147.

Getting the Lesson Started

> "The first graders were doing a warm up game at the beginning of class and one student must have tweaked his ankle because he came limping off and said he needed to sit out because he broke his foot. About 3 minutes later he jumped up and said, "My foot is fixed, I can come back now."

Dan Fallon,
Conway Elementary School,
Conway, New Hampshire

After reading this chapter, you should be able to do the following:

- Describe techniques for involving students in activity as soon as they enter the gym or playground.
- Present the pros and cons of instant activity.
- Explain the purpose of and techniques related to set induction and lesson scaffolding.
- Discuss the roles of calisthenics and lap running as introductory activities.

The children are in their classroom. Eyes glance at the clock. It's 10:25 a.m. PE begins at 10:30. Then they'll have 30 minutes to move, play, and escape the confines of the classroom. Hearts beat faster as they move toward the gym. Some feel as if they are going to burst with excitement as they anticipate exploding into movement.

These feelings are characteristic of some elementary school children (we hope the majority) immediately before physical education class. The way the teacher begins the lesson will determine how the children feel in a few minutes.

Just like elementary school children, some teens are also eager for physical education class to begin. Others, however, may be less eager, and a few may be unhappy that they have to endure another physical education class. Thus, at the middle and high school levels, the beginning of a lesson is equally, or more, important for students (Smith & St. Pierre, 2009). This chapter explores successful ways of beginning physical education classes.

Instant Activity

Most children, and hopefully most teens, come to physical education class ready to move. They want to be active, not to listen to the teacher talk. Others, particularly middle and high school students, come to PE feeling tired and lethargic. An instant activity is a great way to wake students up, warm them up, or get the wiggles out. As soon as they arrive at the gym door or in the outdoor space, encourage them to begin moving. This is one of the protocols to teach at the beginning of the year (chapter 2).

The content of the instant activity may be related to that day's lesson, or it may be a review of something done in the past. You can use the introductory activity to provide skills or routine practice in relatively short spurts (e.g., jumping rope) or as a warm-up for the lesson.

Why Instant Activity?

Some physical educators are concerned that students will be out of control if they don't enter the gym and sit down quietly before moving. As we watch teachers who begin their classes with instant activity, we rarely find this to be true. After a few minutes of vigorous activity, students seem far more ready to listen to instruction. Instant activities also encourage teens to leave the locker room and start the lesson, especially if there are choices that appeal to a wide range of abilities and interests. It's important to remember, however, that you need to have taught your students how to begin each lesson during the first few days of the school year (chapter 2).

In contrast, we have observed teachers require students to enter the gym or outdoor space and sit quietly on a line, or in squads, before any activity can begin. Often, several minutes are wasted because students are so eager to begin moving that their squirming and fidgeting leads to talking and pushing, which means they have to try to sit quietly even longer.

Another advantage of instant activity is that it can be a time for students to talk to you and even one another without disrupting the entire class. As any elementary teacher will attest, especially in the primary grades, there is always a child or two who wants to tell you about something that happened at home since the last class: the new TV, the lost tooth, the baby sister, the puppies, the accident down the street, the game over the weekend, or a new video game.

Teens often want to share their experiences or concerns. Some want to share what happened at a hockey tournament the past weekend, whereas others want to share some of the problems they're having with their friends or family, how they struggled on their driving test, or even concerns about climate change. A few minutes of activity at the beginning of the class allow some students to share a few moments with you privately while the rest of the class is moving.

How Long Should the Instant Activity Last?

The short answer is "As long as it takes." Other than waking up or warming up students or getting their wiggles out, the instant activity is intended to prepare them to learn. In general, a couple of minutes can do it, although sometimes you may need the instant activity to run five minutes or more. Other times, one minute of high-intensity activity is what it takes for your students to be ready to focus on the day's lesson. It all depends on your students, although some things, whether superstition or reality, can dictate how long your instant activity lasts. It may need to last longer when there's a full moon, on windy days, on November 1 (the day after Halloween), following a long weekend, as a holiday approaches, close to homecoming, on picture day, on rainy days, or before a big football game for the school team. Just be ready to make that decision according to your observation prior to class starting and during the instant activity—don't feel you have to follow a set formula for length.

TECH TIPS QR Codes for Instant Activities

Using QR codes to introduce instant activities is a good way to get students moving as soon as they enter the gym and keep them on task for the next several minutes. Post four to six QR codes of various colors around the room. Assign students a color to begin, and instruct them to rotate around the gym counterclockwise, completing each activity described by the QR code. You will need a smart device provided by the school (e.g., iPad, iPod, smartphones) and a free QR reader downloaded from the device app store (some schools allow students to carry and use their personal devices, which can be used for this as well). Make sure there are enough smart devices for every student. Consider having students work in groups to reduce the number of devices needed. Creating QR codes is simple and quick. Visit any free QR generator site (www.qrstuff.com) and enjoy making your own codes. *Helpful hint:* If you have limited Wi-Fi access, create text QR codes only; these can also be used outside.

Communicating the Instant Activity to Students

You can use posters, bulletin boards, verbal reminders, student-designed routines, and music to involve your students in activity as quickly as possible.

Posters and Bulletin Boards

Depending on the physical setting, you can post bulletin boards inside the gym that tell students how to begin (e.g., *Get a rope and work on your jump rope routine*). You can also use posters with instructions such as these posted outside the gym:

Poster Instructions for Elementary School Students
- If your last name begins with the letters A to L, practice your partner sequence on the mats.
- If your last name begins with M to Z, find a ball and practice a dribbling routine.
- When the music stops, put equipment away and sit on the center circle.

Poster Instructions for Middle School and High School Students

- Get any equipment you like from the equipment at the four corners of the gym and get active on your own or with one or more of your classmates.
- When you hear the signal, begin the team warm-ups that you designed last class.

Written instructions work well. One of the advantages of providing a variety of tasks (rather than the same task for the entire class) is that it encourages students to read the poster or bulletin board rather than simply checking to see what the first few to arrive are doing.

 Instant Activity The web resource includes a video that provides a brief description of instant activity along with examples of how teachers direct youngsters to begin the class.

Verbal Reminders

Of course, many younger children are not yet reading. In this case, make sure to use instant activities the students are familiar with and can begin quickly without instruction. Verbal reminders of how students will begin the next class, given at the end of the lesson, can also work well. For example, you might say: "Next class, the scoops and the balls will be against the wall. As soon as you come in, find a scoop and a ball and start throwing and catching to yourself." Depending on the number of days between classes, some students will forget. But there are always a few who will remember, and they quickly remind the others. This is one of the routines you should practice at the beginning of the year, so youngsters learn to listen carefully so they can remember how the next class will start.

Like younger children, some teens will remember instructions from the preceding class, and some won't. For example, during the first two lessons in a mountain bike unit, you might teach students how to conduct a safety check and ride. Students learn to check their bikes' brakes, chain, and tires and the condition of their helmets prior to riding a short safety loop on flat ground to verify the safe working condition of their bike. At the beginning of the following class, you can then give a verbal reminder such as "safety check and ride" to prompt the students to use that routine as the instant activity.

Student-Designed Routines

The instant activity routine can also be designed by students. At the elementary school, teachers often have students design their own games that make for fun instant activities. For example, during a lesson on throwing, you could give each group of students a box of equipment (five balls of different kinds, six cones, three jump ropes, two rubber chickens, eight spots) with the instructions to design and name their own throwing games. On arriving to class the following day or week, prompt the students to pick up their boxes of equipment and play the games they designed during the last class for the instant activity.

The same approach can be taken with secondary students. Each student can develop and write up a personal warm-up routine that includes some running and a circuit of exercises such as crunches, push-ups, pull-ups, and box jumps. They can then use their routines as the instant activity for the remaining days of that unit. As part of a lacrosse unit, teams that you assign might develop and write out their own 5- to 10-minute practices on one day of the unit. They can then use these team practices as the instant activity for subsequent lessons in the unit.

Music

Another option is to start your classes with music. The music is on when students arrive, and they do the instant activity until the music stops. An advantage to using music is that it provides a relatively consistent guide for the length of an introductory activity. Most songs range from two to three minutes, which is adequate time for students to move before beginning the instructional part of the lesson. This is also a time-saving opportunity to take attendance in secondary schools. Music motivates most students and therefore helps to get them moving, but remember to select music wisely by reviewing for inappropriate lyrics. Allowing a student to select the music for the next class can be an effective reward for good behavior, but make sure to review all music before incorporating it into your lesson. PE Central, a website for K-12 physical educators (www.pecentral.org), contains a variety of instant activity suggestions.

Communicating the Purpose of the Lesson

After a few minutes, the instant activity ends. Students should then gather around you and listen quietly for instruction about the day's lesson. As part of your protocol for beginning a class, you might have students sit in a circle with you. Another option is to simply ask the students to come over and stand or sit by you. This is the time to explain the purpose of the day's lesson (Dyson & Pine, 1996).

Set induction and scaffolding aid students in understanding how lessons interconnect and how they relate to their lives today—and still will in 20 years. These strategies shouldn't take much time but are most helpful in answering these important questions: "What is the purpose of physical education?" and "Why are we doing this stuff?"

Set Induction

To be a successful teacher, you need to do more than simply tell your students what they will be doing in the lesson. You must find ways to provoke their interest and enthusiasm so that they are eager to become involved in your lessons. The technical term for this teaching strategy is *set induction* (it is also called *cognitive set* or *anticipatory set*).

 Set Induction The web resource that accompanies this text provides a brief description of the set induction along with examples of different set inductions delivered by K-12 teachers.

The purpose of set induction is to motivate students so that they become interested in the lesson and understand its purpose, thereby encouraging them to practice efficiently and eagerly. Set induction has the advantage of helping them understand why they will be doing certain activities or tasks during a lesson. In some ways it is also a preview to the lesson (Dyson & Pine, 1996). Others suggest that it is a way of marketing the lesson to a class (Weiller, 1992).

TECH TIPS Create Animated Presentations

Do you want to use a short presentation on your Smart Board to introduce the lesson content? As an alternative to PowerPoint, try PowToon, a free source that allows you to create a two- to three-minute animated presentation. PowToon allows you to use its bank of images, sounds, and words as well as upload your own music, pictures, and even voice. Students also enjoy creating PowToons.

The following are examples of set inductions teachers have used to heighten students' interest in a lesson:

- "When you jump, how quietly can you land? Can you land as quietly as a cat? A feather? Today I want to help you practice quiet landings."
- "Do you remember which test we did last week? Right. The pull-up test to assess upper-body strength. The purpose of today's lesson is to find ways we can improve our upper-body strength when we're at home watching TV."
- "When you play a basketball game, does anyone ever steal the ball from you? In today's lesson we are going to practice two secrets to help you keep others from stealing the ball."
- Stand 10 feet (3 m) from a wall and hit a ball to the wall with a racket 10 times without a miss. Then say, "In today's lesson I want to show you two cues that helped me become a good tennis player."
- "Do you ever get mad at your friends when you're playing a game? Do you ever say mean things to one another? The purpose of today's lesson is to understand why we say mean things to others and to find some ways to avoid making our friends feel bad."
- "If someone told you they'd give you $5 if you made a basket from anywhere you like, where would you choose to shoot from? Why? Your odds of making a shot are much better the closer you are to the hoop. The purpose of today's lesson is to use screens and offensive strategies so that your team can get a shot closer to the hoop during game play."
- Sticking three pencils in a ball of clay, ask the class what you can do to make the object stand up in a strong position. Students eventually come to widening the base of support and lowering the ball of clay. Then say, "In today's lesson, we are going to use these same ideas of base of support and center of gravity for partner balances and stunts."

All too often, teachers know the purpose of the lesson, but the students don't. You may discover this at the end of a lesson during closure (chapter 7) when you are sitting and talking with the class. You may discover that the students didn't really understand the purpose of the lesson and that they can't recall the key points of the objectives.

Using set inductions well can be difficult because you may teach so many classes a day, often on the same topic. After teaching four or five gymnastics lessons in a row, you may be ready to get on with the lesson rather than thinking about how to stimulate the interest of the students. You need to remember that the lesson is new for them, no matter how many times you have taught it.

What's Going on Here?

Watch the first five minutes of a PE lesson, either recorded or live. Try to enter the world of the students and view the beginning of the lesson from their eyes. Is the purpose of the lesson clear? Do you know what is going on? Would you be excited about the lesson?

Scaffolding

Have you ever been a student in a class and wondered, *What are we doing? I have no idea what the purpose of this lesson is and what point the teacher is trying to make. I'm lost.* Along with set induction, scaffolding is designed to communicate the purpose of a lesson and its relationship to past and future lessons. Scaffolding links a series of lessons in a unit or skill theme or, in some instances, the year. It is often difficult for students to realize that lessons are designed sequentially to help them better understand skills or concepts or sports (i.e., to realize that one lesson is related to another). By relating a lesson to past experiences, you help students understand it and place it in perspective.

This is especially important for children and youth because they live so much in the present. Children have difficulty understanding that practicing striking a ball with a racket might someday lead to easier, faster progress in tennis, badminton, or racquetball, or for teens to see the link between a sport and becoming or remaining active and fit for life. When you show them the interconnectedness of these activities, however, much as a scaffold is erected outside a building at the beginning of construction, you help them develop a schema (a mental outline) of the overall purpose of the series of lessons on a particular topic. If you have the advantage of teaching many students over several years, you can gradually fill in this scaffolding as you revisit lessons and units from year to year.

You can erect a physical education scaffolding for students in several ways, including posting your yearly plan, teaching PE vocabulary, and having students keep PE notebooks or logs.

Scaffolding   The web resource includes video demonstrations of scaffolding along with a brief description of this teaching technique.

Post the Yearly Plan

Some teachers, typically those who have taught at the same school for several years, post the yearly schedule (curriculum scope and sequence; see chapter 3) on a bulletin board. Doing this shows students the entire sequence of lessons and, with guidance, how they connect over the year. It also minimizes one of the most often-asked questions of physical education teachers as they interact with students in the halls and cafeteria: What are we going to do today in PE? As students enter the gym, a quick glance at the topic for the day tells them quickly what will be happening.

Although the idea of posting a yearly schedule is logical, you might have difficulty knowing exactly how long you will spend in activities throughout the year, especially if you are a beginning teacher or new to a school. After several years at the same school, however, you will develop a reasonably accurate portrait of the time needed to develop particular themes or units.

Physical Education Vocabulary

Another technique that helps youngsters, especially children, understand scaffolding for physical education is to display the program vocabulary on the wall of a gym or on a physical education bulletin board. This permits you not only to verbally tell the children about the lesson but also to show them the written terms. This is especially helpful when referring later to terms the students studied months earlier. It is also valuable for students who are just learning to read. You can share this vocabulary with classroom teachers to assist them in integrating physical education into the classroom.

Notebooks

If you teach in the upper grades (i.e., grade 4 and higher), you can have your students keep PE notebooks or logs. These have a variety of uses, but one is that they help students link lessons (units) by using the same terminology and concepts over a number of lessons.

Notebooks are useful for storing and referring to the following:

- Written descriptions or drawings of student-designed games, sequences, or dances that can be recalled in future lessons
- Completed worksheets on topics studied throughout the year (e.g., the names of muscles and bones)
- Individual heart rate monitor or pedometer results that can be used as a benchmark for measuring individual improvement
- Descriptions of how students feel about themselves and physical activity at various times
- Records of activity performed at home (e.g., minutes of physical activity versus minutes of watching television or playing video games)

Obviously, notebooks can be used at various times and in various ways. They are an aid to understanding the scaffolding of the overall physical education program and, in turn, the entire curriculum.

Traditional Ways to Start a Lesson

In concluding this chapter, we want to comment on how teachers have traditionally started lessons—with calisthenics and laps—and explain why some believe that we have better ways to begin physical education classes. Historically, some physical educators have started every class by having their students run a lap and then do calisthenics such as 20 jumping jacks, 20 push-ups, and 20 sit ups. Technically, this might be considered an instant activity. Clearly, however, there are many more enjoyable, developmentally appropriate, and effective ways to start a lesson than running laps and performing the same boring calisthenics all year long. Although some might argue that calisthenics and running laps have physical fitness benefits, the purpose of the instant activity is to make a transition from the classroom to the gym or outdoor space and to prepare students to learn.

TECH TIPS Attendance Apps

Taking attendance requires time, and time is nothing to waste when your students are with you for such a short period of time. Many attendance apps allow you to quickly mark students who are present that day, tardy, disruptive, and more. One example is the user-friendly Attendance app.

Calisthenics

Research has caused many to question the value of calisthenics as they were done in the past (i.e., the same calisthenics done as a warm-up routine to every class) (Branner, 1989; Graham et al., 1992). Calisthenics are a combination of stretching (traditionally static) and muscle exercises that do not require equipment (e.g., sit-ups, push-ups, jumping jacks, planks). We know today that there are many ways to warm up the body and that, ideally, calisthenics and stretches should be designed to prepare students' bodies to participate in a certain type of activity (Anderson, 1980).

We also know that some calisthenics, as done in the past, are simply bad practice, no matter when they're done. Straight-legged toe touches, straight-legged sit-ups, and sit-ups with the hands clasped behind the head are potentially harmful to children, and

adults for that matter (Anderson, 1980; Branner, 1989). Research has shown that static stretching before activity does not prevent injury (Weerapong, Hume, & Kolt, 2004). Also, many experts today recommend that stretching be performed as a cool-down to a lesson rather than as a warm-up. It can also help students relax or settle down before returning to class and has some fitness benefits such as increased flexibility.

As a result of this research, and also the limited amount of time available for physical education in many schools, some teachers simply skip calisthenics. Their instant activities serve as warm-ups for their lessons. Rather than doing calisthenics because they have traditionally been done at the beginning of physical education lessons, you can use them only when they have value for student learning. You should teach your students the correct way to use calisthenics as well as the reasons to use (or not use) them. For example, when teaching students about stretching and flexibility, you may focus on the difference between long, slow, static stretches and dynamic stretching movements, and when both are most appropriate (S3.M9.8; SHAPE America, 2014). High school classes may incorporate certain types of calisthenics in Tabata sets, high-intensity fitness workouts, or fitness stations. We are not saying that all calisthenics are bad. We are advocating for their use in appropriate contexts, not as instant activities to begin lessons.

Laps

Some teachers also question the value of running laps as a way to start physical education lessons. Three to five minutes of jogging (as in running laps), although perhaps beneficial as a warm-up, does not lead to improved cardiorespiratory fitness—that would take at least 15 minutes and perhaps more (S3.H10.L2; SHAPE America, 2014). Obviously, then, the purpose of running laps as a warm-up for your PE class is not to improve cardiorespiratory endurance. An instant activity can be a good alternative to running laps. Simply running not only is boring to students but also wastes time because students aren't really learning anything or benefiting from the activity.

You can have your students run laps to teach them to pace themselves so that they can run or jog for an extended period of time. As anyone who has ever tested students on a distance run will recall, those who haven't learned about pacing will run the first lap or so quickly, only to end up walking the last half of the distance. Focusing on pacing in running helps students understand the concept of running slowly at the beginning to avoid having to walk at the end.

Increasingly, elementary schools are providing opportunities for children to jog or walk vigorously at the beginning of the school day. Rather than having children sit for 15 or 20 minutes when they arrive at school, you can outline a course for children to walk or jog, and encourage them to do so. Such a program allows you to focus on the important skills, knowledge, dispositions, and behaviors that children need to learn. Parents and guardians, classroom teachers, and paraprofessionals are quite capable of supervising these before-school walk-jog programs.

As with calisthenics, we are not suggesting that running or jogging is not appropriate for your PE program. It most certainly is an important skill to teach, beginning with grade 2 when children are learning to run with a mature pattern (S1.E2.2a; SHAPE America, 2014) and to understand the difference between jogging and sprinting, and on to grade 8 when students should participate in a variety of self-selected aerobic activities outside of school and plan a program of cross-training that includes aerobic activity (S3. M4.8; SHAPE America, 2014). Running can be incorporated into a variety of fitness lessons, such as high-intensity training sessions with bouts of aerobic exercise coupled with strengthening exercise for high school students. The purpose of this section is to encourage you to think about why you are choosing calisthenics and laps—is it because it's the traditional way to begin your lesson, or do they have a purpose for student learning?

Summary

The first few minutes of a physical education lesson are important. When students come to class and their curiosity and understanding are stimulated immediately, the odds are increased that they will not only be eager participants but also learn from the lesson. Starting class with an instant activity helps by waking students up, getting the wiggles out, and getting them warmed up. A variety of methods can get your students into an instant activity, including posters, verbal reminders, student-designed routines, and music. Once students are ready to learn, tell them what they are going to learn and why during a set induction. The ways you involve your students in lessons, provoke their curiosity and intellect, and stimulate them to learn and practice go a long way toward setting the tone for your entire lesson—and your entire program.

Methods such as websites, bulletin boards, and student notebooks help to scaffold instruction for the entire year and program. This helps students grasp where they started and where they're going in class. Finally, it's important to remember that just because physical education classes have started a certain way in the past doesn't make it the best approach in today's schools. There are more efficient ways to take role, and starting classes with laps or calisthenics can be replaced by more developmentally and instructionally appropriate strategies that are considerate of every student's interests and abilities.

The examples and discussion in this chapter represent only a few of the ways you might begin a lesson and provoke your students' interest and involvement. We do not mean to suggest that there is one right way to begin a physical education lesson. There are many ways. The essence of this chapter is that the beginning of a lesson is important and that successful teachers devote time and energy to ensure that the opening relates to that day's lesson, lessons from the past, and future lessons. You can provoke students' eagerness for the day's lesson while also helping them understand how the lesson connects with what they did in past lessons and where the lesson will lead in the future.

Questions for Reflection

1. Try to recall how you felt when you had been in a classroom for several hours and it was finally time to go outside or to the gym. Describe your feelings and how you would react to instant activity as compared to having to sit and listen for the first few minutes.

2. Some teachers feel uncomfortable having students enter a gym and begin activity immediately without first talking to them. Why do you think this is true? How would teachers who ask their students to begin activity immediately differ in their feelings?

3. Set induction is commonly found in many aspects of our lives, including television, books, and lectures. Provide three examples that were motivating to you as a child and three that were motivating to you as a teen.

4. Think about the concept of set induction and how it might be used to stimulate students' interest in a lesson. What types of things do teachers say and do that students of different ages find interesting and exciting?

5. The strategy of providing students with a scaffold to help them understand the overall curriculum is something that good teachers do. Can you recall teachers who provided scaffolds? Do you remember some who didn't? Describe and analyze the differences for you as a learner.

6. What is your view of calisthenics and laps as ways to start a physical education lesson? Try to find someone with a contrasting view, and discuss your reasons for beginning lessons in a certain way.

References

Anderson, B. (1980). *Stretching*. Bolinas, CA: Shelter.

Branner, T.T. (1989). *The safe exercise handbook*. Dubuque, IA: Kendall/Hunt.

Dyson, B., & Pine, S. (1996). Start and end class right. *Strategies, 9* (6), 5-9.

Graham, G., Castenada, R., Hopple, C., Manross, M., & Sanders, S. (1992). Developmentally appropriate physical education for children: A position statement of the Council on Physical Education for Children (COPEC). Reston, VA: National Association for Sport and Physical Education.

SHAPE America. (2014). *National standards & grade-level outcomes for K-12 physical education*. Champaign, IL: Human Kinetics.

Smith, M.A., & St. Pierre, P.E. (2009). Secondary students' perceptions of enjoyment in physical education: An American and English perspective. *Physical Educator, 66* (4), 209-221.

Weerapong, P., Hume, P.A., & Kolt, G.S. (2004). Stretching: Mechanisms and benefits for sport performance and injury prevention. *Physical Therapy Reviews, 9* (4), 189-206.

Weiller, K.H. (1992). Successful learning = clear objectives. *Strategies, 5* (5), 5-8.

Instructing and Demonstrating

" I was teaching a lesson on the respiratory system and when we got to "epiglottis" a student raised his hand and said, "Miss Brooker, Epiglottis sounds like it should be on the menu at a fancy Italian Restaurant." "

Amanda Brooker,
Teague Park,
Caribou, Maine

Reprinted with permission from PE Central
(www.pecentral.org).

After reading this chapter, you should be able to do the following:

- Explain the differences between the two types of instruction: organizational and informational.
- List the guidelines for effective informational instruction.
- Describe the characteristics of effective demonstrations by teachers and students.
- Analyze the way classes spend their time in lessons.
- Explain pinpointing and how to use it effectively.
- Describe the technique of checking for understanding and its role in instructing and demonstrating.
- Discuss the role of play-teach-play as part of the instruction and demonstration process.
- Explain how videos and other technologies can heighten students' interest and understanding in physical education settings.

The lesson is four minutes old. As soon as the second-graders arrived at the playground, they were challenged to run and find different ways to jump over the carpet squares spread over the blacktop. The torrent of energy stored up after three hours in the classroom has erupted. Bursts of running interspersed with leaps, hops, giggles, and jumps demonstrate the children's exuberance at being outside in a space where movement is not only allowed but encouraged. To be able to move—unrestricted, free, emancipated for a few minutes from the confines imposed by walls, tables, and chairs—creates genuine joy. The song that has been playing on the tape player, "Jump" by Van Halen, ends. The children know this is the signal to stop and assemble around the teacher. They do so quickly, realizing that the teacher will not talk long and that they will be able to move shortly thereafter. Set induction and scaffolding are followed by a brief period of instruction and demonstration to help the children understand exactly what and how to practice. The children have no questions. On the signal "Go," they quickly gather their equipment and begin the first task.

This chapter focuses on two of the teaching skills used by the teacher in the preceding vignette: instructing and demonstrating. The ideas presented in the previous chapters, when implemented effectively, will help you arrive at the point in a lesson at which you can provide effective instruction and demonstration. As you have surely noticed, however, when students don't listen or stop when requested, the quality of instruction is virtually irrelevant—the students simply don't hear it. Before instruction and demonstration can be successful, no matter how adept you may be at this part of the teaching process, the students must have learned to pay attention to you—and they must be ready to do so. Once you have laid the groundwork (chapter 2), the students are ready to benefit from your information and demonstrations.

Instructing

Instructing is the process of providing information to the students primarily, but not exclusively, through talking. Over the years, many studies have analyzed physical education lessons. These studies, individually and collectively, present a clear picture: many PE teachers spend a lot of time talking, and many students spend a lot of time listening, waiting, and getting organized rather than in meaningful physical activity (Fairclough & Stratton, 2006; Metzler, 1985; Siedentop & Tannehill, 2000). Teachers need to talk, but in physical education classes, students need to move. This chapter addresses ways to communicate so that your students understand and learn without subtracting a lot of time from their opportunities to move.

For purposes of discussion, we have artificially divided instruction into two categories: organizational and informational. This is an oversimplification and also a false division, because the two are often intertwined. We hope, however, that this division will clarify the process teachers use to provide information to their students.

Organizational Instruction

One of the challenges of teaching physical education is organizing large groups of students in undefined spaces. Classrooms have chairs and desks—obvious places to sit. In contrast, outdoor spaces and gyms have lines and walls; grassy fields have a few trees and perhaps a backstop. What are the boundaries in a gym or on a playground or field? Where do students go for instruction? How do they avoid running into one another?

One type of instruction, organizational instruction, tells students what to do, with whom, where, and with what equipment. This is necessary at the beginning of most lessons and typically occurs after an introductory activity. When it is done with clarity, students understand and can proceed quickly to activity. You must, however, make sure your students have learned the management protocols outlined in chapter 2. If they haven't learned to follow protocols, have them practice them, because instructions and demonstrations will be ineffective if students are talking to their friends, playing with equipment, or moving around the gym.

Into the Great Beyond

One of the things taught in educational psychology classes is that young children have yet to develop adult concepts of space awareness. We are always reminded of this when we watch elementary school teachers describe a rather poorly marked general space. Typically, after the explanation, the teacher asks the children, "Do you understand where the boundaries are?" Twenty-nine six-year-old heads all bob "uh-huh" in unison. The teacher says, "Go." Ten seconds later, seven children are happily traveling beyond the boundaries without realizing they are out of bounds. A better way to check for understanding of boundaries might be to say, "When I say 'Go,' stand on a boundary line for today's lesson."

Organizational instruction doesn't tell students anything about how to throw a ball or perform a static stretch. It does tell them how activities can be done without interruption safely and enjoyably. Effective organizational instruction answers the Who? What? Where? and With whom? questions:

- Where will I do the activity? What are the boundaries?
- Will I do it alone or with others? How will my group be formed?
- Do I need any equipment? Where will I find it?
- When will I start? Stop? What do I do if I finish early?
- What if I have a question?

Obviously, this is a lot of information for any student—especially young children or those who are new to a program. One technique that will help you enhance the clarity of organizational instruction is to ask one or more students (depending on the activity) to show others how the task is done.

Asking students to walk through the organization might sound like a waste of time. In fact, it often saves time because the students can visualize how the activity is organized. This has the advantage of providing information both verbally (teacher explanation) and visually (student demonstration). This technique is critical for young children, especially at the beginning of the school year, and can also be helpful for secondary students in certain situations (Valentin, 2004; Weiss, Ebbeck, & Rose, 1992; Wiese-Bjornstal, 1993).

For example, after telling a class of third-graders that they will need to choose a partner, a ball, two cones, and a space away from others to begin their game, you can call on two of the students and talk them through the beginning of the task. You might say something like this:

Lois, would you please show us how to begin? Right. First she picks a partner—McKenzie. Now she and McKenzie pick a ball from the pile, get two cones, and find a spot by themselves. Now they're ready to begin their game. Thank you for showing us how to get organized for the game. When I walk by and tap you on the shoulder, please select your partner and begin.

The decision of whether to provide a student demonstration depends on the task and the class. If the class has done the task before and the students are good listeners, you may not need a demonstration.

In general, however, instructions about organization are clarified by demonstration. Good teachers often simultaneously show and tell organizational directions (i.e., they demonstrate while they talk). In time, students learn the shortcuts. The other day, for example, at the end of a lesson I (GG) was observing, the teacher said, "Now I need you in two seated lines." I wondered which of the many lines in the gym he meant. The children knew exactly. They quickly sat on two red lines by the door ready to move into the hallway.

TECH TIPS QR Codes for Video Demonstrations

During station work to practice skills, you can post QR codes that are linked to short video clips of the skill, including your own prerecorded instructions. This prevents you from having to repeat directions and gives the students an ongoing reminder of the station tasks and a visual image of correct execution.

Informational Instruction

Organizational instruction tells students what they are going to be doing. It doesn't tell them how to do the activity, however. Instruction about how to land from a jump, make a symmetrical shape, pace a distance run, play zone defense, or form a group we have classified as informational instruction. It has also been termed lesson presentation (Mustain, 1990).

Successful teachers follow four guidelines in providing skill (informational) instruction.

Teaching Is More Than Instructing

Instructing is one aspect of teaching. However, the general public considers it the total process of teaching. A teacher who is clever and witty is often considered effective. What experienced teachers know is that the real measure of success as a teacher is what the students are doing—and how they feel about what they are doing. This is what makes the difference in developing a love for physical activity. Motivating students to work hard and continue to practice requires much more than simply providing a clever set of instructions. If teaching and instructing were synonymous, this might be a book with one chapter!

1. One Idea at a Time

The first of the four guidelines is to keep it simple. For a novice, an explanation of how to grip a racket, how to move to the ball and prepare to swing, and then how to actually swing—in the same minilecture—is information overload, even for an adult (Schmidt & Wrisberg, 2008). You may have almost been hit by a car driven by someone who was texting while driving. The erratic driving occurred because the person couldn't focus on both texting and driving at the same time. We can switch our attention from one thing to another, but we cannot actually concentrate on two things at once. When you explain and demonstrate one idea at a time (e.g., a level swing), learners can better remember the concept and begin to incorporate it into their schemas. When you explain several concepts simultaneously, students can't figure out which one they should think about as they practice. Instruction about one idea at a time is especially effective when you then provide feedback about how students are (or are not) swinging (i.e., feedback that is congruent with the instruction; see chapter 9).

Obviously, in some instances you can successfully present more than one concept, especially when one of them is a review of a past lesson. Too often, however, teachers give learners far more information than they can process—even if they are trying to remember it all. The critical point here is that you are not demonstrating an entire skill or concept but rather one specific part (Oslin, Stroot, & Siedentop, 1997; Parson, 1998). This is not to say, however, that you should teach only one idea or concept in a lesson; you may teach several—but one at a time. Move to another concept based on your observations of your students.

2. Keep It Brief

Another advantage of explaining one idea at a time is that the instruction can be brief, a second principle of effective instruction. Students are far more willing to listen when they know that an explanation will be quick and they can return to activity. Think about how you might limit your instruction to 60 seconds or less, perhaps alternating short bouts of instruction with all students demonstrating an understanding of the skill or concept.

In keeping with this guideline, avoid falling into the habit of repeating an explanation two or three times. Beginning teachers are particularly prone to this habit as they try to find words to enhance their explanation or notice confused looks on students' faces. This is because, in many instances, they haven't talked about the ideas they are attempting to teach—the content is new to them as teachers (Brown & Brown, 1996). Consequently, some students tend to hear the first explanation and not bother to listen to the next one; some might prefer to wait until the second or third explanation because they know the idea will be explained more than once. Once again, using a showing-while-telling approach often leads to more clear directions the first time and reduces student confusion.

Uhs, Ums, OKs, and *You Knows*

It's common for teachers, especially early in their careers when they are unaccustomed to public speaking and are presenting information for the first time, to use certain phrases or filler words that are distracting to listeners. The most common are *uh, um, OK,* and *you know,* but others also creep in. There is a reason for using these words—they allow you to stall for time as you think about what you want to say next. It's natural. It's also distracting. One of the quickest ways to discover these habits is to record a lesson to see whether any of these habits have crept into your instruction. If they have, simply becoming aware of them can be enough to eliminate them from your speech. In some cases, however, a habit has become so ingrained that it won't go away. Fortunately, there is a good way to eliminate these habits. Select a class you work well with, and ask the students to help you eliminate your habit. They will already be aware of it. Ask them to repeat the distracting phrase to you every time you say it. For example, every time you say, "OK," ask them all to say "OK?" back to you. Although the lesson you are instructing might not be very good, you will quickly stop using that word. It works—and students really enjoy helping you change the habit.

3. Reminder Word or Phrase

Our explanations, of necessity, require a number of words. When we can provide children with a reminder word or phrase, it helps students recall the idea more easily, which is a third component of effective instruction (Buchanan & Briggs, 1998; Dillard, 2003; Melville, 1988; Parson, 1998). Reminder words and phrases present easily remembered mind pictures. For example, the cue often used with beginners when striking a ball with a racket is that the side of the body (as opposed to the front of the body) should be facing the target when the ball is struck. The word *side* can serve as a shortcut to remembering this concept (Dillard, 2003). This also makes providing feedback easy because you can simply say "Side" to remind a student to turn the side toward the target. Although this might not seem important at the beginning of the day, after seven or eight classes, a shortcut like this can be very helpful (table 7.1).

When reminder words are not easy to create, students can sometimes help. For example, the cue for bending the knees, hips, and ankles when landing from a jump was identified by students as squashing the landing.

Knuckle of the Big Toe

A soccer player was trying to help another student with a soccer-style kick for distance. The player didn't want the other student to use his toe, but she didn't want him to use the inside of his foot either. In attempting to describe that location on the foot between the toes and the inside middle of the foot (actually, the joint of the first metatarsal), she came up with the term *knuckle of your big toe.* Perhaps not quite accurate, but easy to remember.

4. Based on Observation

As explained previously, classes' needs differ. Effective teachers can observe a class, reflect on the students' movements, and then select the appropriate cue from their repertoire of understanding about that skill and how it is learned. Observation is the fourth principle of effective instruction. In teaching dribbling with the hands, for example, the following cues (chapter 4) might be helpful:

TABLE 7.1   **Sample Verbal Cues for Motor Skills**

Skill	Verbal cues
Dodging	
Use a quick change of direction and speed to avoid a chaser or object.	Dart, or change
Jumping	
Land from a jump with bent knees to absorb the force and maintain balance.	Squash
When jumping over a single rope, make small, springy jumps with very little height.	Jump, jump
Dribbling	
Dribble by pushing with the soft part of the fingers.	Finger pads
Protect the ball by keeping your body between the ball and the defender.	Protect the ball
Rolling	
When rolling while traveling, jumping, or dismounting, round your back and tuck your chin and knees.	Round body
Striking	
When traveling while striking a ball or puck with a hockey stick, use both sides of the stick to move around obstacles.	Both sides
Return a volley to your opponent's weak side (most often the backhand).	Hit to weakness
Game strategies	
Keep moving even when you don't have the ball or disc to get open and create space for your teammate.	Move away from the ball (or disc)
Position yourself with your back to the goal to see the ball and your "man" while defending to disrupt passing lanes and opponent movement.	Back to the goal

Cues adapted from G. Graham, S. Holt/Hale, and M. Parker, 2012, *Children moving: A reflective approach to teaching physical education*, 9th ed. (New York, NY: McGraw-Hill).

- Use the finger pads.
- Push the ball—don't slap it.
- Look away from the ball.
- Dribble low.
- Keep the ball on the side away from the opponent (SHAPE America, 2014).

With beginning students, you might emphasize the first two or three cues one at a time. A class of more skillful students would benefit from the latter two cues. You should base your decision of which cue or refinement to emphasize (chapter 4) on your observations, however, not on a preset notion of what, say, all third-graders need (chapter 5). Then combine that information with your knowledge of the cues students find most beneficial. In some instances, your students will have already learned the cues, albeit with a different skill, in which case you can spend less time explaining and demonstrating it. For example, the overhand throwing motion is in the same family of skills as the overhand volleyball serve, the tennis serve, and the badminton overhead clear (Wilkinson, 2000).

Observing a class and making these decisions are not skills that come easily. As with many of the tools in the pedagogy toolbox, learning takes time and practice. In the beginning, it is helpful to have several cues in mind and then scan the class to determine which will be most beneficial to this class. If the majority of students are gripping their rackets correctly, then it is of little use to explain the grip to the entire class. You can do it individually. In contrast, if most of the students are swinging their rackets in uneven pathways, causing them to miss or mis-hit the ball, then you need to spend time on their swing pathways. This decision is best made through observation.

One of the mistakes many secondary teachers make is not carefully observing their students and then explaining and demonstrating a cue or concept they have already learned. Consider how many times you were taught the basics of dribbling a basketball or throwing a ball in your physical education classes over a 9- or 10-year period.

Demonstrating

Demonstrating is typically a part of instruction in which a movement is shown rather than described. Demonstration is especially important for young children, who might have difficulty understanding verbal explanations of the concepts (Valentin, 2004). Demonstration is also crucial in schools with students who aren't fluent in English or who have hearing impairments.

Much of your teaching involves using words to describe how to perform motor skills. Words are helpful, but they are not as efficient as demonstrating a skill. The same is true for music or art. Words are helpful, but listening to a symphony or seeing a portrait in an art gallery is far more instructive than trying to explain a work of art or piece of music. Words are obviously effective in focusing our attention on particular aspects, phases, or sequences of a movement—and even more so when combined with a demonstration. As with instruction, a good demonstration has four components (Adams, 1993; Darden, 1997; Rink & Werner, 1987; Wiese-Bjornstal, 1993).

Location

When demonstrating, stand in a location that allows all students to see you easily without distraction. If you're outside, stand so the sun isn't in their eyes. When sharing outdoor or indoor space with other classes, keep your back to a wall or building so that other classes are working behind your students rather than behind you. Also be sure that you can see all your students. This is obvious, yet from time to time forgotten. There's really not much more we can say about this aspect—it's simply a matter of trying to be aware of students and what they are seeing and hearing.

Whole or Part

Generally, the first demonstration should be of the entire movement or task, whether informational or organizational. This allows students to form a complete mental picture of the skill (Darden, 1997; Housner & Griffey, 1994; Rink & Werner, 1987), the second component of an effective demonstration. If the skill is passing a volleyball to a setter, you (or a skilled student) should demonstrate the entire pass. The next phase of the demonstration focuses on the part (e.g., showing the shoulders squared to the target, a setter). You may or may not follow this with another demonstration of the whole. It's important to verbally highlight the critical element, or cue, before the demonstration so that the students know what to pay attention to as they are watching the demonstration (Valentin, 2004). When this is not done, students tend to focus more on the outcome of the movement (the product) rather than on the cue (the process) you are trying to emphasize.

 Demonstrating The web resource includes a brief video explanation of the process of demonstrating and examples of effective demonstrations.

Normal or Slow

Sometimes students need to see a skill at normal speed; other times it helps to slow it down, often when the cue is demonstrated. Demonstrating at a normal or slow speed is the third component of good demonstrations. Many students cannot see the movement unless it is slowed down. For example, watching the hips rotate through when throwing a ball or swinging a golf club is difficult to observe at full speed. The movement is simply a blur. This is especially true when attempting to refine a complex sport skill in higher-skilled students (e.g., swinging a golf club or racket, or throwing). The focus may be on how the hips, arms, and shoulders move in relation to one another.

What if I Can't Perform the Skill to Be Demonstrated?

A question often raised by beginning teachers is "What do I do if I'm not skilled enough to demonstrate?" Our answer is "Don't." Most of the time, you will know a student or two in the class who can demonstrate the whole skill. That same student can then demonstrate the part of the skill you want to emphasize, often in slow motion. Evidence suggests that peer modeling is more motivating to youngsters because the movement appears more like their own than that of an adult or expert does (Darden, 1997). Although you may be uncomfortable with the fact that you are not highly skilled in everything you teach, students won't find this especially troublesome if you are honest about it. Such situations are excellent times to point out how long it takes to become proficient at a skill and how few people are proficient at every skill. In fact, one of the aspects of teaching we enjoy most is when students attempt to teach us a skill we are not very good at. The sharing, the compassion, and the support they provide as they try to teach us to do a handstand or twirl a hoop around one leg create an environment in which it's OK not to know everything. We all learn that it's fun to learn and to try, and that our class is a place we can all feel comfortable trying and failing—because failure is a part of learning.

Verbal Focus

Finally, to benefit from a demonstration, students need to know what to look for during the demonstration (e.g., "Watch the plant foot; notice that it is placed alongside the ball"). This fourth component of good demonstrations is about focusing students' attention. If this isn't done, as the ball is kicked, many students will watch the flight of the ball, oohing and aahing as it sails away (the product) and forgetting to notice where the foot was planted (the process).

Pinpointing

Pinpointing is a technique to use after you have explained and demonstrated a skill and some students are either having a hard time understanding or focusing more on the outcome than the cue. To pinpoint, select two or more students who are correctly using the component and ask them to demonstrate for their classmates. Say, for example: "Stop. Now I want you to watch Starla and Todd. Notice how their arms are fully stretched to help them keep their balance as they walk along the beam." Starla and Todd might not be the most skilled students in the class, but they can show the correct use of the critical element (in this instance, fully stretched arms).

Pinpointing reinforces instruction and demonstration and tells students that you are more interested in how they are balancing (the technique) rather than in whether they are falling off the beam (Darden, 1997). Pinpointing two or more students at once seems to work best. Students often don't like to perform solo in front of the class. Fear of embarrassment is reduced when several students are moving at the same time. Try to avoid always pinpointing the highly skilled students—even less-skilled students, who might not have the best balance, can demonstrate how to stretch their arms to maintain their balance. This indirectly says to the students: "Even though you might not be highly skilled, you can learn to do this part, and I am more interested in how you do the skill than in the results." It also allows you to reinforce the students who are trying hard but have yet to put it all together (chapter 12).

In a study of students' perspectives on teaching strategies (Cothran & Kulinna, 2006, p. 177), a student named Jessica had this insight related to the pedagogical skill of pinpointing: "Teenagers sometimes have a tendency to not listen to adults when they actually

say it, but if a kid, you know, tells them how they are doing or how better to move they actually listen and try to like the ideas they give them." Nick agreed: "Kids really more listen to other kids than they do to adults." This appears to be especially true for older children and adolescents.

 Pinpointing   The web resource includes several video examples of pinpointing.

Checking for Understanding

At the culmination of an instruction–demonstration episode, a good technique is to quickly test students to be sure they understand the instruction and the demonstration. A variety of techniques are available to ascertain whether students have grasped the concept you are attempting to convey (Wiese-Bjornstal, 1993). The decision on which technique to use depends largely on the developmental level of the students, the time available, and the content you are teaching. Three checking-for-understanding techniques are recognition, verbal, and performance.

Recognition Check

One of the quickest ways to check for understanding is to demonstrate a movement and then ask students to raise their hands, give a thumbs-up sign, or indicate in some other way that the movement was performed correctly or incorrectly. For example, you might say, "Thumbs up if my elbow is in middle level; thumbs down if it is not in middle level." The problem with this technique, of course, is that students often check with other students before providing their own responses. Be sure to mix up the questions so that your demonstration is not always correct.

Verbal Check

A second way to check for understanding is to ask students to verbally tell you the cue or concept you are teaching. Ideally, you can ask several students at a time to tell you, for example, three cues they have learned for catching a ball, although you may not have taught all of the cues in that lesson. Although you could ask the whole class at the same time, when 25 students are talking at once, it is impossible to know which of them have really grasped the concept. Another technique is to ask youngsters to explain in their own words a concept taught during the lesson as they exit the gym or playground. This allows you to quickly interact with each student in the class while assessing their overall understanding.

 Checking for Understanding   The web resource includes video clips of teachers checking for understanding.

Performance Check

"Show me how to squash a landing after a jump" or "Show me where not to put your arms when you do a crunch" are examples of performance checks, the third technique of checking for understanding. Asking students to demonstrate their understanding works especially well in physical education because you are teaching movement, and you can quickly scan the class to see whether their demonstrations indicate that they have understood the concept.

Checking performance provides a way of evaluating students' comprehension of the functional use of a cue. Given the number of classes typically taught by elementary school physical education specialists and the difficulty of evaluating 300 to 600 children, this technique can be helpful for assessing your students' progress. Scanning the class to see how many have understood the instruction and the demonstration can be done relatively easily and quickly. It also shows you whether students are just memorizing concepts or truly understanding why a cue or concept is important. Checking performance early in the lesson will help you ensure that your students understand what to focus on throughout the lesson. Imagine waiting until the end of the lesson to check for understanding, only to learn that a majority of your students misunderstood! Of the three techniques discussed, the performance check is probably the most important because it allows you to quickly scan the class to see whether the students can demonstrate their understanding of the cue or concept.

Closure

A good time to check for understanding is during the lesson closure, which is typically brief—ideally two or three minutes long. It helps to conclude the day's lesson by inviting students to reflect on what they have learned and how it relates to a bigger picture (i.e., scaffolding).

At the end of a physical education class, you might bring your students close to you and have them sit down. You might then do one or more of the following:

- Quickly review the key points of the lesson—usually the critical elements or concepts that were emphasized. This can take the form of a verbal summary, or you could ask questions about the lesson using one of the four checking-for-understanding techniques described earlier.

- Have the students complete a quick written assessment related to the lesson (chapter 13).

- Comment on the behavior of the class during the lesson. This typically should occur more in the beginning of the school year when you are establishing protocols. Many teachers, however, use this as a time to compliment the entire class when the students have worked hard and appropriately during the lesson.

- Assign homework. Here are some examples:
  ◦ Practice dribbling a ball for at least 10 minutes before the next class.
  ◦ Stretch (do crunches, push-ups) during at least three television commercials before the next class.
  ◦ Locate (identify) at least one place in the community where they might go to practice their racket skills (e.g., tennis or racquetball courts, badminton net in a neighbor's backyard).
- Remind the students about the instant activity (chapter 6) for next class. You might say: "On Wednesday when you come to class, find a ball and practice your dribbling, or a jump rope and practice jumping. As soon as the music stops, put your equipment away and come stand by me. Who thinks they can remember? OK, we'll see."

Closure also serves as a brief break from physical activity and allows students to wind down before returning to the classroom. Educational psychologists tell us that this is a valuable learning time because learners are more likely to recall what happens at the end—and beginning—of lessons. Closure doesn't need to be lengthy, just two to three minutes, but it is an important part of a lesson.

 Closure   The web resource contains several examples of closure.

Play-Teach-Play

As you know, students don't want to listen to long explanations. They want to be active. This fact is compounded by youngsters' focus on the present (i.e., they rarely see the long-term benefits of practicing a skill). It's hard for them to make the connection between practice today and proficiency several years from now. They want to *play*, not practice. As a result, they are often reluctant to pay attention to instructions and demonstrations. In addition to pinpointing and checking for understanding, another effective technique that is part of the instruction and demonstration process is play-teach-play. Although this technique can be used with any age, it is typically used with children in upper elementary grades and beyond who are interested in playing a game rather than spending time in practice—although they might need the practice. Play-teach-play has two advantages:

- It heightens students' interest because instruction and demonstration can be related to the game (or activity) that just concluded. This is similar to fixing a flat tire. If we include a section on changing a flat tire, you might skip over it. If you have a flat tire on the freeway, however, your interest in the instructions and demonstration would be much greater. When students know that they will be returning to a game and you are describing a way to increase their success in that game, they will be more interested in listening to you.
- Students practice tasks in the actual context in which they will be used, so activities are more meaningful. This is especially true of secondary students who are into playing the game.

Historically, we have structured units (lessons) so that the practice (drill) occurs first, followed by a game. Adolescents especially want to play the game rather than practice because the two seem unconnected in their minds. In play-teach-play, connections between practice and play are made clearer by initially playing a small-sided version of the game (participating in the complete sequence or combination of skills); this helps both the students and the teacher understand and decide on the skills or combinations of skills to practice.

In many throwing and catching games, students have difficulty throwing a ball while moving. Often, the receiver (the intended target) is also moving and perhaps guarded. When students are initially involved in a game that requires moving to throw and catch, and when they are continually unsuccessful, instruction in this skill (and opportunities to practice) makes much more sense to them. The practice is related to the context of the game, not isolated and unconnected from it. After having an opportunity to practice, students can resume the game. They play, practice some more, and then play again.

Obviously, throwing and catching while moving isn't learned in a few minutes of practice, so you may have to stop the game frequently to provide more practice. The advantage of this approach is that the students can clearly see what and why they need to practice.

This isn't always the case when practice is removed from the context of the game. Let's look at dribbling with the hands. When students are practicing on their own with no opponents, they typically dribble the ball waist high and in front of them. As soon as someone tries to steal the ball, however, they dribble lower and often to the side. When you point this out, the dribbling practice seems far more useful. This is especially true when the students realize that in a few minutes they will be back in a game in which someone is going to try to steal the ball once again.

You determine the frequency and timing of playing, practicing (instructing and demonstrating), and playing. In some instances, the playing may be rather brief; in others, it may be longer. At times the play-teach-play cycle may be repeated several times; at other times the complete cycle might not be used because practice is productive and interesting to students, so there is no need to return to the game. As with so much of teaching, these decisions should be based on the characteristics of your classes.

Play-teach-play seems especially helpful with a class of students who are accustomed to playing games every day as a major part of the lesson. When the game is played first, you are no longer besieged by the question "When do we get to play the game?" The class can clearly recognize that certain skills need to be practiced for the game to truly be a game.

Serve–Chase–Serve–Chase

This section reminds me (GG) of the volleyball games I have observed in which students can neither serve nor volley. How dull the game becomes when it consists of serve, chase the ball, serve, chase the ball, serve, miss a volley, chase the ball. This pattern is often seen in tennis matches played by unskilled students. The advantage of placing the class in the game context initially is that they can immediately see the need for practicing the serve and the techniques for receiving the serve.

Play-teach-play, as with so many of the ideas discussed in this book, is helpful for some classes some of the time. Our experience has been that as students become accustomed to instructional physical education (emphasizing learning through practice) rather than recreational physical education (playing games with minimal instruction), the technique of play-teach-play is used less frequently, if at all, because students understand that physical education is a time to learn (instruction) rather than a time to play with no instruction (recreation).

Using Video Technology

Another technique that can heighten students' interest in instruction and demonstration is video recording. Increasingly, commercial companies are developing and marketing online resources for use in physical activity instruction. Privately developed resources are also widely available through sites such as YouTube. It is important that you screen and select appropriate videos and materials, especially when they are created for the general public, to make sure the content is safe, appropriate, and accurate. As with any product, the range of quality is broad, and resources designed for adults are rarely appropriate for children.

Recent advances in technology provide opportunities to make videos for your own programs. iPads and other devices with video recording capabilities are now commonly used in schools. Teachers have found a wide range of uses for videos made during physical education classes. Following are some examples:

- Show segments of programs on YouTube or other websites to your classes to demonstrate aspects of a particular skill, sequence, or game or to motivate students to practice more diligently, as a part of the set induction (chapter 6).

- Have students record one another and then immediately watch themselves to analyze their movements or assess their skill execution.

- Make videos of classes of older students to show younger students movements or routines (Melville, 1993).

- Use videos to provide instruction when you will be absent and a substitute teacher is responsible for your classes. This allows the sub to simply play your instructions, thereby minimizing the off-task behavior students can get into with subs.

- Given the increasing specter of malpractice lawsuits haunting teachers today, consider recording your management protocols, rules, and expectations as you explain them at the beginning of the year (Adams, 1993). You might also require new students to view the video before participating in physical education class.

- In a similar vein, record yourself as you explain routines and rules for certain activities that tend to be classified as high risk (e.g., climbing ropes, adventure activities, use of equipment in gymnastics) (Adams, 1993). In this way you have a visual record of the guidelines you provided to your classes for participating in these activities (chapter 2).

- Allow your students to record their own creations and show them to others. This can be both instructional and motivational. It also gives you the opportunity to select the most interesting sequences and creations for future showings.

- Record segments of lessons to present examples of classes, lessons, and teaching techniques to other teachers, parents and guardians, and administrators.

TECH TIPS Add Questions to Videos

Zaption is a free website that allows you to post videos that include questions to check for student understanding. You might post a one-minute video demonstrating the overhand throw. The students view it once; the second time they watch, the video pauses and your questions about the proper cues for performing the overhand throw appear.

Analyzing Students' Use of Time

As we conclude this chapter, we are concerned that it might appear that a substantial part of each lesson is devoted to instructing, demonstrating, pinpointing, checking for understanding, and so on. We hope not. Experts recommend that students be physically active for at least 50 percent of a lesson. We agree!

In this final section, we describe a technique for analyzing how students spend time in a lesson so that you can be certain that they are spending the majority of the time actually moving. We encourage our undergraduate students to instruct, demonstrate, and check for understanding in less than 60 seconds. This is obviously an arbitrary limit, but it reinforces the point that the entire cycle can be completed in one minute or less for many skills or activities—and be easily understood by students. The time analysis form presented in this section will help you systematically observe your own teaching to learn how your students are spending their time (e.g., listening to you talk versus actively moving).

Definition of Categories

Time analysis is also referred to as duration recording (Siedentop & Tannehill, 2000). The form in figure 7.1 is frequently used for time analysis, although it provides a rough rather than precise estimate. You can use it to sort your students' class time into four categories:

- Management—time spent getting out and putting away equipment, organizing into groups, and the like
- Activity—time spent moving as they perform activities consistent with the purpose of the lesson (ideally more than 50 percent of the lesson)
- Instruction—time spent listening to instruction, watching a demonstration, pinpointing, answering questions verbally, listening to other students talk
- Waiting—time spent waiting for a turn or to get the ball in a game, waiting for the teacher to get out the equipment or find the right song on a playlist, and so on

Coding the Time Students Spend in a Lesson

To record the time spent in a lesson, use a stopwatch and a reproduction of figure 7.1. (A blank copy of the time analysis form is in the web resource.) Start the stopwatch when students enter the outdoor space or gym. Each slash mark represents 15 seconds, and each number represents one minute. This form allows you to code a 30-minute lesson. In doing this analysis, focus on what the majority (51 percent) of the students are doing. Be certain to focus on the students, not yourself. For example, if you are talking but the students are moving, you would record that time as activity, not instruction. Record what 51 percent of the students are doing at any given time by making a slash mark and then indicating what the students spent the previous seconds doing by using an A for activity, an I (for instruction) if they are listening to you but not moving, an M (for management) if they are getting out equipment or organizing into groups, and a W if they are waiting for you to get equipment or if more than half of the students are waiting for a turn as in a relay race. Refer to figure 7.1 for the following example:

- If they spend the first 30 seconds of the class getting a piece of equipment, make a slash mark and then place an M to indicate that students had spent that time managing.

- If they spend the next 180 seconds (three minutes) in activity, place an A over that section.
- If the next 30 seconds are spent listening to you talk (and the students are not moving), place an I over that section.

Obviously, students do not change categories exactly at 15-second intervals. Make the best estimate of when the category changed and put your slash there.

You can analyze lessons or videos to determine how students spend their time. If you are analyzing a video-recorded lesson, you will have to make judgments about 51 percent of the students, based on which ones are visible at any given time.

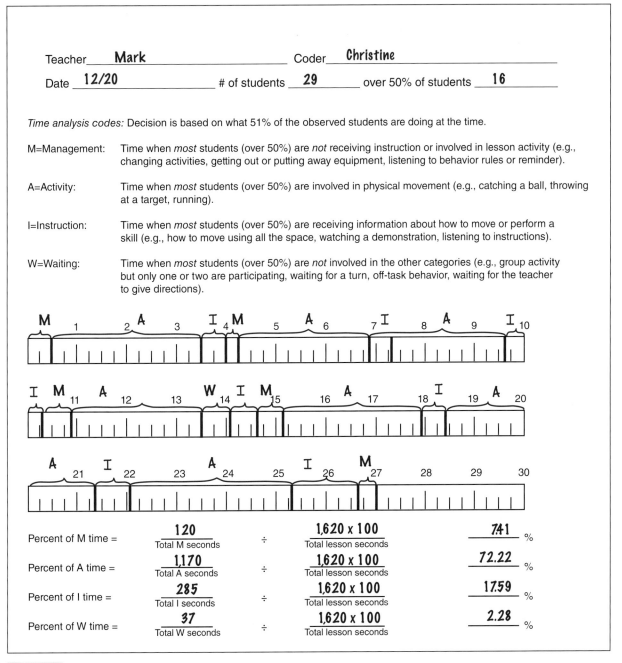

Teacher **Mark** Coder **Christine**

Date **12/20** # of students **29** over 50% of students **16**

Time analysis codes: Decision is based on what 51% of the observed students are doing at the time.

M=Management: Time when *most* students (over 50%) are *not* receiving instruction or involved in lesson activity (e.g., changing activities, getting out or putting away equipment, listening to behavior rules or reminder).

A=Activity: Time when *most* students (over 50%) are involved in physical movement (e.g., catching a ball, throwing at a target, running).

I=Instruction: Time when *most* students (over 50%) are receiving information about how to move or perform a skill (e.g., how to move using all the space, watching a demonstration, listening to instructions).

W=Waiting: Time when *most* students (over 50%) are *not* involved in the other categories (e.g., group activity but only one or two are participating, waiting for a turn, off-task behavior, waiting for the teacher to give directions).

Percent of M time =	120 / Total M seconds	÷	1,620 x 100 / Total lesson seconds	7.41 %
Percent of A time =	1,170 / Total A seconds	÷	1,620 x 100 / Total lesson seconds	72.22 %
Percent of I time =	285 / Total I seconds	÷	1,620 x 100 / Total lesson seconds	17.59 %
Percent of W time =	37 / Total W seconds	÷	1,620 x 100 / Total lesson seconds	2.28 %

Figure 7.1 Form for coding students' use of time.

Analyzing and Interpreting the Results

When a lesson has ended or your observation has ceased, the first step is to total the number of seconds for the entire lesson. In the example in figure 7.1, the lesson was 27 minutes long (1,620 seconds). All calculations are done in seconds, so the denominator for each of the four categories is 1,620. Total the number of seconds students spent in each of the four categories, and write it in the appropriate place on the form. Divide the number of seconds for each category by the total length of the lesson (in seconds) and multiply by 100 to determine the percentage for each of the four categories. In this lesson, for example, students spent 1,170 seconds in activity, which amounted to 72.22 percent of the lesson. Less than 3 percent of this lesson was spent in waiting.

Obviously, there are many ways to interpret the time students spend in a lesson. Some lessons require more instruction than others, for example. Thus, you must always interpret the form in terms of the lesson content, the class taught, the grade level, and so on. Generally, however, we encourage our undergraduate students to try to design and teach their lessons so that students are active at least 60 percent of the time. We also encourage our students to aim for no waiting time at all. We assume that virtually every lesson will include some instruction and some management time.

Summary

Implementing effective instructing and demonstrating strategies is critical to a quality program. Two instructional processes are organizational instruction (telling students what to do, with whom, where, and with what equipment) and informational instruction (telling students how to complete the task correctly). Four guidelines in providing informational instruction are presenting one idea at a time, keeping it brief, using a reminder word or phrase, and basing instruction on observation. Demonstrating is a part of instruction, and good demonstrations address a location for demonstrating, demonstrating the whole and parts of a skill, demonstrating at normal and slow speeds, and providing a verbal focus. Other techniques are pinpointing students to demonstrate, checking for understanding, play-teach-play, closure, and using video technology.

An analysis tool can help you determine how students spend their time in your classes. You can see how much time they spend being active, waiting, managing, and listening to instructions. This is important information to help you ensure that students are active for the majority of the class period with little or no wait time, and that you are not spending too much time instructing and demonstrating.

Questions for Reflection

1. Why do you think the distinction between organizational and informational instruction is necessary?

2. Physical education instructors tend to tell students far more than they need to know or are able to comprehend. Why do you think this is the case? Why is it so hard to limit instruction to one cue at a time?

3. It seems that physical education teachers don't demonstrate as often as they might. Can you explain why this might be true?

4. Some lessons might require more instruction or demonstration than others. Think of examples—consider the time of year, grade level, and lesson content.

5. Pinpointing is another form of demonstration. In what way is it an effective supplement to teacher demonstration?

6. Checking for understanding is a useful technique. Interestingly, it isn't employed as often as it could be—why might this be true?

7. Play-teach-play is a technique with advantages and disadvantages. Describe one of each and suggest when it might be effective and when it might not be effective.

8. Pull out your crystal ball and look for ways you might use video in your classes in the future. Don't worry about cost; imagine that your budget is unlimited. Don't neglect Internet possibilities.

References

Adams, S.H. (1993). Duty to properly instruct. *Journal of Physical Education, Recreation and Dance, 64* (2), 22-23.

Brown, S.C., & Brown, D.G. (1996). Giving directions: It's how you say it. *Journal of Physical Education, Recreation and Dance, 67* (6), 22-24.

Buchanan, A., & Briggs, J. (1998). Making cues meaningful: A guide for creating your own. *Teaching Elementary Physical Education, 9* (3), 16-18.

Cothran, D.J., & Kulinna, P.H. (2006). Students' perspectives on direct, peer, and inquiry teaching strategies. *Journal of Teaching in Physical Education, 25*, 166-181.

Darden, G. (1997). Demonstrating motor skills: Rethinking that expert demonstration. *Journal of Physical Education, Recreation and Dance, 68* (6), 31-35.

Dillard, K. (2003, November/December). Using key words to develop sport skills. *Strategies*, 32-34.

Fairclough, S.J., & Stratton, G. (2006). A review of physical activity levels during elementary school physical education. *Journal of Teaching in Physical Education, 25* (2), 239-257.

Graham, G., Holt/Hale, S., & Parker, M. (2012). *Children moving: A reflective approach to teaching physical education* (9th ed.). New York, NY: McGraw-Hill.

Housner, L.D., & Griffey, D.C. (1994). Wax on, wax off: Pedagogical content knowledge in motor skill instruction. *Journal of Physical Education, Recreation and Dance, 65* (2), 63-68.

Melville, S. (1988). Thinking and moving. *Strategies, 2* (1), 18-20.

Melville, S. (1993). Videotaping: An assist for large classes. *Strategies, 6* (4), 26-28.

Metzler, M. (1985). An overview of academic learning time research in physical education. In C. Vendien & J. Nixon (Eds.), *Physical education teacher education* (pp. 147-152). New York: Wiley.

Mustain, W. (1990). Are you the best teacher you can be? *Journal of Physical Education, Recreation and Dance, 61* (2), 69-73.

Oslin, J.L., Stroot, S., & Siedentop, D. (1997). Use of component-specific instruction to promote development of the overarm throw. *Journal of Teaching in Physical Education, 16* (3), 340-356.

Parson, M.L. (1998). Focus student attention with verbal cues. *Strategies, 11* (3), 30-33.

Rink, J., & Werner, P. (1987). Student responses as a measure of teacher effectiveness. In G. Barrette, R. Feingold, C. Rees, & M. Pieron (Eds.), *Myths, models and methods in sport pedagogy* (pp. 199-206). Champaign, IL: Human Kinetics.

Schmidt, R.A., & Wrisberg, C.A. (2008). *Motor learning and performance* (4th ed.). Champaign, IL: Human Kinetics.

SHAPE America. (2014). *National standards & grade-level outcomes for K-12 physical education.* Champaign, IL: Human Kinetics.

Siedentop, D., & Tannehill, D. (2000). *Developing teaching skills in physical education* (4th ed.). Palo Alto, CA: Mayfield.

Valentin, N. (2004). Visual cues, verbal cues and child development. *Strategies, 17* (3), 21-23.

Weiss, M.R., Ebbeck, V., & Rose, D.J. (1992). Show and tell in the gymnasium revisited: Developmental differences in modeling and verbal rehearsal effects on motor skill learning and performance. *Research Quarterly for Exercise and Sport, 63* (3), 292-301.

Wiese-Bjornstal, D.M. (1993). Giving and evaluating demonstrations. *Strategies, 6* (7), 13-15.

Wilkinson, S. (2000). Transfer of qualitative skill analysis ability to similar sport-specific skills. *Journal of Physical Education, Recreation and Dance, 71* (2), 16-18, 23.

Motivating Students to Practice

After reading this chapter, you should be able to do the following:

- List and provide examples of three keys to motivating students to practice.
- Explain how to use teaching by invitation to motivate youngsters.
- Discuss the differences between teaching by invitation and intratask variation.
- Describe how task sheets, learning centers, student-designed activities, and peer tutoring can heighten student motivation.
- Discuss the use of student-designed activities and videos to involve students.
- Explain why helping youngsters to set realistic expectations might be motivating.

Parents and guardians understand the challenge of motivating children to become and stay involved in productive and worthwhile activities (only on rare occasions do they classify television and video games as worthwhile). Teachers understand how much harder it is to keep 25 or more students eagerly involved in the same activity—and this feeling is supported by researchers who study motivation (Bagøien, Halvari, & Nesheim, 2010; Ryan & Deci, 2000). This chapter focuses on ideas for motivating youngsters to become and remain involved in practice that leads to learning and understanding.

Mentoring

We are often struck by the fact that teaching is neither terribly difficult nor mysterious when it is one-on-one tutoring (e.g., a mother and daughter, an older and a younger brother, a grandparent and grandchild). Tasks can easily be changed and accommodated to suit the needs and interests of the learner. The challenge in schools is that teachers are responsible for many students, have limited resources, and work in confined spaces—an awesome task that, viewed in perspective, most teachers do remarkably well.

Three Keys to Motivating Youngsters

It's common knowledge that children learn by doing. Research on teacher effectiveness clearly supports this premise. The challenge for teachers is to involve all of their students most of the time in activities that are appropriate for their varying skill levels. Successful teachers motivate children and adolescents by creating learning environments in which the tasks or activities are success oriented, autonomy supportive, and developmentally appropriate (Block, 1995; Hastie, Rudisill, & Wadsworth, 2013; Tjeerdsma, 1995).

Success Oriented

Failure, especially when we have never had much success, makes us want to quit trying. If we have never succeeded, there's no reason to believe that continuing to try, and failing, will eventually lead to improvement. This rationale is quite typical of young learners who have yet to make the connection between lots of practice and success (Lee, 2004). To motivate students to practice, the task needs to be one at which they can be successful— highly successful. The research literature, as well as common sense, suggests that when we're learning a new skill, success rates close to 80 percent are appropriate (Brophy & Good, 1986; Pellet & Harrison, 1996; Siedentop & Tannehill, 2000; Tjeerdsma, 1995).

With experience and age, we start to make the connection between practice and expertise (Lee, 2004). For example, an adult might think, *If I want to be a good skater, I will need to practice a lot. It will probably take months or even years.* In contrast a child might think, *I want to be a good skater. I tried it today. I fell down a lot. I can't skate.*

To be a successful physical educator, you need to create and change tasks so that your students succeed at high rates. The variety of tasks described in chapter 4 provide the opportunity to accommodate a wide variety of skill levels in your class. You can also encourage your students to modify tasks on their own to make them easier or harder to better match their abilities. At the same time, discourage them from making social comparisons (Lee, 2004). Finally, try to make tasks fun so that your students enjoy doing them without necessarily realizing that they are leading to improvement. The following three examples, taken from actual classes, show how to design tasks so that youngsters can succeed.

Self-Adjusting Target Throwing

Each student has a beanbag and a cardboard box. Challenge them to throw the beanbag into the box but don't tell them how far away from the box to stand. Watch how they adjust the distance based on their ability. The less skilled stand closer to their boxes; the more skilled stand farther away. Several successful throws might result in students moving farther away; several failures might result in taking a few steps closer to the box. Notice, too, that the more highly skilled children tolerate a lower rate of success than the less-skilled children (Rogers, Ponish, & Sawyers, 1991). This example focuses on elementary school children, but it can also apply to adolescents. For example, when teaching volleyball, you can allow students to choose the spot from which they serve the ball; in soccer, you can have students set cone goals up on their own and thus self-adjust the size of the goal by how far apart the cones are.

Self-Adjusting Shampoo

One morning as I (GG) was showering, I read the label on the shampoo bottle. It claimed that the shampoo was self-adjusting—it would adjust its cleaning action to the particular needs of each person's hair. I thought, *That's exactly what we need for our classes—self-adjusting tasks that change based on the abilities and interests of the students in the class!*

Slanty Rope

Here's another example of designing a task to promote success. For elementary classes, set up two ropes on the floor in a slanty rope design (Mosston & Ashworth, 2002). At one end, the ropes are close together. At the other end, the ropes are much farther apart. Challenge students to jump over the river (the ropes) without landing in the water. Observe how they choose the location at which they jump to match their ability to jump for distance—the less skilled jump the river at the narrower end, and the better jumpers jump at the wider end.

The slanty rope principle can also be used with middle and high school students. For example, a traverse climbing wall (students climb sideways with their feet never more than 3 feet [1 m] above the floor) has many holds. Low-skilled students can climb using any holds they like. More skillful students can be given specific routes marked with

colored tape that use smaller and more difficult holds. Even the highest-skilled climbers can find appropriately challenging routes. At any time, students can choose a more easily accessible or larger hold.

The point is that a large range of task difficulty is available. Students have the option to choose where along the slanty rope to jump or which route is best for them for climbing.

Varied Basketball Goal Heights

A third example of students wanting to be successful can be observed when several basketball goals are set at various heights for elementary school children. If given a choice, many choose to play at the lowest goal, thereby increasing their chances for success. Equipment manufacturers have recognized this and now sell adjustable basketball goals.

You can apply the same principle with middle and high school students. For example, in a volleyball, lacrosse, or field hockey unit, give students a choice of leagues in which to sign up. Volleyball leagues can include recreation (modified rules such as allowing the volleyball to bounce, playing with a volley trainer, using a lower net, and serving from anywhere), city (no calling double hits, serving from anywhere, letting the server choose the ball to use), and professional (calling double hits, playing by official rules). Students choose the league that is best for them, and they can also move from league to league.

● ● ● ●

It's interesting to take any of the preceding examples and compare the involvement and interest of students when they have no choice (i.e., when the distance or height is the same for everyone). Typically, practice decreases and off-task behavior increases. The low-skilled student becomes frustrated; the higher-skilled ones become bored (Mandigo & Thompson, 1998). The purpose of designing and adjusting tasks so that students can be successful is to encourage them to continue trying. That is true in class and out of class. In math homework, for example, experts recommend that problems assigned to young learners allow them to succeed at a 100 percent success rate, thereby increasing their motivation to do the homework.

I (GG) wish I had had math teachers who provided math homework assignments at which I could have succeeded. My memories are still vivid of the frustration, leading to exasperation, when I could do only 2 of 10 math homework problems. I wonder how much that contributed to my feelings of incompetence in math today.

Obviously, not every task you design can be self-adjusting and allow students to be continually successful. The principle, however, is that success is fun and motivating—and you want them to feel good about their physical abilities. They will have plenty of opportunities to experience failure and frustration—you don't need to intentionally create them.

How Successful Are the Students?

One way to determine the success rate of your students is to use a coding form to provide objective evidence (figure 8.1). The form is easy to use; in fact, some children use it quite well (Wolfe & Sharpe, 1996). It is most effective, however, with practice attempts that are easily counted. Lessons emphasizing throwing, catching, kicking, and serving a volleyball are ideal. By counting the successful and unsuccessful tries for a low- and a higher-skilled student, you can obtain a reasonably accurate estimate of their success rates. Remember, however, that 80 percent is a general target and may not be the appropriate success rate for some students. Once again, observe and get to know your students. A youngster becoming off task is often an indication that the success rate isn't optimal and the task is either too hard or too easy.

Autonomy Supportive

In addition to creating success-oriented environments, you should try to find ways to help your students develop an intrinsic motivation for participating. This is called autonomy-supportive teaching.

Autonomy refers to a person's sense of control. We know that students who feel autonomous during physical education are more actively engaged in learning activities and are more physically active during physical education and outside of school (Bagøien & Halvari, 2005; Halvari et al., 2009). Teachers who are autonomy supportive display many of the pedagogical skills described in this book. Providing a motivating set induction that captures student interest (chapter 6), scaffolding instruction so that students see the relevance of what they are learning (chapter 6), and developing a safe learning

FIGURE 8.1 Form for Analyzing Practice Opportunities and Success Rate

Teacher's name _____ Observer's name _____

Directions: Select two children (preferably one high skilled and one low skilled). Each time they attempt the skill presented in the task (kick with the instep, catch a ball, etc.) mark an S if the attempt is successful and a U if the attempt is unsuccessful. Switch your observation from one child to the other every other minute.

Criterion skill: _____

Child 1

Total successful _____

Total unsuccessful _____

Total attempts _____

(Total successful ÷ total attempts) _____

Child 2

Total successful _____

Total unsuccessful _____

Total attempts _____

(Total successful ÷ total attempts) _____

environment with clear protocols and rules (chapter 2) are all characteristics of autonomy-supportive teaching. To create an autonomy-supportive environment, give your students the following:

- A variety of tasks
- Opportunities to make decisions about the tasks
- Feedback (private recognition and evaluation) of performance
- Self-paced instruction and choices of tasks
- Ways to measure personal improvement and avoid social comparisons
- Opportunities for experimentation and self-initiation
- Cooperative learning opportunities

An autonomy-supportive learning environment encourages students to develop a high sense of independence, thereby encouraging intrinsic motivation (Valentini & Rudisill, 2004). You can help your students build and sustain intrinsic motivation by avoiding social comparisons, both with others in the class and with externally validated norms. Avoid contests that determine who can make the most shots, do the most sit-ups, or score the most points. Discourage your students from comparing their performances with state or national fitness test norms. Rather, invite them to compare their current and past performances to recognize how they are improving and to show them that practice and hard work eventually pay off (Alderman, Beighle, & Pangrazi, 2006; Lee, 2004; Rink, 2004; Valentini & Rudisill, 2004).

TECH TIPS Tracking Participation

Use pedometers, MOVbands, Sqord Boosters, or some other cost-effective tool (approximately $20-$30 each) to record student participation. MOVbands and Sqord Boosters allow students to quickly upload their movements to a website that both you and they can monitor. You can set challenges for individual students or entire classes. Sqord Boosters allow students to create avatars who grow stronger as the students increase their own activity.

Perhaps the emphasis on intrinsic motivation can best be understood when placed in the context of a popular activity such as jogging (Xiang, Chen, & Bruene, 2005). Most adults don't start jogging because they expect to win races or set records. They jog because they feel good about improving their fitness and perhaps losing weight. If they want to, they can chart their improvement using a wearable physical activity tracker (e.g., Fitbit, pedometer, GPS device, tracking app). If they were forced to run races and have their times published in the newspaper, we suspect many would quit jogging. From time to time, however, many choose to enter races. The important point is that they choose to enter races for their own reasons. They don't have to. Shouldn't children and adolescents have the same choices?

There is no way to prevent students from comparing their performances with those of others. They do compare accomplishments, especially the highly skilled. Nevertheless, you can encourage students to succeed on their own by downplaying comparisons and avoiding creating competitive situations.

As with virtually any endeavor, the higher-skilled seek extrinsic motivation by comparing themselves with others, typically through competition. You can make these opportunities available, but again, only for those who choose to compete.

Ban the Spelling Bee

One of the most blatant violations of the idea that children should be allowed to choose whether they want to compete and have their performances compared with others is the spelling bee. For the few good spellers in a class, it's a marvelous competition. For the remainder of the students, who know they are not good spellers, not only is the spelling bee humiliating but it also publicly reinforces what they have been thinking all along: they can't spell—and now the whole class knows it (Valentini & Rudisill, 2004). The United States has had spelling bees for years, culminating in a national competition every year in Washington, DC. Has this resulted in a nation of good spellers?

Developmentally Appropriate

A third characteristic of a motivating learning environment is that it reflects age-related and physical differences. An environment that is developmentally appropriate encourages students to work hard and remain on task (Graham et al., 1992; National Association for Sport and Physical Education [NASPE], 2009; Stork & Sanders, 1996).

As children develop, they are motivated by different opportunities and experiences. Primary-grade youngsters, for example, are eager to please the teacher and are therefore motivated by teacher praise and encouragement. Observe any kindergarten class and you will hear children saying, "Watch me! Watch me!" all day long. Furthermore, if children haven't learned to remain in one location, teachers will continually be trailed by five-year-olds wanting them to say "Wonderful!" after every attempt they make to jump over a rope or throw a beanbag into a box.

As children grow older, the desire to please the teacher is accompanied (in some cases apparently replaced) by a desire to please their peers. They also refine their ability to distinguish between motor skill ability and effort (how hard they try) (Lee, 2004). Attention and respect from peers play an important role in the motivation of middle school youngsters. The opportunity to work in groups to design activities or solve problems is often motivating for adolescents who are interested in peer interaction. Examples include designing a game, dance, or movement sequence and making a video, perhaps to show to classmates (Valentini & Rudisill, 2004).

In addition to age-related differences (Garcia, 1994), skill level influences the type of support that is effective. Youngsters who are only minimally successful even when tasks are adjusted for them need lots of praise and encouragement to continue to work hard and to try. They also need help understanding that proficiency in motor skills requires a lot of appropriate practice (Rink, 2004).

Highly skilled students who receive satisfaction from succeeding at various tasks seem to be motivated by praise focused on the way they perform the task (sometimes the results), rather than by the fact that they are working hard. In fact, being praised for succeeding at tasks that are relatively easy for them might give highly skilled students the impression that PE is really for the poorly skilled. We believe that this occurs with many athletes who are not challenged in physical education classes. They receive a lot of praise for accomplishments that are much better than those of others in the class but that represent a relatively minimal effort on their part.

Eight Techniques for Motivating Students

Teachers use a variety of techniques to motivate their students by creating learning environments that provide high rates of success, avoid social comparisons, and accommodate individual differences. These include teaching by invitation, intratask variation, task sheets, peer tutoring and cooperative learning, stations or learning centers, student-designed activities, video recording, and homework practice.

Teaching by Invitation

Youngsters like to have choices, especially as they get older (Hastie, Rudisill, & Wadsworth, 2013; Prusak et al., 2004). A great technique for adjusting tasks or activities to allow for individual differences is teaching by invitation. It involves providing two or more tasks and letting the students decide which best suits their abilities. Here are several examples:

- "You might want to strike a balloon, a vinyl ball, or a playground ball."
- "If this is easy for you, try turning when you are in the air so that you land facing in a different direction."
- "When you and your partner can catch the ball 10 times in a row, you might want to move your carpet squares farther apart."
- "Now I am going to put on some music. If you and your partner are ready, you can try to match your routine to the music."
- "I want you to do at least 25 sit-ups today [you know that every student can do at least that many]. If you want to do more than that, go ahead."
- "You might want to work alone or with a partner."
- "In your game you might want to keep score or not. You decide."
- "As you ride your mountain bike up to each obstacle, you can choose to go over it or around it."
- "Inline skate between or around the outside of the cones."

When teaching by invitation, be careful not to make one alternative appear or sound better than the other. Neither is better. It's simply a way of allowing students to adjust the task so they can be successful—and challenged—and enjoy practicing. You may find that your students automatically adjust the tasks to better match their abilities. Actually, some do this even when you don't teach by invitation.

Teaching by Invitation The web resource includes several video examples of teaching by invitation preceded by a brief description of the process.

It's always interesting to watch youngsters decide which invitation to accept. Some choose to put down a balloon to work with a foam ball. If they aren't successful, they quickly return to the balloon. The same is true for the choice between punting a round ball or a foam football (Pease & Lively, 1994).

Older children and adolescents typically choose to work with a partner or a group if they have a choice—but not always. On a number of occasions, we have students who normally choose to work with a partner choose to work alone one day. When we ask whether they feel all right, some admit to not feeling very well; others just prefer to be alone. We have days like that, too.

Obviously, teaching by invitation is only one technique in your toolbox. At times safety concerns, for example, may make it inappropriate to use teaching by invitation. At other times you may have a reason for having the entire class work on the same task at the same time.

Intratask Variation

Like teaching by invitation, the technique of intratask variation is appropriate for some classes and some lessons. It also allows you to modify a task based on the abilities and interests of your students, or when students have chosen tasks (teaching by invitation) that are inappropriate for their ability levels. Intratask variation differs from teaching by invitation in that you make the decision for the students (i.e., you decide that a task needs to be easier or harder for a student or a group of students) (Pellet & Harrison, 1996; Tjeerdsma, 1995). This teaching technique may be more difficult because you must observe the students and then make a series of decisions based on your perceptions. Typically, intratask variation is used to make a task easier for the lower skilled (e.g., using a different type of ball, landing on two feet instead of one, not turning when they jump, playing in a less skilled league) or harder for the higher skilled.

Intratask variation provides highly skilled students, who don't need basic skill practice, the opportunity to play a game they are ready for. For example, a secondary school class working on the forearm pass in volleyball may include four or five club volleyball players. The highly skilled players can be instructed to pepper (i.e., partner 1 forearm passes the ball to partner 2, who sets the ball back to partner 1, who hits the ball to player 2, who then passes the ball, and the rotation continues), while the rest of the students work on forearm passing to a wall or with a partner.

TECH TIPS   Activity Tracking Devices and Apps

A plethora of physical activity tracking devices (e.g., Fitbit) and apps (e.g., Map-MyRun) are available to motivate students to practice both inside and outside of PE. Introduce them to your students; they can then choose the best one to help them monitor their daily physical activity and attain their goals. Many of these apps allow users to share data with others (e.g., teachers or friends).

An example from my (GG) teaching illustrates the use of intratask variation. I was teaching hand dribbling to a class of fifth-graders. Most of the students were at the stage at which dribbling and traveling at the same time was challenging. A few were well past this stage because they had been playing basketball on teams for several years. After presenting the entire class with the task of dribbling slowly in general space, I called six students over who were highly skilled. My instructions were: "Go down to the other half of the playground. Get a game going that has dribbling in it. As long as you get along and don't make a lot of noise when I stop the rest of the class to talk to them, you can continue with your game." Several things happened:

- As you might imagine, the six decided to play a modified version of basketball. They played the entire time. Several times I offered suggestions for dribbling more effectively.
- The remainder of the class continued to practice dribbling and traveling and dribbling and trying to keep the ball away from an opponent.
- Some asked why they couldn't play with the other six. I told them that they could when they were able to dribble well enough, and I encouraged them to practice hard—not only at school, but also at home.

Intratask variation allows you to match the tasks to the variety of skill levels in virtually every class you teach. This is especially appropriate for highly skilled youngsters, who frequently want to play a game. The fact is that in many cases they are ready to benefit from playing a game. You may be thinking that some students might feel it is not fair when others in class get to play different variations of a game or task. Youngsters generally become accustomed to intratask variation because they realize that the same students are not always chosen to participate in the modified or adjusted activities. This is especially important to avoid stereotyping lower-skilled youngsters. We have also found that the less skilled are delighted not to always have the highly skilled athletes with them as they learn new skills.

Most of the time, you can use intratask variation with individuals or small groups, and others in the class won't even be aware that the task has changed. To use the dribbling example again, if you didn't want to set up a game for the higher-skilled students, you might challenge them privately as you move through the class: "Can you dribble it behind your back? Between your legs? Make a figure eight?" At the same time, you might make the task easier for the lower-skilled students: "Try dribbling the ball more in front of you. It's OK if you use two hands every once in a while." The point is that in every class skill level varies. Both intratask variation (modified tasks for individuals) and teaching by invitation (modifications suggested to the whole class) acknowledge differences by attempting to match tasks to students' skill levels, thereby minimizing the boredom or frustration that occurs when all 25 youngsters are required to do the same task.

Intratask Variation   The web resource includes video examples of teachers using intratask variation in different lessons.

Task Sheets

A third approach to increasing students' success rates and allowing them to progress at their own pace is task sheets (Iserbyt & Byra, 2013). These are especially helpful with activities that lend themselves to self-testing (e.g., jump rope and balance activities), but they can also be used with individual sports (e.g., inline skating, climbing, mountain biking) and team sports (e.g., basketball, ultimate, softball) (Kozub, 2001). Typically, the task sheet lists a progression from simple to complex, and youngsters work at their own pace (see figure 8.2). Task sheets usually list individual skills rather than partner or group skills.

 FIGURE 8.2   Tasks for Striking With Paddles

Directions: This task sheet lists 15 tasks. Some will be easy. Some will be hard. When you get to a task you cannot do, that is the one to spend time practicing. Don't worry about others in the class. Just try to practice a lot so that you can improve. I will help you as you practice. When you can do a task, write your initials beside it. You will need a foam paddle for each task.

1. ___ I can strike a balloon with a paddle 10 times in a row without the balloon hitting the floor.

2. ___ I can strike a balloon with a paddle 15 times and remain on my carpet square.

3. ___ I can spell my first and last name by saying a letter each time the ball hits the paddle—without a miss.

4. ___ I can strike a foam ball 20 times in a row without leaving my carpet square or the ball hitting the floor.

5. ___ I can strike the ball to the ground (dribble) 16 times in a row without a miss.

6. ___ I can strike a foam ball 18 times in a row doing "flip-flops"—one side of the paddle, then the other.

7. ___ I can spell the entire city I live in by saying one letter each time the paddle strikes the shuttlecock.

8. ___ I can hit a ball against a wall 13 times in a row without letting the ball bounce twice.

9. ___ I can hit a ball against a wall 9 times in a row without letting the ball hit the floor once.

10. ___ I can hit a ball against a wall without letting the ball hit the floor once and not leave my carpet square.

11. ___ My partner and I can hit the ball back and forth 9 times in a row without letting the ball bounce twice.

12. ___ My partner and I can hit the ball back and forth 11 times in a row without letting the ball touch the floor.

13. ___ I can hit a forehand, backhand, forehand, backhand against the wall 14 times without letting the ball bounce twice in a row.

14. ___ My partner and I can hit the shuttlecock across the net 21 times in a row without a miss.

15. ___ My partner and I can hit the ball to each other 25 times in a row without having the ball hit the floor. Each time I hit I have to change from a forehand to a backhand to a forehand to a . . . .

Remember: This is not a race! Take your time and try to do each task well. I will be here to help you. We will use this task sheet several more times this year.

You can devise a way to hold students accountable for their progress. You can also design the task sheets so that partners can observe each other. If a task is done correctly, the observing partner initials the task sheet to indicate that the task has been accomplished. You may prefer to have your students show you when they are ready to be checked off on a task.

As with virtually every idea mentioned in this book, this approach works better with some classes and teachers than with others. Obviously, students need to be able to read and work reasonably well on their own (i.e., be self-directed) to use task sheets. Also, focusing on the quality of the movement is difficult with task sheets—the emphasis is on results rather than on the process, which might lead to the development of inefficient movement habits.

Newsome (2005) suggested that task sheets be designed so that even the lowest skilled in a class can accomplish at least a few of the tasks. He also recommended listing more skills than anyone in the class could possibly finish in the allocated time while reassuring the students that they are not expected to complete the task sheet in one class period. This gives you an opportunity to stress honesty and integrity when completing the tasks (Newsome, 2005). Figure 8.3 is a task sheet for orienteering. Each course is progressively more difficult than the one before it, and students can progress at their own pace.

Task sheets are best used over a period of several months during which students revisit them from time to time. This encourages them to practice on their own because they know the task sheet will be used again later. You can easily store the task sheets in a manila folder for later use.

Another advantage of task sheets is that they are marvelous assessments of progress that you can share with parents and guardians at the end of the year. If you work in a school with low turnover rates, you can use the same task sheets for several years.

PE Central Challenges

PE Central (www.pecchallenge.org) has two challenges that can be easily adapted as task sheets over a period of months or even years. One challenge focuses on six basic motor skill tasks, including throwing, catching, and striking with a paddle. The other challenge focuses on physical fitness and includes six tasks such as partner sit-ups and push-ups. Many of the challenges focus on working with partners to promote teamwork and peer encouragement.

Peer Tutors and Reciprocal Teaching

Peer tutoring and reciprocal teaching, which often work well in conjunction with task sheets, are other ways to motivate youngsters to practice and work hard (Block, 1995, 1996; Ellery, 1995; Kolovelonis & Goudas, 2012). A peer tutoring program can be especially motivating for students with special needs who are included within physical education classes and for low-skilled students. If you plan to institute peer tutoring into your program, select the tutors carefully (Ellery, 1995); then teach them how to tutor (Block, 1995, 1996). Ellery (1995) suggested the following criteria for selecting peer tutors:

- Age—they should be the same age or slightly older than the students they will be tutoring.
- Maturity level—they should be able to cope with peers who learn at slower rates and remain positive and encouraging.

FIGURE 8.3   Task Sheet for Orienteering

Course 1

120°	10 steps
240°	10 steps
0°	10 steps

Course 2

300°	8 steps
60°	8 steps
180°	8 steps

Course 3

90°	12 steps
180°	12 steps
270°	12 steps
0°	12 steps

Course 4

90°	6 steps
180°	8 steps
330°	10 steps

Course 5

130°	3 steps
220°	4 steps
310°	6 steps
100°	5 steps

Course 6

110°	6 steps
120°	8 steps
290°	12 steps
80°	10 steps

Compass Cues

1. Turn the compass dial to the desired bearing.
2. Connect the back of the compass to your belly button.
3. Park your red car in the garage (turn your body in a circle until the red magnetic needle lines up with the arrow inside the compass dial).
4. Choose a reference point that your directional arrow points to.
5. Put the compass in your pocket and walk to your reference point.

If you finish all of these, try making your own course!

- Communication skills—they should have good verbal and nonverbal skills.
- Physical skill level—they often need to demonstrate, so they should be skilled enough to provide demonstrations.
- Desire to volunteer—they should want to serve in this role.

Once you have selected tutors, you need to teach them how to tutor. They need to learn the skill components (motor skill cues) to look for so that they will be able to provide helpful feedback to the students they are tutoring (Block, 1995).

Another form of peer tutoring, called reciprocal teaching, can also motivate students (Kraft, Smith, & Buzby, 1997; Mosston & Ashworth, 2002). In this process one student assumes a tutor role and the other assumes a learner role. However, they take turns serving as tutor and learner. Reciprocal teaching is often used with task sheets as students work together to help each other improve. Figure 8.4 provides a reciprocal task sheet for students to use to evaluate each other on a baseball or softball swing. The cues on a reciprocal teaching task sheet must have been covered so that the students are familiar with them. Both peer tutoring and reciprocal teaching can be very motivating. As with any of the

---

FIGURE 8.4 Softball Swing Reciprocal Task Sheet

Name _____ Partner's name _____

With your partner, get 10 balls, a baseball bat, and one tee (or do self-toss). One partner (the batter) hits the ball with the bat, trying to hit line drives. The other partner (the coach) gives feedback as follows:

- Remember, start with something your partner is doing right.

- Feedback might sound like this: "I like the way you're keeping your eye on the ball, but make sure to step with your front foot only 3 to 6 inches [8-15 cm]—you're stepping, like, 2 feet [60 cm]."

- Keep track of your partner's performance on the following cues. Mark at least two cues on each swing.

Cue	Yes	No
Stance—sideways to target, feet slightly wider than shoulders, weight on balls of feet.		
Back hand on top, front shoulder slightly lower than back shoulder.		
Step 3 to 6 inches (8-15 cm) toward pitcher or target before starting swing.		
Start with chin on front shoulder; swing to chin on back shoulder.		
Hips rotate to face pitcher or target.		
Follow through—top hand rolls over bottom hand.		

concepts suggested in this book, however, success depends on you, your students, and your school environment.

Stations, or Learning Centers

Another frequently used approach that can be motivating is stations, or learning centers. A number of activities are set up around the gym or outside. The space for each activity is defined by cones or lines on the floor, posters describing the activities are often displayed at the stations, and the equipment for each activity is provided. Students rotate from one activity to another, spending several minutes at each. Obviously, stations can be used in a variety of ways and for a variety of reasons in physical education classes. Consider the following:

- Stations are great for reviewing skills. Set up five or six stations that revisit skills the students have practiced over the past few lessons or weeks (e.g., rolling, dribbling, striking with paddles).

- Stations also work well for fitness workouts. Set up 15 or so stations that students visit for short periods because the activities are intense (e.g., bench step-ups, sit-ups, jumping rope, jumping into and out of hoops).

- Stations are great in primary grades. Young children often lose interest in an activity quickly because their skill levels are low and there isn't much variety. Stations give them an opportunity for variety even though they may all address the same skill. One station might involve throwing a ball at a square on the wall; another might require throwing beanbags into a box; a third might challenge them to throw tennis balls to knock down bowling pins.

- Stations are also helpful when equipment is limited. Waiting for a turn can be eliminated because different equipment can be used at different stations.

 Instant Activity   Fitness stations are illustrated in the instant activity section of the web resource.

As with so many other topics taught in physical education, students initially need to learn the protocol (chapter 2) for using stations. Typically the protocol focuses on the following:

- Putting equipment where it was before rotating

- Learning where to rotate next (from station 1 to station 2) to avoid mass confusion

- Reading the poster at each station before beginning (especially important when students have a choice of several activities at the same station based on their ability levels)

TECH TIPS **Apps to Keep Students Motivated**

Many great apps and programs are available to keep students motivated. You can vary your lesson by using QR codes, augmented reality, or even Google Drive. All of these tools allow students to practice independently on their skill activities by scanning the QR codes or augmented reality sheets that best fit their skill levels. Google Drive folders are another beneficial tool. For example, for a gymnastics unit, you can have an iPad at each station with multiple levels of gymnastics skills demonstrated through pictures and videos. The students can then progress through the unit at their own pace and skill level.

Student-Designed Activities

Older youngsters often enjoy the opportunity to work in small groups to design their own games, dances, gymnastics sequences, or team practices. The worksheet in figure 8.5 directs middle school students to design their own softball practices. This is motivating because they are working with their peers and encouraged to use their own creative abilities to solve the problem or meet the challenge.

Kinetic sculpturing is a good example of a student-designed activity in which students work together to solve a problem. Groups of four to six are challenged to create a group sculpture that moves. For example, the students might be challenged to create a kinetic sculpture that does one of the following:

- Moves symmetrically or asymmetrically.
- Moves fast or slow.
- Is interpretive (e.g., their version of an escalator, a bicycle, a volcano) or improvisational (simply an interesting movement).

No special type of movement is required, so the low- and high-skilled students can work in the same groups as integral parts of the sculpture. With older students, responsibility becomes an important learning outcome. A game, practice, or gymnastics routine task might include making sure all group members are included and appropriately challenged.

It can be fascinating to assign, rather than have students choose, groups for kinetic sculptures and watch them accommodate the various ability levels. In a group of five, two higher-skilled youngsters might be in handstands at the ends of the sculpture, supporting their legs on the two students next to them. In the middle might be the lower-skilled student on his hands and knees, as all five sway slowly back and forth as a single unit. When groups have achieved solutions, feelings are often very positive and motivating. All group members feel good about their work together.

 Problem Solving Examples of youngsters designing their own games and activities are illustrated in the problem-solving section of the web resource.

Video Recording

When students cooperate in groups on a project such as kinetic sculpturing, positive feelings often result. However, you may feel that the movement lacks quality. Students can have a hard time working toward a finished product. For example, when students present their creations, they never do them the same way twice. It's hard to motivate them to refine their dances or sequences beyond simply combining a few movements.

Video recording can be a valuable tool for aiding this process, because students can observe and analyze their creations and begin to actually refine their work so that it achieves a level of quality—the slows are truly slow; the movements, truly synchronous. As they see their work evolve into an interesting design, in synchrony with others, they are often motivated to continue to practice. Without this visual feedback, they might be reluctant to work beyond the initial creation of a sequence to truly develop it into a work of art.

Video recording is also motivating because students can watch their performances of skills such as batting, kicking, rolling, and playing zone defense. They can see how well they are doing and also where they can improve. No topic is more interesting to youngsters than their own performances. Video recording allows you to take advantage of this human characteristic and channel it into a motivational tool in physical education.

FIGURE 8.5 Worksheet for Student-Designed Softball Practice

Softball Practice

Team members' names _____

Design a practice that you can do on one half of a field.

1. Identify skills your team wants to focus on.
2. Select activities from the list to use in your practice. You must select at least one activity from each skill category and six activities overall.
3. Identify how long you will spend on that activity.
4. Identify the cues you will focus on in that activity.
5. Each person on your team must be active and have the same number of practice tries.

Hitting tasks	Cues
Hit off tee.	Stance, front shoulder lower, step, roll hands over, hips first
Partner soft toss, hit to curtain.	Hit to open space
Bounce ball, hit to curtain.	
Pitch friendly ball, hit to curtain.	
Play over-the-line game.	

Fielding tasks	Cues
Play catch.	Watch the ball, catch on throwing side, two hands, give with ball
Play catch, throwing both ground balls and fly balls.	Quick transition to throwing hand, quick feet to get side to target
One member hits grounder or fly ball to fielder. Rotate.	
Play over-the-line game (batters who miss throw ball to fielder).	

Throwing tasks	Cues
Play catch and throw. How many throws can you make in one minute?	Step, transfer weight, side to target, elbow up
Do group juggle in large space.	Quick feet, hips first
Do throwing relay.	
Catch fly ball or grounder; then throw as quickly as possible to partner.	

Practice Outline

Activity	Time	Cues

Homework Practice

The last of the eight techniques that can be motivating for some youngsters in some school settings is homework practice (Kraft, Smith, & Buzby, 1997). You can provide a homework task card listing a series of tasks for them to work on with a parent or guardian. Figure 8.6 is a task card for the volleyball forearm pass. Middle or high school students can have homework that requires them to walk, skate, bike, or scooter with a friend or sibling around the neighborhood. They can create a map that identifies accessible and safe parks and play spaces of other facilities where they can be physically active (figure 8.7). You may want to lend equipment (e.g., foam rackets, hockey sticks, juggling scarves) to those who do not have them at home. There is no guarantee that everything will be returned, but it is certainly worth a try if it encourages them to become physically active outside of school.

Developing Realistic Expectations

The eight techniques for motivating youngsters described so far can be used when teaching entire classes. Obviously, you can vary them in many ways. A more long-term approach that doesn't fit neatly into the category of a technique is guiding youngsters to

FIGURE 8.6   Homework Task Card

Dear Parent or Guardian:

A volleyball has been checked out to your child to use for homework in physical education. Your child must complete the list of tasks below and return the volleyball to the physical education teacher in three school days. We ask you to please initial below to confirm that your child has completed each task.

Student name: _____   Grade: _____

Classroom teacher: _____   Date ball is checked out: _____

Directions: Complete the following tasks using the volleyball. Have your parent or guardian sign at the bottom once you've completed them all. Make sure you show your parent or guardian how you did!

- Toss the ball up, bump it once with your arms, and then catch it.

- Toss it up, bump it twice, and then catch it.

- Try to bump the ball as many times in a row as you can. How many did you get? _____

- Toss the ball to the wall, bump it to the wall, and then catch it.

- Try to bump the ball off the wall as many times in a row as you can. How many did you get? _____

- With a family member, bump back and forth as many times as you can. How many did you get? _____

Parent/Guardian signature: _____

Adapted from Kraft, Smith, and Buzby 1997.

FIGURE 8.7 Homework Practice for Activity Route Mapping

Name _____ Class period _____

This PE homework assignment is worth 15 points and is due on _____.

From your house, where can you safely ride? Are there places to go? What bike route would you take to get there? For this assignment, do the following:

1. Create a map from your house of where you can ride your bike by drawing a route on a separate sheet of paper or on the back of this paper. Make up a name for your route.

2. Do the following:
   a. Label trail and street names.
   b. Mark the streets or trails you will have to cross with an X.
   c. Draw a continuous line to show the route, and indicate the right side of the road with a different colored pen or marker.
   d. Estimate the total mileage of the route and how long it might take you to complete it. Include this at the top of your map.

3. Discuss with a parent or guardian your mapped route. Have him or her answer the following questions:
   a. How would I safely go about riding this route?
   b. What other obstacles or challenges do you know about that I may have forgotten to include on the map?
   c. Would you allow me to safely test the route? If so, what would be your guidelines for me? If not, why not?

4. Have a parent or guardian sign the bottom of your map to verify that you completed the project.

Parent or guardian signature _____

Parent or Guardian, please indicate whether you feel comfortable with your child actually using this physical activity plan:

_____

_____

_____

create and understand realistic expectations about the length of time and the amount of practice required to learn a skill.

Too often, children and adolescents expect to learn to perform a skill well in a single 30-minute lesson. You might provide clear and interesting instructions and a good demonstration, but you may neglect to tell them that the skill can't be learned in 20 minutes or after 35 throws—it takes much longer than that. When students are continually reminded that it takes a long time to learn a motor skill, they understand better that they're not failing (Rink, 2004; Schmidt & Wrisberg, 2013). It takes a lot of practice to learn a skill. This may also help them understand the need to practice beyond class. Following are concepts students can learn relatively quickly:

- Use the underhand throw for accuracy or when you are close to a target, and the overhand throw for distance or force.
- A wide base of support results in a more stable balance than a narrow one.
- Moving continuously when playing soccer, even when you don't have the ball, makes it harder for a defender to cover you and makes it easier to create open lanes to receive a pass.
- A leap means taking off from one foot and landing on the other.
- Taking a ball away from someone who is dribbling at a low level is harder than taking it away from someone who is dribbling at a high level.

The idea that it takes a lot of practice and time to master a motor skill is one that apparently many adults don't understand either. Observe a foursome of golfers. If one is less skilled than the other three, watch how the skilled golfers continually provide tips to the poorer golfer. The assumption seems to be that if they could just provide the magic cue, the less-skilled golfer would instantly become a good golfer (see chapter 4).

As physical educators, we know that someone doesn't suddenly become a good golfer because of a magic cue. It might be the appropriate cue, but it takes a long time before it is incorporated into a golf swing schema that integrates the cue into a functional motor plan (Schmidt & Wrisberg, 2013). One of your goals as a teacher is to help youngsters understand this important concept: those who are good at sports practice and practice and practice—they weren't born that way.

Physical Education Dropouts

Sometimes we wonder whether one of the contributing factors to youngsters dropping out of or losing interest in physical education early is unrealistic expectations. Others in the class who play on teams or in the neighborhood after school have learned a variety of skills—but not in physical education. If youngsters expect to become as good as their classmates in relatively few lessons, it's no wonder they become frustrated and conclude early that they're no good at physical activity.

Teacher as Cheerleader

We want to comment on the idea that youngsters can be motivated by teachers who are cheerleaders. Cheerleader teachers buzz around the gym shouting things like "Terrific! Outstanding! Fantastic! Awesome!" as they encourage their students to continue working and trying. This is a great technique with some obvious limitations.

The first limitation is that some of us are not cheerleaders. Even if we wanted to be, we couldn't keep it up for 10 classes a day for 30 years. The second limitation is that if students come to expect this type of extrinsic motivation from a teacher, they rely on the teacher rather than on themselves for encouragement and a sense of improvement.

TECH TIPS Showcase Your Students!

You can post student pictures and video clips (with parents' or guardians' permission) to the school website to showcase your program. Students are motivated by being the star of the week for physical education. Perhaps the cafeteria has a monitor you could use to showcase your students and their work.

Fortunately, students aren't always taught by teachers who can or want to serve as the total source of motivation for their classes, even if they could. Given this reality, it is important for youngsters to develop the inner satisfaction that comes from continuing to try and recognizing that, as a result of their effort, they are improving. You can help your students recognize that they are getting better, not as quickly as they might like, perhaps, but gradually. In so doing, you can make an especially significant contribution to their eventual enjoyment of and satisfaction through physical activity. That's not to say that for some students, some classes, and some topics, cheerleading isn't important. It is, but students also need to experience the satisfaction that results from their own desire and motivation to continue working and trying.

Summary

One of the key challenges you face as a teacher is motivating your students so that they want to continue learning independently of you. Three keys to motivating students are providing tasks that are success oriented, autonomy supportive, and developmentally appropriate. Motivational strategies include teaching by invitation, intratask variation, task sheets, stations or learning centers, homework practice, and video recording. Guiding students in designing their own games, tasks, and activities can also motivate them to engage in physical activities. Most of these techniques give you opportunities to present all students with tasks that are appropriate for them—and that's important because every student in your classes is unique.

As is true of so much of teaching, one technique alone won't continually motivate students. You need to create an ambiance, an environment, that makes youngsters want to learn—not because of your personality but because the lessons are designed so that they succeed and feel good about their progress.

Questions for Reflection

1. Think about what motivates you to practice—success or failure? Is it different for different sports or activities? Has it changed with experience? With age?

2. Some teachers describe their classes as no-fault zones. How might this concept apply to the ideas discussed in this chapter?

3. This chapter describes techniques for modifying tasks to increase success. Can you think of ways you change tasks (or bend the rules) so that you can succeed?

4. Observe youngsters playing together. Notice how they invent and change the rules of play. Why do you think they do this? When do adults modify rules when they play together?

5. Which of the techniques described in this chapter do you feel most comfortable with as a teacher? Least comfortable? Why do you think this is so?

6. Do your students rely on you for their motivation? Do you want them to? Have you found ways to help them develop realistic expectations and intrinsic motivation? Explain your answers.

References

Alderman, B.L., Beighle, A., & Pangrazi, R.P. (2006). Enhancing motivation in physical education. *Journal of Physical Education, Recreation and Dance, 77* (2), 41-45, 51.

Bagøien, T.E., & Halvari, H. (2005). Autonomous motivation: Involvement in physical activity, and perceived sport competence: Structural and mediator models. *Perceptual and Motor Skills, 100* (1), 3-21.

Bagøien, T.E., Halvari, H., & Nesheim, H. (2010). Self-determined motivation in physical education and its links to motivation for leisure-time physical activity, physical activity, and well-being in general. *Perceptual and Motor Skills, 111* (2), 407-432.

Block, M.E. (1995). Use peer tutors and task sheets. *Strategies, 8* (7), 9-11.

Block, M.E. (1996). Modify instruction: Include all students. *Strategies, 9* (4), 9-12.

Brophy, J., & Good, T.L. (1986). Teacher behavior and student achievement. In C.M. Wittrock (Ed.), *Handbook of research on teaching* (3rd ed., pp. 328-375). New York: Macmillan.

Ellery, P.J. (1995). Peer tutors work. *Strategies, 8* (7), 12-14.

Garcia, C. (1994). Gender differences in young children's interactions when learning motor skills. *Research Quarterly for Exercise and Sport, 65* (3), 213-225.

Graham, G., Castenada, R., Hopple, C., Manross, M., & Sanders, S. (1992). Developmentally appropriate physical education for children: A position statement of the Council on Physical Education for Children (COPEC). Reston, VA: National Association for Sport and Physical Education.

Halvari, H., Ulstad, S.O., Bagøien, T.E., & Skjesol, K. (2009). Autonomy support and its links to physical activity and competitive performance: Mediations through motivation, competence, action orientation and harmonious passion, and the moderator role of autonomy support by perceived competence. *Scandinavian Journal of Educational Research, 53* (6), 533-555.

Hastie, P.A., Rudisill, M.E., & Wadsworth, D.D. (2013). Providing students with voice and choice: Lessons from intervention research on autonomy-supportive climates in physical education. *Sport, Education & Society, 18* (1), 38-56.

Iserbyt, P., & Byra, M. (2013). Design and use of task cards in the reciprocal style of teaching. *Journal of Physical Education, Recreation and Dance, 84* (2), 20-26.

Kolovelonis, A., & Goudas, M. (2012). Students' recording accuracy in the reciprocal and the self-check teaching styles in physical education. *Educational Research & Evaluation, 18* (8), 733-747.

Kozub, F.M. (2001). Using task cards to help beginner basketball players self-assess. *Strategies, 14* (5), 18-22.

Kraft, R.E., Smith, J.A., & Buzby, J.H. (1997). Teach throwing and catching to large classes. *Strategies, 10* (3), 12-15.

Lee, A.M. (2004). Promoting lifelong physical activity through quality physical education. *Journal of Physical Education, Recreation and Dance, 75* (5), 21-24.

Mandigo, J.L., & Thompson, L.P. (1998). Go with their flow: How flow theory can help practitioners to intrinsically motivate children to be physically active. *Physical Educator, 55* (3), 145.

Mosston, M., & Ashworth, S. (2002). *Teaching physical education* (5th ed.). Columbus, OH: Bell & Howell.

National Association for Sport and Physical Education (NASPE). (2009). *Appropriate practices in physical education.* Reston, VA: AAHPERD.

Newsome, J.A. (2005). Task sheets and stations: Busy, happy and learning. *Strategies, 18* (6), 22-23, 31.

Pease, D.A., & Lively, M.J.A. (1994). Variation: A tool for teachers. *Strategies, 7* (4), 5-8.

Pellet, T.L., & Harrison, J.M. (1996). Individualize to maximize student success. *Strategies, 9* (7), 20-22.

Prusak, K.A., Treasure, D.C., Darst, P.W., & Pangrazi, R.P. (2004). The effects of choice on the motivation of adolescent girls in physical education. *Journal of Teaching in Physical Education, 23*, 19-29.

Rink, J.E. (2004). It's okay to be a beginner. *Journal of Physical Education, Recreation and Dance, 75* (6), 31-34.

Rogers, C.S., Ponish, K.P., & Sawyers, J.K. (1991). Control of level of challenge: Effects in intrinsic motivation to play. Unpublished manuscript.

Ryan, R.M., & Deci, E.L. (2000). Self-determination theory and the facilitation of intrinsic motivation, social development, and well-being. *American Psychologist, 55* (1), 68-78.

Schmidt, R.A., & Wrisberg, C.A. (2013). *Motor learning and performance* (5th ed.). Champaign, IL: Human Kinetics.

Siedentop, D., & Tannehill, D. (2000). *Developing teaching skills in physical education* (4th ed.). Palo Alto, CA: Mayfield.

Stork, S., & Sanders, S. (1996). Developmentally appropriate physical education: A rating scale. *Journal of Physical Education, Recreation and Dance, 67* (6), 52-58.

Tjeerdsma, B.L. (1995). How to motivate students . . . without standing on your head! *Journal of Physical Education, Recreation and Dance, 66* (5), 36-39.

Valentini, N., & Rudisill, M. (2004). Motivational climate, motor-skill development, and perceived competence: Two studies of developmentally delayed kindergarten children. *Journal of Teaching in Physical Education, 23*, 216-234.

Wolfe, P., & Sharpe, T. (1996). Improve your teaching with student coders. *Strategies, 9* (7), 5-9.

Xiang, P., Chen, A., & Bruene, A. (2005). Interactive impact of intrinsic motivators and extrinsic rewards on behavior and motivation outcomes. *Journal of Teaching in Physical Education, 24*, 179-197.

Providing Feedback

THAT TIME YOU REALLY USED 'QUICK FEET' GREAT!

"We were beginning striking with paddles in the kindergarten classes. The classes were receiving instruction on how to keep the wrist stiff when contacting the piece of equipment being struck. The classroom teacher came to pick them up and one student proceeded to exclaim, with much excitement, "I had fun playing with those 'skillets!'" I guess the association came from the use of "flipping pancakes" while we were tossing and catching beanbags with a stiff wrist. "

Paula Green,
Price's Fork Elementary School,
Blacksburg, Virginia

Reprinted with permission from PE Central
(www.pecentral.org).

After reading this chapter, you should be able to do the following:

- Describe the advantages and uses of feedback.
- Assess which students are receiving feedback.
- Analyze types of feedback.
- Explain the value of feedback in physical education.

During a physical education class, when you observe that

- the task is appropriate for the students,
- they don't need a challenge because they are practicing the task as intended, and
- they understand the cue, or critical element,

that is a good time to provide feedback. Observe the students individually and apprise them of how they are moving and what they can do to improve. Student feedback has several advantages:

- Feedback encourages students to continue practicing because they know you are watching them move (Silverman, Tyson, & Krampitz, 1992).
- Feedback plus practice increases students' skill and knowledge acquisition (SHAPE America, 2014).
- When providing feedback, you tend to travel around the teaching area, as opposed to standing in one spot, which is an effective teaching behavior (chapter 10).
- Feedback helps students better assess their own performances.
- Feedback lets you assess individual students to determine how quickly (and correctly) they are learning skills (Stroot & Oslin, 1993).
- Feedback increases engagement in uninterested learners (Pollock, 2011).
- Feedback not only contributes to a student's functional understanding of a motor skill and performance but also is a motivational influence on learning (Wulf, Shea, & Lewthwaite, 2010).

Types of Feedback

Successful teachers provide various amounts and types of feedback to accomplish the purposes just listed (Nicaise et al., 2006). Typically, quality feedback is categorized as specific, congruent, simple, and generally positive or neutral (Sharpe, 1993).

KP or KR

Feedback can be classified in many ways (Lee, Keh, & Magill, 1993; Schmidt & Wrisberg, 2013; Silverman, Tyson, & Krampitz, 1992). One of the more common distinctions is between knowledge of performance (KP) and knowledge of results (KR). Knowledge of results refers to the outcome, or product, of the movement (e.g., the ball hits the target). Knowledge of performance refers to the characteristics of the movement (the cues, or critical elements), which is also referred to as the process of the movement (Boyce et al., 1996; Schmidt & Wrisberg, 2013). This chapter focuses on knowledge of performance, or the movement process.

Specific Feedback

Feedback is specific when it tells learners exactly what they need to practice or how they are moving (Claxton & Fredenburg, 1989; Mustain, 1990; Pellett & Harrison, 1995; Rink & Werner, 1987; Silverman, Tyson, & Krampitz, 1992; Wiggins, 2012). Feedback is general when it does not refer to any one factor; it might refer to the learner's movement, behavior, or dress.

Probably the most commonly used expression of general feedback in education today is *Good!* Unfortunately, this doesn't provide information students need to improve. They

are left wondering whether the outcome, result, or process (performance) was good. Or was it simply a good try?

Expressions such as *Good, Great, Terrific, Wow,* and *All right* are helpful for promoting a positive and warm learning environment, especially with young children who desire teacher approval and have yet to achieve the skill level that allows them to obtain intrinsic satisfaction from moving in accomplished ways (Sharpe, 1993). General feedback is good for encouraging children to continue to move and continue to try.

As children mature, they benefit from the information teachers provide that they can't obtain themselves. They know, for example, that the ball isn't going where they want it to—they just don't know what they need to do differently. Specific feedback tells them exactly what they need to focus on to get the ball into the air or to make it go straight. Effective feedback is specific and actionable. Students should know from your feedback what specifically they should try to do the next time.

Here are some examples of specific feedback (knowledge of performance):

- "This time see if you can bend both your knees and your ankles."
- "Be sure to turn your side toward the target."
- "Great. That time you both started at the same time."
- "Can you make your shape even wider?"
- "This time see if you can make the slow part even slower."
- "Try to follow through so that your hand and arm go right to the target."

At times, when students are familiar with the terminology, one or two reminder words (cues, or critical elements; chapter 4) can provide specific feedback about how they are moving. This is best done when the feedback relates to a cue or refinement that you explained recently.

TECH TIPS Video Analysis Apps

Students can give themselves or their partners specific feedback by using a video analysis app such as Coach's Eye or Hudl Technique. Students can record skills or activities; then analyze the video using stop motion technology, add audio narration, and even draw on the screen. This creates a new video that can be assessed by the student, peers, or a teacher to provide appropriate feedback.

Congruent Feedback

Feedback that focuses on the cue or refinement just explained (chapter 4) and often demonstrated to the entire class (chapter 7) is called congruent feedback. It corresponds to the idea just presented that, ideally, they are thinking about as they move (Masser, 1993; Pellett & Harrison, 1995; Rink & Werner, 1987). An example will help make the point.

Consider a lesson focused on learning to strike with a paddle. The task the fourth-graders have been working on is striking the ball back and forth with a partner (S1.E24.4b). The teacher stops the class and demonstrates the concept of quick feet (moving quickly to be in a position to hit the ball). He then asks them to continue striking with their partners and thinking about quick feet as he begins to circulate and provide feedback. Congruent feedback would consist of telling students how they are (or are not) using quick feet to move to the ball.

Incongruent feedback might be about how to hold the paddle, watching the ball, following through, extending the elbow, and other important critical elements related to striking with paddles. These examples of incongruent feedback are not wrong—just incongruent because they are not about what the students have been asked to think about and pay attention to as they practice.

To provide congruent feedback, limit your statements to the information you most recently provided when you explained the cue to the entire class. This doesn't mean that some learners don't need feedback about other cues—often they do. Congruent feedback, however, lets them know how their practice of the cue is going; they receive feedback about what they are thinking and practicing. You can reinforce it through pinpointing (chapter 7), in which you ask certain students to demonstrate the cue to the entire class.

TECH TIPS Using Video Delay

The BaM Video Delay app is a great tool to help students see and reflect on the skills they are performing. This app is always recording at a station, but the video is delayed. When the students finish performing, they can go to the iPad to analyze their form. You can also use it to provide feedback to individual students during the next lesson.

 Teacher Feedback   The web resource provides videos of several teachers providing feedback.

Simple Feedback

One of the advantages to you of providing congruent feedback is that it helps you focus on only one component at a time (chapter 7). This is referred to as simple feedback. Providing simple feedback is far easier and no doubt more accurate than attempting to do a complete biomechanical analysis of all students in the class as you move around, including analyzing the correct use of four, six, or even eight critical elements.

In addition to being easier for you, the students benefit from simple feedback because they hear the cue repeatedly as you move about. Obviously, this repetition promotes learning (Sharpe, 1993). It also gives you a better idea of when to change the cue because you can notice when students are incorporating it into their movements.

Let's look at an example of simple feedback. If the most recently taught cue relates to the use of the finger pads in dribbling, this might be the feedback pattern:

- "Pads, Mark."
- "Nice pads, Rosa."
- "Ferman, are those your finger pads?"
- "Liz, good pads."
- "Pads, Verenda."
- "Use your pads, Shawn."

Simple feedback can often consist of a word or two; you can use the reminder words you used to describe the cue during instruction (chapter 7) as feedback. When you provide specific, congruent, simple feedback, students (anyone really) can tell what you are emphasizing. You might find yourself saying "Pads" hundreds of times during eight or more classes and be sick of the word by the end of the day. However, you have the satisfaction of knowing that when the 200 to 300 students you taught that day go home, they can answer the question "What did you learn in PE today?" Well, realistically, many of them will be able to answer the question.

Positive and Neutral Feedback

Overall, the best feedback is positive feedback (Schmidt & Wrisberg, 2013; Sharpe, 1993; Silverman, Tyson, & Krampitz, 1992). It is encouraging and creates a warm, pleasant atmosphere as compared to a nagging, harsh environment in which youngsters feel that they are continually doing something wrong. Review the previous feedback examples, and you will notice that they are either positive ("Nice, good") or neutral ("Pads"). Few teachers use negative feedback (Silverman, Tyson, & Krampitz, 1992). Overall, you should vary the affective message of your feedback: sometimes positive, sometimes neutral, occasionally negative (Kniffen, 1988). Providing feedback both verbally and visually by demonstrating a skill and, when appropriate, physically guiding the student through a movement is helpful (Sharpe, 1993). This way you can ensure that students are truly grasping the concepts.

In addition to influencing skill performance, feedback might also affect perceived competence (Nicaise et al., 2006). Feedback from teachers, parents or guardians, and coaches can influence how children and adolescents feel about their ability to perform a task or assume a role in a game or group work. This is another reason to be sensitive to the type, and tone, of the feedback you give to children and adolescents.

Coaches' Feedback

My (GG) recollection of the type of feedback I received from coaches in team sports is that it was predominantly negative. If I did something right, I didn't hear much about it. But if I messed up, I sure received feedback in a hurry, and it was often negative—and loud! Why was that so? Are athletes on a team different from students in a physical education class? Does one's skill level influence the type of feedback that might be useful? Are coaches today different from the coaches of 20 years ago?

Although negative feedback is rarely recommended, we find that teachers who provide feedback that is specific, congruent, and simple can use negative feedback occasionally to let their students know that they still aren't using a cue correctly. Although this feedback is negative, our experience suggests that it can be done in such a way that it is helpful, not damaging. A private statement such as "Jenelle, those are your fingertips, not your pads" or "Mike, remember that you should not stop your racket motion short of a complete follow-through" are technically negative but realistically helpful.

Negative feedback is especially useful for students who just don't understand the cue and fail to realize, after repeated feedback, that they are still not using the cue. It's also particularly useful for the occasional youngster who is an athlete or highly skilled and doesn't bother to listen carefully to a teacher. He may have played on the basketball team since second grade and thinks he knows everything there is to know about the game and certainly everything about a simple skill such as dribbling. This might sound harsh if you are an inexperienced teacher, but if you are a veteran, you most likely recognize our characterization of the athlete who supposedly knows it all.

Brophy and Good (1986), as part of an analysis of effective teaching, provided guidelines for praising children effectively (table 9.1). The table summarizes many of the principles described in this chapter for effective feedback—specific, simple, congruent, and generally positive.

To this point, we have addressed feedback directed to individual students when you are nearby. That is often the case, but at times feedback may be directed to a single student, or a group of students, from across the room so that the other students can hear it (Ryan & Ratliffe, 2000). This type of feedback, called cross-group feedback, has the advantage of focusing students on the cue and also reminding them that you are watching their practice attempts. Group-specific feedback is also sometimes appropriate when you observe that most students in a class need corrective feedback on a specific cue. Stop the class, provide specific feedback on how to correct the problem, and then provide more practice opportunities so that students can work to correct the performance error (SHAPE America, 2014). Both cross-group and group-specific feedback are good tools to have in your teacher toolbox.

TECH TIPS Using Google Forms

Google Forms provides a very easy way to collect information from students through surveys, quizzes, and tests. Because you receive responses from Google Forms right after the students submit their information, you can provide quick feedback.

TABLE 9.1 **Guidelines for Effective Praise**

Effective praise	Ineffective praise
Is delivered contingently	Is delivered randomly or unsystematically
Specifies the particulars of the accomplishment	Is restricted to global reactions
Shows spontaneity, variety, and other signs of credibility; suggests clear attention to the students' accomplishments	Shows a bland uniformity that suggests a conditioned response made with minimal attention
Rewards attainment of specified performance criteria (which can include effort criteria, however)	Rewards mere participation, without consideration of performance processes or outcomes
Provides information to students about their competence or the value of their accomplishments	Provides no information at all nor gives students information about their status
Orients students toward better appreciation of their own task-related behavior and thinking about problem solving	Orients students toward comparing themselves with others and thinking about competing
Uses students' own prior accomplishments as the context for describing present accomplishments	Uses the accomplishments of peers as the context for describing students' present accomplishments
Is given in recognition of noteworthy effort or success at difficult (for *this* student) tasks	Is given without regard to the effort expended or the meaning of the accomplishment
Attributes success to effort and ability, implying that similar successes can be expected in the future	Attributes success to ability alone or to external factors such as luck or low task difficulty
Fosters endogenous attributions (students believe that they expend effort on the task because they enjoy the task and/or want to develop task-relevant skills)	Fosters exogenous attributions (students believe that they expend effort on the task for external reasons—to please the teacher, to win a competition or reward, etc.)
Focuses students' attention on their own task-relevant behavior	Focuses students' attention on the teacher as an external authority figure who is manipulating them
Fosters appreciation of, and desirable attributions about, task-relevant behavior after the process is completed	Intrudes into the ongoing process, distracting attention from task-relevant behavior

Reproduced from J. Brophy, 1981, "Teacher praise: A functional analysis," *Review of Educational Research* 51(1): 5-32.

Analyzing Your Feedback

Figure 9.1 is a completed example of a form to help you analyze your feedback—which students are getting your feedback, what type of feedback you are giving, and how much feedback you are providing in a lesson. (A blank version of this form is available on the

FIGURE 9.1 Feedback Analysis Form

Date __11/20__   Class __Ms. Brown__   Grade __Second__

Feedback Analysis Form

What is the primary focus of the lesson (the cue[s] you are teaching)?

Throwing—side to the target (S1.E14.2)

Your feedback (in each space, write an instance of feedback given and to whom)	Type of feedback			
1. Xavier, side to the target.	**X** Skill __Behavior	__General **X** Specific	__Negative __Positive **X** Neutral	**X** Congruent __Incongruent
2. Cathy, please don't run into others as you move.	__Skill **X** Behavior	__General **X** Specific	**X** Negative __Positive __Neutral	__Congruent **X** Incongruent
3. When you throw, always remember side to the target.	**X** Skill __Behavior	__General **X** Specific	__Negative __Positive **X** Neutral	**X** Congruent __Incongruent
4. Sofia, I like the way you're following through.	**X** Skill __Behavior	__General **X** Specific	__Negative **X** Positive __Neutral	__Congruent **X** Incongruent
5. Great side to the target! (to Quinn and Spencer)	**X** Skill __Behavior	__General **X** Specific	__Negative **X** Positive __Neutral	**X** Congruent __Incongruent
6. Good work, class.	**X** Skill **X** Behavior	**X** General __Specific	__Negative **X** Positive __Neutral	__Congruent **X** Incongruent
7. Great!	**X** Skill **X** Behavior	**X** General __Specific	__Negative **X** Positive __Neutral	__Congruent **X** Incongruent
8. Side, Makayla.	**X** Skill __Behavior	__General **X** Specific	__Negative __Positive **X** Neutral	**X** Congruent __Incongruent
9. Think about your side. (to Ethan)	**X** Skill __Behavior	__General **X** Specific	__Negative __Positive **X** Neutral	**X** Congruent __Incongruent
10. You don't have your side to the target, Devin.	**X** Skill __Behavior	__General **X** Specific	**X** Negative __Positive __Neutral	**X** Congruent __Incongruent
11. Follow through, Mike.	**X** Skill __Behavior	__General **X** Specific	__Negative __Positive **X** Neutral	__Congruent **X** Incongruent
12. Please keep the balls out of the bleachers, guys.	__Skill **X** Behavior	__General **X** Specific	__Negative __Positive **X** Neutral	__Congruent **X** Incongruent
13. Terrific job today, class, staying on task.	__Skill **X** Behavior	**X** General __Specific	__Negative **X** Positive __Neutral	__Congruent **X** Incongruent

web resource.) To use this form, record yourself teaching a class (if possible, using a wireless microphone so you can hear your interactions with individual students). Analyze the video, and list all the feedback you gave during the lesson. List each feedback instance, indicating the student or group receiving it or whether it was given to the entire class. Next, indicate whether it was related to a skill or behavior (e.g., off-task or inappropriate behavior). Then record whether the feedback was general or specific; positive, neutral, or negative; and congruent or incongruent with the lesson focus (cue, or learnable piece).

Who Gets Your Feedback?

If you're honest with yourself, you probably notice that you tend to favor one type of student over another. You may prefer to teach the highly skilled or the less skilled. Ideally, you would provide equal amounts of feedback to students of all skill levels (Sharpe, 1993; Tjeerdsma, 1997). Physical attractiveness may also influence your feedback tendencies. Martinek (1983), for example, found that attractive children tend to get more teacher attention than unattractive children. Some teachers provide more feedback to boys; others give more to girls. Who gets your feedback? Do you need to practice giving equal amounts of feedback to all students in your class?

Once you have reviewed the entire lesson and analyzed your feedback, consider these questions:

- How many times did you give feedback to an individual student? Which (if any) students did not receive feedback from you?
- Did you tend to favor any particular group—the highly skilled, the more personable students, boys, girls (Nicaise et al., 2006)?
- How many times did you give feedback to the entire class? Was it more likely to be skill or behavior related? Was it appropriate and congruent?
- Do you tend to use specific or general feedback? How might you make your feedback more specific?
- How many times did you give feedback that was congruent with your cues?
- Are you satisfied with the ratio of positive to neutral to negative?
- Did you vary your use of positive terms? Or did *Good* or *All right* predominate?
- What did you do well in providing feedback? What could you do differently?

Obviously, you could also ask a number of other questions about your feedback. This type of analysis, done periodically, helps you better understand and analyze your teaching.

Research on Physical Education Teacher Feedback

Historically, physical education teachers have been taught that teacher feedback is an important technique to help students learn motor skills. No doubt this is true. But some suggest that feedback might be overrated in terms of its value as a teaching skill (Lee, Keh, & Magill, 1993; Nicaise et al., 2006; Silverman, Tyson, & Krampitz, 1992).

Motor learning researchers have documented the value of feedback in laboratories (Lee, Keh, & Magill, 1993; Schmidt & Wrisberg, 2013; Silverman, Tyson, & Krampitz, 1992). They created settings in which subjects received absolutely no feedback whatsoever. The subject pressed a button, for example, and had no idea whether she pressed it too soon or too late. The researchers then provided whatever type of feedback they were testing. These studies revealed that any feedback is superior to no feedback.

In contrast, when students are learning a motor skill on the playground, they always receive some type of internal feedback—they know, for example, where the ball went, how far it went, or how high. If they were rolling or jumping, they have some sense of how it felt and where they ended up. Although different from feedback provided by a teacher or researcher, students' knowledge of results lets them know how they are moving.

Some of the feedback studies done in gyms and on playgrounds have also suggested that feedback is valuable (Pellett & Harrison, 1995; Sharpe, 1993; Silverman, Tyson, & Krampitz, 1992; Stroot & Oslin, 1993). Unfortunately, controlling for the amount of practice the students receive is often difficult. Typically, when teachers are providing feedback, students are practicing. Thus students who received higher amounts of feedback sometimes learned more—or better. They also practiced more, however, making it difficult for the researchers to know whether their improvement was a result of teacher feedback or simply more practice opportunities. As more researchers begin to control the amount of practice so it is equal for students under varying practice conditions (Goldberger, Gerney, & Chamberlin, 1982) and to set their studies in the real world of physical education, we will gain an increased understanding of teacher feedback and its contribution to student learning.

Today, we believe that teacher feedback is important, especially when it is specific, congruent, simple, and mostly positive and neutral. We know, however, that lots of practice at high rates of success contributes to student learning and feelings of satisfaction and enjoyment. Keeping this in mind, you should first make sure that all your students are practicing appropriately. Only then should you provide individual feedback. Spending time with individual students while many of the others drift off task is probably counterproductive.

Video Games Are a Great Example

Consider a video game you play or are familiar with (e.g., Angry Birds, Candy Crush). When you play, you get constant feedback in real time; it's both timely and ongoing. If you fail, you are given an opportunity to start again, and with your new knowledge from the previous feedback, you will most likely perform better. The same applies to your physical education students. By giving them continual feedback during a lesson, they have opportunities to learn from your feedback and improve their performance (Wiggins, 2012).

Summary

Providing feedback has many advantages, including encouraging and motivating students to stay engaged and to continue to practice. This helps them increase their skills and knowledge. This chapter discussed feedback focused on knowledge of performance (the movement process).

All students should receive reasonable amounts of feedback from their teachers. Feedback that is specific (rather than general), congruent (rather than incongruent), simple (rather than complex), and positive or neutral (rather than negative) is most effective. Students should also be praised appropriately. Analyzing your feedback will help you know what types of feedback you are providing, which students are getting your feedback, and how much feedback you are giving in a lesson. Feedback analysis should be done periodically to remind you of the areas in which you are doing well and those that could use improvement. Feedback analysis is also a helpful tool to have in your teaching toolbox.

Questions for Reflection

1. Why is providing feedback an important teaching skill? What is the impact when a teacher provides no feedback at all to students?

2. Can you think of some instances in which general feedback might be useful to the entire class? Provide several examples.

3. Think of your physical education experiences as a student. Was feedback important to you? Can you remember the types of feedback you received? If you were an athlete, it might be interesting to compare the feedback you received from a coach to that from a teacher.

4. Why is congruent, simple feedback so rare in physical activity lessons? Why do instructors tend to overload students?

5. Can you think of several instances in which a lot of feedback might not be beneficial for a particular lesson? To certain learners?

6. Analyze the feedback you give during a lesson using the form in this chapter. What did you do well? Where could you improve?

7. Devise a plan to use feedback analyses in your teaching to help you become a more effective teacher. What will it look like (how, when, where)?

8. What do you think about the use of negative feedback? Should it never be used? Used sparingly? Is it damaging to a learner's self-concept? How much depends on the way you provide it? What is an example of a situation in which negative feedback would be harmful?

References

Boyce, B.A., Markos, N.J., Jenkins, D.W., & Loftus, J.R. (1996). How should feedback be delivered? *Journal of Physical Education, Recreation and Dance, 67* (1), 18-22.

Brophy, J. (1981). Teacher praise: A functional analysis. *Review of Educational Research, 51* (1), 5-32.

Brophy, J., & Good, T.L. (1986). Teacher behavior and student achievement. In C.M. Wittrock (Ed.), *Handbook of research on teaching* (3rd ed., pp. 328-375). New York: Macmillan.

Claxton, D., & Fredenburg, K. (1989). Coaching young athletes: Strategies for success. *Strategies, 2* (2), 5-8, 19.

Goldberger, M., Gerney, P., & Chamberlin, J. (1982). The effects of three styles of teaching on the psychomotor performance and social skill development of fifth grade children. *Research Quarterly for Exercise and Sport, 53,* 116-124.

Kniffen, M. (1988). Instructional skills for student teachers. *Strategies, 1,* 5-10.

Lee, A.M., Keh, N.C., & Magill, R.A. (1993). Instructional effects of teacher feedback in physical education. *Journal of Teaching in Physical Education, 12* (3), 228-243.

Martinek, T. (1983). Creating Golem and Goleta effects during physical education instruction: A social psychological perspective. In T. Templin & J. Olson (Eds.), *Teaching in physical education* (pp. 59-70). Champaign, IL: Human Kinetics.

Masser, L. (1993). Critical cues help first-grade students' achievement in handstands and forward rolls. *Journal of Teaching in Physical Education, 12* (3), 301-312.

Mustain, W. (1990). Are you the best teacher you can be? *Journal of Physical Education, Recreation and Dance, 61* (2), 69-73.

Nicaise, V., Cogerino, G., Bois, J., & Amorose, A.J. (2006). Students' perception of teacher feedback and physical competence in physical education classes: Gender effects. *Journal of Teaching in Physical Education, 25* (1), 36-57.

Pellett, T.L., & Harrison, J.M. (1995). The influence of a teacher's specific, congruent, and corrective feedback on female junior high school students' immediate volleyball practice success. *Journal of Teaching in Physical Education, 15* (1), 53-63.

Pollock, J. (2011). *Feedback: The hinge that joins teaching and learning.* Thousand Oaks, CA: Corwin.

Rink, J., & Werner, P. (1987). Student responses as a measure of teacher effectiveness. In G.T. Barrette, R.S. Feingold, C.R. Rees, & M. Pieron (Eds.), *Myths, models, and methods in sport pedagogy* (pp. 199-206). Champaign, IL: Human Kinetics.

Ryan, S., & Ratliffe, T. (2000, July/August). Keeping kids on-task with crossgroup feedback. *Strategies,* 34-35.

Schmidt, R.A., & Wrisberg, C.A. (2013). *Motor learning and performance* (5th ed.). Champaign, IL: Human Kinetics.

SHAPE America. (2014). *National standards & grade-level outcomes for K-12 physical education.* Champaign, IL: Human Kinetics.

Sharpe, T. (1993). What are some guidelines on giving feedback to students in physical education? *Journal of Physical Education, Recreation and Dance, 64* (9), 13.

Silverman, S., Tyson, L., & Krampitz, J. (1992). Teacher feedback and achievement in physical education. *Teaching and Teacher Education, 8* (4), 333-334.

Stroot, S.A., & Oslin, J.L. (1993). Use of instructional statements by preservice teachers for overhand throwing performance of children. *Journal of Teaching in Physical Education, 13* (1), 24-25.

Tjeerdsma, B.L. (1997). A comparison of teacher and student perspectives of tasks and feedback. *Journal of Teaching in Physical Education, 16* (4), 388-400.

Wiggins, G. (2012). Seven keys to effective feedback. *Educational Leadership, 70* (1). Retrieved from www.ascd.org/publications/educational-leadership/sept12/vol70/num01/Seven-Keys-to-Effective-Feedback.aspx

Wulf, G., Shea, C., & Lewthwaite, R. (2010). Motor skill learning and performance: A review of influential factors. *Medical Education, 44* (1): 75-84.

Minimizing Off-Task Behavior and Discipline Problems

During an exercise unit, I asked a 1st grade class, "What makes our heart beat faster?" Without skipping a beat, a boy sitting next to me whispered in my ear "My girlfriend." "

Sabrina Larmer,
Thomson Estates Elementary,
Elkton, Maryland

Reprinted with permission from PE Central
(www.pecentral.org).

After reading this chapter, you should be able to do the following:

- Describe strategies to minimize off-task behavior.
- Explain the general concepts of two discipline systems used in schools today: Canter's assertive discipline model and Hellison's personal and social responsibility model.
- Discuss the role of parents and guardians, principals, and classroom teachers in supporting a discipline system.
- Describe the feelings and strategies of teachers during discipline confrontations.

Wouldn't it be great if you could just teach—no one misbehaving, no one off task, everyone eager to listen and learn? It would be, but that's a dream. Even teachers who develop the management protocols described in chapter 2 still have some students who misbehave. The reality of teaching is that there will always be a few students who, for whatever reason, march to the beat of a different drummer. We want to emphasize that the techniques described here are typically necessary for only a few students in a class. Most try to please the teacher, follow the rules, and work hard at their tasks. This chapter describes and analyzes some of the ways to prevent off-task behavior.

Why Do Students Act Out?

Many things can lead to off-task behavior; some are in our control, and some are not. Could it be that students are confused about directions or being asked to do tasks that are too easy, too hard, or too protracted? Could they feel put on the spot or embarrassed for some reason? Could a student be looking for attention, be plain old tired or hungry, or have a learning disorder or developmental challenge that leads to frequent outbursts or frustration? Is a holiday coming up, or did one just end? Are a student's parents going through a divorce, or is something going on at home or with friends that is on his mind?

Our experience suggests that when a class (or a student) that is well behaved most days becomes off task, often the teaching is what needs to be modified. You may have to demonstrate a task or activity again to clear up any confusion about expectations. You could provide a harder task for students who are bored with a task that's too easy for them (we covered this in detail in chapter 5). The point is that you must identify the cause of off-task behavior and, when it's within your control, adjust your teaching to get your students back on task.

Some youngsters, however, have a difficult time staying on task day in and day out. Kulinna, Cothran, and Regualos (2006) reported that the most common misbehaviors reported by teachers are talking, not sitting still, arguing, not paying attention, interrupting, not following directions, seeking attention, giggling, and laziness. As you well know, these misbehaviors may be rooted in situations outside of school; nevertheless, you have the responsibility and the challenge of working with all of the students in your classes.

Strategies for Minimizing Off-Task Behavior

Appropriate on-task behavior is often described as students behaving positively in a way that is consistent with the goals of the educational setting (Siedentop & Tannehill, 2000). A class of students who are on task most of the lesson contributes to a positive learning environment and is unlikely to present discipline problems. Even if you have taught the behavior protocols presented in chapter 2, however, you are still going to have incidences of off-task behavior. Therefore, you need strategies that can minimize the misbehavior of students. Unfortunately, they are just strategies, not guarantees. Some of them succeed with some youngsters some of the time. We wish we knew foolproof strategies that work for all teachers all of the time, but we don't; no one does. Good teachers seem to have a repertoire of strategies that they use, sometimes consciously and sometimes without really thinking about them. They include back to the wall, proximity control, with-it-ness, selective ignoring, overlapping, learning names, and positive pinpointing.

Back to the Wall

One of the simplest strategies is referred to as back to the wall. Teachers use this technique for formative assessment (chapter 5) and also for behavior management. Standing on the outside of the boundaries (the wall in the gym or the edge of the playground) lets you see what is going on in a class. When you stand in the middle of a class, about 50 percent of the class is out of your sight; thus, you may not see off-task behavior until it has gone on for some time.

 Back to the Wall The web resource includes several video examples of teachers using the back-to-the-wall technique.

The ability to detect off-task behavior as soon as it begins appears to be a characteristic of successful teachers. Immediate detection seems to prevent the behavior from escalating. When the behavior persists for several minutes, several students might become involved. Thus, a relatively minor incident can escalate into a major incident (e.g., one student tries to wrestle a ball away from another). This is known as the ripple effect (Kounin, 1970). When you see the beginning of such an incident, you can quickly prevent it from escalating because your targeting and timing are appropriate. You can identify the students correctly and quickly, thus preventing the situation from developing into a crisis.

Proximity Control

One technique that can prevent the ball-taking episode just described from escalating is proximity control—simply walking in the direction of the off-task student to let her know that you see her. Giving her the look will let her know that she's off task.

Veteran teachers know what we mean by the look. It's a certain way a teacher looks at a youngster to say, "You're off task; now get back to work." Obviously, however, you need to be close enough so that the student can see your expressions.

Sometimes the look isn't even necessary. Simply standing by a group of students on the verge of becoming off task is often enough to let them know that you see them and expect them to remain focused.

Proximity control implies that you are moving around the gym. Early in their careers, teachers have a tendency to stand in one place. Although standing in one place may be more comfortable than moving around, it's not as effective. Virtually without exception, good teachers move about the classroom, the gym, and the outdoor space.

With-It-Ness

The strategies of back to the wall and proximity control give the class the impression that you have with-it-ness—it's like having eyes in the back of your head (Kounin, 1970). When he began his series of research studies on discipline, Kounin hypothesized that teachers whose students were well behaved and consistently on task were those who threatened them, basically scaring them into behaving. He discovered that this wasn't true. The teachers with the fewest discipline problems communicated to their classes in a calm and reassuring way that they knew what was going on in their classes, they knew the tricks, and therefore students shouldn't even bother to try them. By keeping their backs to the wall and quickly targeting youngsters tending toward off-task behavior, they convinced their students that indeed they were with it.

With It and Without It

Remembering my (GG) days in elementary school, I can recall a sixth-grade teacher who was particularly with it. She was friendly and warm, yet from the first day, we could tell that she wasn't about to let us get away with anything. It was uncanny how she could identify children who were off-task types and, with looks and proximity control, keep them from misbehaving much of that year. The next year, however, we had a teacher who was "without it"; the same class quickly escalated into a rowdy group of children who were continually yelled at and threatened, though without much success. I am sure we were difficult to teach that year. We were essentially the same children, but, among other things, the teacher was "without it."

Selective Ignoring

Recently, I (GG) watched a first-grade lesson focused on round, narrow, wide, and twisted shapes. At times the children were making shapes in their own space; at other times they were traveling around the gym in their shapes. Whenever the opportunity was given to travel, one of the children, Bryan, ran. My reaction and that of my college students who were also observing was to immediately want to stop Bryan from running. The teacher ignored him, however. As we watched, I realized that Bryan really wasn't bothering other children. In fact, they ignored him also. Another teacher might have considered Bryan's behavior off task; Bryan's teacher didn't. And, after watching the entire lesson, I think she was right. Bryan was one of those high-energy children—some might have labeled him hyperactive. He was doing what the teacher asked but at a fast speed. The teacher obviously saw him but chose to selectively ignore him. It was an effective strategy in that lesson.

Selective ignoring works when students have been helped to understand why a student looks or acts a certain way. The opportunity to learn to accept students who behave in ways outside of the norm has been one of the major advantages of mainstreaming in schools. When we observe students working with those with special needs, we are always warmed by their ability to understand the situation and their genuine willingness to help. This understanding doesn't happen automatically, however. Good teachers intentionally teach their classes to understand and work with special students.

> ### Nick's Insight
>
> When my (GG) oldest son, Nick, was in fourth grade, I remember talking to him about some of his classmates after I had observed his class. I commented on one boy who was off task constantly and obviously annoying the teacher. I said that the boy who was off task seemed to be a distraction to the class and a troublemaker. I expected Nick to agree. He surprised me, however, by providing me with one of those glimpses into how children view the world when he said: "Dad, it's not all his fault. The teacher doesn't understand him. He's really a good guy if you give him a chance. She never really gave him one." I try to remember Nick's insight when a child misbehaves in one of my classes.

Overlapping

Unlike back to the wall, which is an easily learned strategy, overlapping is a skill that is learned with practice. Overlapping is the ability to focus on several things at once and still maintain an intended direction.

As a teacher, you are continually required to deal simultaneously with several students or situations. For example, you may nod your head yes at the youngster who has to go to the bathroom; smile at the child who says "Watch me"; put your hand on the shoulder of the youngster who wants to talk to you to signal "Wait a second"; and continue to observe the whole class as you determine whether to change the task or continue it for several more minutes. Locke's vignette in chapter 1 is another illustration of the need to develop the ability to overlap.

Overlapping is a pedagogical skill learned through experience. It is critical because if you work with 30 or more students in a class, you will have to overlap at times to keep a lesson from coming to a complete stop. Obviously, establishing routines and protocols will minimize the need for overlapping, yet it is needed at times.

TECH TIPS ClassDojo

ClassDojo is a wonderful app that you can use to encourage your students, log classroom behavior, and engage parents and guardians. Compatible with any Apple or Android device, ClassDojo allows you to give behavior or skill feedback instantly to individual students and help them see their progress right away. Parents and guardians can see their children's behavior points on a daily basis, and you can even exchange messages with them through the app to keep them informed and engaged.

Learning Names

Learning students' names can be difficult, but it is possible even if you have 600 or more students. One of the frustrating aspects of teaching is attempting to get the attention of a student whose name you don't know. As you try to find out, you may halt the flow of the lesson as several youngsters volunteer the student's name and then stop moving to watch what you have to say to him. When you know a student's name, you can often speak it across the gym to let him know that you see him and offer praise or remind him to get on task.

Some teachers learn names with relative ease. For others it's a struggle. We have all heard of name-learning techniques (e.g., alliteration, using the name several times in conversation, having the students tell you their names when they enter and leave the gym, and taking photos of students) (Williams, 1995). PE Central (www.pecentral.

org) provides a number of suggestions in the section "Tips for the Beginning Teacher." Increasingly, classroom teachers are making name tags for younger children who then wear them to PE until the teacher has time to learn their names. Learning names is even more challenging for teachers who work in schools with transient populations. Half of the youngsters they teach in September are gone in May, replaced by a new group. We wish we had a magical, instant solution to this challenge of learning several hundred names, but we don't. We do know, however, that it really helps to know students' names when trying to prevent off-task behavior.

Positive Pinpointing

Identifying one or more students and pointing them out to the rest of the class as modeling the desired behavior or skill is called pinpointing. This strategy is common in elementary schools. *I like how Verenda and Tommy are standing quietly* is an example of positive pinpointing. Our experience suggests that this technique is more effective with younger children who want to please the teacher. It can be overused, however. Some youngsters seem to ignore it because the teacher is constantly talking about how well someone is doing something. As with any of these strategies, pinpointing can work depending on the students, the way you use it, and how frequently you use it. Chapter 7 explains how to use pinpointing when teaching motor skills.

Many of these strategies or techniques seem to be innate characteristics of successful teachers. Although they are rarely taught or discussed, many teachers use them. But not all do—especially in the beginning of their careers. Beginning teachers are often anchored in the same location throughout their lessons, or fail to see students misbehave because their backs are turned. As with so many of the skills discussed in this book, it's easy to write about them and far more challenging to actually use them when teaching. We hope, however, that you will reflect on the subtle orchestration of teaching skills and strategies and their value for minimizing off-task behavior, whether you are a beginning or an experienced teacher (Downing, Keating, & Bennett, 2005). No matter how well you use these strategies, and others, some students will simply refuse to do what you ask (Timmreck, 1978). Such students are not off task; they have become discipline problems.

All teachers experience discipline problems in their classrooms from time to time. Some minimize the problems, however. What strategies do successful teachers use to minimize discipline problems? To begin with, they spend the first few days of the school year establishing the routines and teaching the management protocols described in chapter 2; they insist that the students learn these routines. They also use many of the strategies previously mentioned for minimizing off-task behavior. In addition, when inappropriate behavior occurs, good teachers examine their own performance. Is the lesson appropriate for the level of the student(s)? Has their behavior instigated student misbehavior? Have they engaged in negative interactions or differential treatment? Is the environment less than positive? Are they reactive rather than proactive?

Proactive or Reactive?

Proactive teachers focus on strategies to maintain or increase positive behavior, such as having established rules, planning appropriate lessons, and praising students who are following expectations (positive pinpointing). Proactive teachers try to avoid discipline problems before they happen. Ideally, we strive to be proactive!

Reactive teachers focus on strategies to stop inappropriate behavior once it has occurred, such as expressing dissatisfaction or imposing an appropriate consequence. Reactive teachers respond after an incident happens to try to avoid further discipline problems. We all must be reactive at times, and with a good discipline system in place, we know the consequences—and so do the students.

Discipline Systems

Most schools have discipline systems that clearly communicate to students and staff both acceptable and unacceptable behaviors and the consequences of misbehavior. Discipline systems widely used in schools generally fit into either an extrinsic or intrinsic category. Extrinsic discipline systems encourage or reinforce appropriate behavior through external rewards or consequences. Intrinsic systems encourage youth to engage in appropriate behavior for internal reasons (i.e., it's the right thing to do) rather than to avoid a punishment or receive a reward. This chapter focuses on two widely used discipline systems: Canter's assertive discipline model (extrinsic system) and Hellison's personal and social responsibility model (intrinsic system). These systems are based on the assumption that some students will misbehave and that teachers need ways to deal with misbehavior for the sake of the students who are misbehaving as well as the others in the class.

Discipline systems should be taught from the beginning of the year and used as needed (Downing, 1996). This is in contrast to hoping students don't misbehave, and when one does, trying to invent a solution on the spot. As any educator will attest, teachers who can continually invent ways to deter off-task behavior amid all the goings-on in a class can be found only in the movies and on television (Kulinna, Cothran, & Regualos, 2006). The advantage of a discipline system is that it gives you a structure for making decisions related to discipline—so that you don't find yourself in the unenviable situation of wondering, *How can I get this student to stop talking (or interrupting, or not following directions) when I have 29 others who need my attention?*

Assertive Discipline

One trend in schools across the United States has been the inception of schoolwide discipline plans relying on extrinsic rewards and consequences. Assertive discipline is one example of a popular, albeit controversial, schoolwide discipline plan that has been used for years and adapted in many schools (Canter, 2010; Hill, 1990; Moone, 1997; Sander, 1989). Art, music, and physical education teachers find schoolwide plans especially helpful because these instructors teach so many different classes in a day and for relatively short periods of time. When a schoolwide program is in place, these teachers have a general idea of the expectations and understanding that the students have been taught regarding behavior in other classes. When all the teachers in a school agree on the rules for behavior, and the consequences of misbehavior, the atmosphere is more consistent for students and somewhat easier for specialist teachers because, at least in theory, they will spend less time teaching their own discipline systems. The major concepts of Canter's assertive discipline model are outlined in figure 10.1.

We realize that adopting a schoolwide discipline plan doesn't necessarily mean that it will be uniformly enforced. The ability to be critically demanding and to have expectations (chapter 2) varies from one teacher to another, as do the students in a class. The concept of schoolwide discipline, however, heightens the chance that teachers in a school will be more consistent with their rules and consequences, thereby providing a more secure environment for the students, who know what to expect from all teachers.

In addition to agreeing on how students should behave throughout the school, there is also agreement on the consequences for misbehavior. Figure 10.2 provides examples of the consequences that are part of an assertive discipline plan (Hill, 1990).

In some schools PE teachers implement their own systems of discipline. In schools with a schoolwide discipline system, PE teachers provide a record of checks for misbehavior to the classroom teachers, who then add them to their checks for the week. The use of bonus or free time on Friday is widespread, although some teachers, partic-

---

FIGURE 10.1　Canter's Assertive Discipline Model: Major Concepts

1. All students can behave responsibly.

2. Firm control (not passive or hostile) is fair.

3. Reasonable expectations (rules, appropriate behavior, etc.) should be clearly communicated.

4. Teachers should expect appropriate behavior from students and receive administrative and parental support to stimulate it.

5. Appropriate behavior should be reinforced; inappropriate behavior should be met with logical consequences.

6. Logical consequences for not meeting expectations should be clearly communicated.

7. Consequences should be consistently reinforced without bias.

8. All verbal and nonverbal communication to students should be firm with definite teacher-student eye contact.

9. Teachers should mentally practice expectations and consequences for consistent use with students.

"Class management skills," A.N. Sander, *Strategies*, 1989, 2(3): 15, reprinted by permission of Taylor & Francis (Taylor & Francis Ltd, http://www.tandfonline.com).

FIGURE 10.2   Consequences for Misbehavior

Elementary

☐ First time a student breaks a rule—student is warned.

☐ Second time a student breaks a rule—student is given a 5-minute time-out.

☐ Third time a student breaks a rule—student is given a 10-minute time-out.

☐ Fourth time a student breaks a rule—teacher calls parents or guardians.

☐ Fifth time a student breaks a rule—student is sent to the principal.

Secondary

☐ First time a student breaks a rule—student is warned.

☐ Second time a student breaks a rule—student loses a grade for the day, sits out the activity, and receives a detention slip.

☐ Third time a student breaks a rule—student receives detention, student is removed from the class or activity, and a parent or guardian is notified.

☐ *Note:* For serious infractions such as fighting and destroying property, the student should be sent directly to the principal's office.

☐ It is important to remember that, each day, the student begins with a clean slate. Thus, regardless of what happened the day or week before, for the first misbehavior of the day, the student is given a warning.

---

ularly those with classes that tend toward misbehavior, use a daily plan rather than a weekly plan, allowing students a few minutes at the end of a class to choose from among several activities. Students who earned checks must work on an activity chosen by the teacher.

Time-Out

Not every teacher and every school uses a formalized discipline system. Other strategies to prevent misbehavior may or may not be a part of an overall plan. Time-out, part of the assertive discipline system, is probably one of the most commonly used techniques in physical education outside of an actual discipline system. It is especially effective because of the subject matter: youngsters might see time away from math or science as a bonus, but they enjoy physical activity, so time-out can be a rather potent technique (Johnson, 1999). Other students might prefer to sit out of physical education, thus making time-out ineffective. In these cases, you can apply other punitive consequences such as grade reductions to make time-out effective. Be careful with reducing grades, however. Grades in physical education, just as in all other subjects, should be based on student learning and performance rather than on effort, participation, or good behavior. When reducing a grade along with having a student sit out, frame it as the student losing the opportunity to demonstrate learning.

Before sending a student to sit out, provide a warning (Moone, 1997)—for example, "If you talk again when I am talking, you will be in time-out." If the undesirable behavior happens again, tell the student to take a time-out or to sit out. Borrowing from the assertive discipline approach, time-out is most effective when you assume that some students will

be in time-out at various times during the year. Teach about time-out at the beginning of the year, almost as one of the management protocols, so that the students clearly understand the process. You can place time-out numbers at various locations on the walls or on the playground and tell a misbehaving student to take a time-out at number 4, for example. This prevents several students from getting together to chat during time-out.

You can also use a clock or a kitchen timer for time-out, allowing students to return to the lesson after, say, two minutes. Another option is to provide paper and pencil on a clipboard and have students write the reason they were placed in time-out (e.g., the rule they violated) before returning to the class. PE Central (www.pecentral.org) has several examples of written activities for youngsters to complete when they are in time-out. Look in the section "Paper and Pencil Assessments." You can also require students to explain to you why they were sent to time-out before returning to class.

If a youngster receives a second time-out in the same lesson, consider requiring him to remain out of the lesson for the rest of the class. This might seem harsh, but some students are so disruptive and demanding that the others in the class, who are on task and trying hard, are shortchanged.

Desirable Rewards and Undesirable Consequences

If you choose to use a discipline system (such as assertive discipline) based on extrinsic rewards, the rewards must be desirable to the students and the consequences must be undesirable. Let's illustrate with several examples. Popcorn parties, in some instances, are desirable. We have been in elementary schools, however, in which the air is permeated with the smell of popping popcorn on Friday afternoons. Our guess is that popcorn every Friday is not a very desirable reward—beyond perhaps the first few Fridays. Students begin to take it for granted after a few weeks.

We have also observed teachers who use free time on Friday as a reward. Although this is motivating for some, it seems to be more of a reward for the teacher than for the students. Classes are frequently threatened with a loss of free time, but somehow part of Friday's lesson is always free time. And how can teachers justify free time when there is much for the students to learn and so little time in which to learn it?

It does not seem that popcorn and free time are effective when they are the only rewards. Some teachers create their own awards. The golden sneaker award is a favorite—an old sneaker spray-painted gold and mounted on a board.

In creating an award, the key is to give it value through the presentation. This may require a bit of acting. In addition to old sneakers, some teachers cleverly create awards from old deflated balls, rusty trophies, whistles without peas, worn-out or knotted jump ropes, or other equipment ready for discard. It's the idea of a reward, more than the value of the item, that is important.

Some elementary school teachers use stickers as a way of saying *Good job*; others use nontoxic stamp pads with messages such as *Awesome* or *Super kid* to stamp the back of children's hands. Rewards secondary students appreciate include activity rewards such as open gym time outside of PE, a choice of warm-up music or class activity during PE, and technology raffles for items such as iTunes gift cards. Some like to earn points toward special events such as school dances or extra gym time on Fridays.

Probably the most effective undesirable consequence for younger children is loss of time in physical education. One of the best ways this is used with younger students is when those who have received misbehavior checks are not permitted to participate in an activity they really enjoy. Parachute activities are often used with younger children, and group games with a cage ball are used with older children—those who have misbehaved during the day or week are not allowed to participate in these activities.

Some secondary students would rather be in time-out than participate in PE class, so sitting out of an activity is not always an effective undesirable consequence. However, sometimes removing a student briefly from a lesson will stop undesirable behavior; sometimes just a warning or reinforcing positive behavior with desirable rewards is all it takes to get secondary students engaged. If undesirable behavior continues, other strategies might include early or after-school detention or meeting with or calling parents or guardians (Rosenthal, Pagnano-Richardson, & Burak, 2010).

The important idea here is that extrinsic rewards must motivate the students for the system to succeed. If they do not care about the rewards, the system will not work.

Personal and Social Responsibility Model

Some teachers prefer intrinsic rewards for students (i.e., internally motivated rewards that are derived from working hard and getting along with others). They believe that youngsters naturally want to do well and that extrinsic rewards are, over the long term, counterproductive (Kohn, 1993). These teachers want their students to participate in and enjoy physical activity for its own sake, not because they can earn extrinsic rewards for participating.

A popular intrinsic motivation system in physical education, the personal and social responsibility model, was developed by Don Hellison (Compagnone, 1995; Hartinger, 1997; Hellison, 2011; Hellison & Templin, 1991; Masser, 1990). Essentially, the model is designed to help youngsters understand and practice self-responsibility. The motivating factor is the innate desire of children and adolescents to get along with others and take responsibility for their own behavior, rather than relying on a teacher to reward them for being good. As with other discipline plans, the model should be clearly explained to students, and students should be encouraged to accept responsibility for their own behavior and work with others. Following are the five levels of Hellison's personal and social responsibility model:

Level 0: irresponsibility. At this level students are unable to take responsibility for their own behavior and typically interfere with others by belittling, intimidating, bullying, or verbally or physically abusing their classmates. Students at level 0 can disrupt the learning environment.

Level 1: respect. This is a level of minimal involvement. Students at level 1 are not necessarily engaged in the lesson or activity but demonstrate respect for others by not disrupting the class or keeping others from actively participating.

Level 2: participation. Students at this level become actively involved in the lessons but typically only when they perceive that the teacher is watching. They will do what they are told or what is required but no more.

Level 3: self-direction. This level is the point at which students begin to take responsibility for their own learning. This implies that they do not need to work under direct supervision from the teacher and that they are able to make decisions independently about what they need to learn and how they might go about learning it. At this level, youngsters are often asked to design their own games, sequences, or dances in small groups. Students can remain actively engaged without direct teacher supervision.

Level 4: caring. Students at this level go beyond simply working with others—they genuinely want to support and help others in the class. For example, a student at this level is the one who volunteers to be a partner for a day with an unpopular student without being asked to do so by the teacher.

Needless to say, this model requires more than simply explaining it to a class and then expecting that students will all want to work at level 4. As with the assertive discipline system, you need to teach the levels at the beginning of the year and then use them throughout the year to encourage students to cooperate with both you and their classmates. Lessons can be specifically designed to initially help students engage in behavior at the higher levels. The levels then become a part of the lessons taught throughout the year to reinforce your rules and expectations. For example, you can use level 1 teaching strategies to help students not disrupt class (i.e., students who are at level 0). For some youngsters, providing opportunities to cool down on their own, even if it means not participating in class, is a step in the right direction. Eventually, the goal is for all students to consistently engage in higher-level behaviors. Following are some strategies for teaching using the levels of responsibility (Hellison, 2011):

General—for teaching all levels

- Ask how they think level 0 people would get out equipment. How about level 1? Level 2? Level 3? Level 4? Then ask them to walk over and get their equipment, showing you the level they think they can work at (Masser, 1990).

- Put students into groups, and assign each group a level to act out. Groups then perform their skits for the rest of the class. All students then discuss the levels they observed.

Level 1—to encourage students who tend to disrupt class (level 0) to remove themselves from activity without disrupting class

- Cool-down zone: Students may remove themselves from an activity and go to the cool-down zone to avoid using foul language, disrupting class, or disrespecting someone else.

- Talking bench: Two students fighting over equipment or the use of space (level 0) can be sent to the talking bench. They sit on the bench until they are ready to explain a solution to you. Assuming that the lesson is interesting, most students will want to return quickly, so they will be eager to find a solution to their conflict (Hartinger, 1997).

- Student complaints: When a student complains about another student, ask the student with the complaint to identify the level the other student is functioning at and to suggest ways to deal with others functioning at that level (Masser, 1990).

Level 2—to include students who tend to remove themselves from activity (level 1)

- All-touch rule: Everyone on the team must touch the ball before anyone can shoot on goal.

Level 3—to encourage students to work independently (move from level 2 to level 3)

- Have students complete task sheets on their own.

- When students are learning a new skill, ask them to suggest ways students at the various levels might practice. Then encourage them to work at the upper levels and compliment them for doing so as a group, or use pinpointing (Masser, 1990).

Level 4—to encourage students to take responsibility for others

- Provide students with peer coaching roles that require decision making and responsibility for others.

- Have students work in groups. Before beginning, they should discuss how students at level 4 would work in a group setting. The focus should be on how to work with youngsters who might display level 0 or 1 behavior (Masser, 1990).

Understanding the Levels of Social Responsibility

Once, when I (SP) was teaching a class of seventh-graders, the focus of the lesson was on the levels of responsibility. Although the lesson was part of a fitness and conditioning unit, the real purpose was to see how well my students understood the levels. I handed out written workouts for the students to choose from and told them that they were responsible for being at level 3 for the day (fully involved) as they did their workouts. As the class followed the written workouts, I assisted them with reminders about the levels and also made mental notes about the levels they seemed to be working at—mostly level 2 (partly engaged), I thought. At the end of class, I asked them all to self-assess by showing me with their fingers the level they worked at during a majority of class. Nearly all showed level 3 or 4; my observations were mostly 1s and 2s. In short, the students thought that they were a lot more responsible than I observed, especially given that they spent a lot of time standing around rather than actually doing their workouts. In the lesson closure, I asked if they were being honest with me, or themselves, about their engagement in their workouts during the entire lesson. I also spoke with nearly all of them individually before they left for their next class and shared my observations of their personal levels. Written fitness workouts were also the focus of the next two lessons. Gradually, the students began to understand what the levels really meant and how to assess their involvement more accurately. By the end of the third lesson, all but one student in my seventh-grade class self-assessed the same level I had observed during class.

Characteristics of Effective Discipline Systems

Whether you adopt or adapt a discipline system based on extrinsic motivation (assertive discipline) or intrinsic motivation (personal and social responsibility model), three important factors will contribute to your success. First, you should explain the discipline system carefully at the beginning of the year so that students understand it; second, you must consistently adhere to the criteria; and third, the principal, classroom teachers, other school staff, and parents and guardians must be supportive.

Student Understanding

Discipline plans that work do so because students clearly understand how they operate and why they exist. To make sure your students know this, introduce the system at the beginning of the year, explain it thoroughly with examples, and then practice it. You could use a class meeting format to introduce your discipline system; at the meeting students can ask questions to help them understand why such a plan is necessary. With either type of system (extrinsic or intrinsic), the class should be involved in implementing the plan so that they understand why it is important and how it will be used.

If you don't set your plan in place from the beginning, misbehavior will simply be a judgment call on your part. You will wonder: *What should I do? How severe should I make the penalty for misbehavior? Can I explain level 0 in 30 seconds so the student will understand?*

A discipline system is similar to a system set up to deal with parking violations. Decisions include the length of time permitted to park at a meter and the places cars can and cannot be parked. Once these rules are established, consequences for noncompliance are determined. In the assertive discipline model, the students are helped to understand clearly the consequences for misbehaving (figure 10.2). In the personal and social responsibility model, the levels are explained along with examples.

When a discipline plan is set in place and explained at the beginning of the year, students know exactly what to expect—the violations and the consequences are spelled out. Many believe that this helps prevent misbehavior.

Teacher Consistency

A second characteristic of a quality discipline plan is teacher consistency. Once you have established protocols and rules, you need to use the same standards from one day to the next. This is easy to say, yet so hard to do. Nevertheless, it's important that your students understand exactly what you expect.

Teachers have a tendency toward slippage. You might start off consistently enforcing the protocol, for example, that when you say "Stop," students place the equipment on the floor. After a few lessons, however, you might start to slacken. One student doesn't put the ball down, and you ignore it. Gradually, however, it becomes two or three; then six. You can prevent slippage through consistency (being critically demanding). Your

Speed Limit: 65 mph? Or Is It Really 72 mph?

As I (GG) wrote the section on slippage, I was reminded of the 65 mph speed limit in the United States. Drivers seem to understand that the limit isn't really 65 mph. The conventional wisdom where I live is that the speed limit is really 72 mph. So that's where we set our cruise control—until our radar detector sounds. Then we slow down to 65 mph. Children and adolescents see their parents and guardians drive this way. The message is clear: There are rules, but they can be stretched. The same might be true in our classes. We might establish rules and then allow them to be stretched; that is, we allow slippage. The rule we post on the wall may appear negotiable (Tousignant & Siedentop, 1983). As teachers, we determine whether and how much our rules can be stretched.

students will quickly understand that you are really going to enforce the rules as discussed at the beginning of the year.

Support From School Staff

Occasionally, you encounter students who are unwilling, perhaps even unable, to sit out for a few minutes without disrupting others in the class. The time-out doesn't work, and rewards and consequences don't either. In these instances you have little choice but to remove the youngster from the class. When this happens, the student's classroom teacher, the principal, or a guidance counselor can be helpful in two ways. First, he might be aware of the reason the student misbehaves and provide helpful strategies. He might also help create a location in the school where the youngster can go when she is unable to function in a class without disrupting others.

Clearly, the preference is to keep your students in your physical education classes. The reality, however, is that some days some students are simply unable to work in a group setting. You have no choice but to remove them from the gym or playground. When this happens, the cooperation of others in the school is vital.

Support From Parents or Guardians

Some parents or guardians can be counted on to help when their children are misbehaving. In this case, phone calls or letters home are very effective.

Some teachers make it a weekly practice to telephone the parents or guardians of several hardworking youngsters and tell them how well their children are doing in physical education. They also call the parents or guardians of misbehaving children. When possible, however, they try to call again as soon as possible with good news—that is, that the student's behavior has improved. This is a potent combination.

Whether you decide to write letters or make telephone calls, be specific about the student's behavior, citing specific protocols or rules that they have followed or broken. This is particularly true for the bad news phone calls (Watson & Lounsbery, 2000).

Unfortunately, involving parents and guardians is not effective in every school setting. In some schools, the principal and teacher are forced to work with students during the school day because their parents or guardians cannot be counted on to work with them in desirable ways. When parents or guardians can become involved in situations in which a child is chronically misbehaving, however, this can be very effective.

Post-it Technique

When he was teaching in Dublin, Virginia, John Bowler had children who misbehaved write their name, phone number, misbehavior, and the date on a yellow Post-it note, and then he put the note by the phone in his office for one week. If the child behaved for one week, he threw the note away. If the child misbehaved again, John called the parent or guardian (Watson & Lounsbery, 2000). Having the child fill out the note provided a clear warning of what would happen if the misbehavior recurred. This technique worked very well for John and his students.

Disciplinary Confrontation

The strategies discussed so far are designed to minimize and prevent discipline problems. Nevertheless, even in ideal situations, you will occasionally confront students who have misbehaved. At times, this can be upsetting. Several strategies can make the discipline confrontation less unsettling and ultimately beneficial for both you and the student (Cothran, 1998).

Try to remember that the youngster's misbehavior is not personal. Try not to be upset. In fact, at times it's wise to catch your breath, center yourself, and then deal with the youngster.

These confrontations are often most productive when done in relative privacy. It's not a good idea to yell across the gym at a student. Instead, walk over, call him to the side, and then conduct a brief interaction. Give the other students in the class a task so that they are active instead of standing and watching the confrontation. This makes it easier on the student being confronted, especially if the student is older and more concerned with what his peers will think.

The best strategy is to calmly and quietly use the student's name, explain the rule (protocol) she violated, and then pause. At times it might be wise to ask for the student's input. If you ask whether she has anything to say, listen with respect and try to understand her view of the situation. With some students, however, it might be counterproductive to ask for their version of what happened. When to ask and when not to ask for input can be determined only as you get to know your students. In either case, when the interaction is finished, conclude by telling her the predetermined consequence of her behavior—a check, a time-out, a loss of free time. If you realize that you were wrong or made a mistake, say you're sorry! We are all human, and this lets your students know that you will acknowledge your own mistakes.

Disciplining seems to be most effective when you have thought through the confrontation process ahead of time. Often, when we are upset or excited, anger enters into the confrontation, which makes it less productive than it might be under calmer circumstances. We don't mean to suggest that good teachers never get angry. They do from time to time, but calm interactions seem to be far more productive than angry ones. Although a student has misbehaved, you still want to preserve his dignity. Once the youngster's feelings of hurt, anger, or frustration have somewhat dissipated, you want him to understand that what he did was a violation of the rules, but that he is OK as a person.

Assertive Communication

Communicating well is always a challenge. This is especially true when you are angry or upset. Fernandez-Balboa (1990) suggested strategies that beginning teachers can use to communicate assertively to students when they misbehave:

1. Describe the behavior in a nonjudgmental way—"Austin, you are taking Carter's equipment away from him."
2. Express your feelings as a teacher—"I am annoyed because you haven't been listening."
3. Acknowledge the feelings of the student—"Are you . . . (frustrated, sad, angry)?"
4. Explain the effect the described behavior is having on you and the rest of the class—"When you talk when I am talking, it distracts me and the others in the class."
5. State your expectations for future behavior—"I expect you to listen, and not talk, when I am talking." (pp. 51-52)

Summary

Teachers who minimize off-task behavior and discipline problems have thought through what leads to youth being off task and have developed a number of strategies for preventing problems from escalating into major confrontations. As they teach, they are constantly aware of off-task behavior and employ many strategies to minimize it. These include back to the wall, proximity control, scanning, selective ignoring, positive pinpointing, and overlapping. Together, these help teachers demonstrate with-it-ness. In addition, they typically have implemented a discipline system that the youngsters understand: the teacher's expectations, the consequences of misbehavior, and the benefits of cooperating with the teacher and others. Some discipline systems are based primarily on extrinsic motivation (e.g., Canter's assertive discipline model), and others are designed to develop intrinsic motivation (e.g., Hellison's personal and social responsibility model). Regardless of the type of discipline system you choose, it is imperative that your students clearly understand the system, and that you are consistent and rigorous in implementing it while respecting the dignity and feelings of the students in the class.

Questions for Reflection

1. This chapter describes several teaching strategies to minimize off-task behavior and discipline problems. Think about your own teaching. List three strategies that are most natural to you. List one or two that you are less comfortable using. Can you explain why?

2. Two discipline systems were selected as examples, one extrinsic and the other intrinsic. Which of the two is more appealing to you? Why?

3. Describe aspects of either of these systems used by teachers you had as a student or teachers you know. How effective were they in using them?

4. Think about the use of intrinsic and extrinsic rewards and the reason some teachers might favor one over the other. Select a typical misbehavior that occurs in elementary, middle, or high school physical education. Describe how a teacher using an

extrinsic discipline system would handle the misbehavior. Then describe how a teacher using an intrinsic discipline system would handle the same misbehavior.

5. If you have a video of yourself teaching a lesson, analyze your use of the following teaching skills: back to the wall, proximity control, with-it-ness, selective ignoring, overlapping, and positive pinpointing. How might these skills help you to minimize discipline problems if you used them differently?

6. From time to time teachers do get angry at a student or a class. Can you understand and explain the reasons for this? How do teachers avoid becoming angry at certain misbehaviors?

7. What are the consequences of believing that youngsters today are harder to teach than they were in the past? How might that belief be reflected in the way we deal with students who are off task?

8. What things might lead to students being off task? Which can you control, and which are out of your control?

9. If you were going to use an extrinsic system, what rewards and consequences would work with middle or high school students?

References

Canter, L. (2010). *Assertive discipline: Positive behavior management for today's classroom* (4th ed.). Bloomington, IN: Solution Tree Press.

Compagnone, N. (1995). Teaching responsibility to rural elementary youth. *Journal of Physical Education, Recreation and Dance, 66* (6), 58-63.

Cothran, D.J. (1998). Anger management in the gym. *Strategies, 12* (2), 16-18.

Downing, J.H. (1996). Establishing a discipline plan in elementary physical education. *Journal of Physical Education, Recreation and Dance, 67* (6), 25-30.

Downing, J., Keating, T., & Bennett, C. (2005). Effective reinforcement techniques in elementary physical education: The key to behavior management. *Physical Educator, 62* (3), 114-122.

Fernandez-Balboa, J.M. (1990). Helping novice teachers handle discipline problems. *Journal of Physical Education, Recreation and Dance, 67* (2), 50-54.

Hartinger, K. (1997). Teaching responsibility. *Teaching Secondary Physical Education, 3* (5), 15-17.

Hellison, D.R. (2011). *Teaching personal and social responsibility through physical activity* (3rd ed.). Champaign, IL: Human Kinetics.

Hellison, D.R., & Templin, T.J. (1991). *A reflective approach to teaching physical education.* Champaign, IL: Human Kinetics.

Hill, D. (1990, April). Order in the classroom. *Teacher,* 70-77.

Johnson, R. (1999). Time-out: Can it control misbehavior? *Journal of Physical Education, Recreation and Dance, 70* (8), 32-34, 42.

Kohn, A. (1993). *Punished by rewards: The trouble with gold stars, incentive plans, A's, praise, and other bribes.* Boston: Houghton Mifflin.

Kounin, J.S. (1970). *Discipline and group management in classrooms.* New York: Holt, Rinehart and Winston.

Kulinna, P.H., Cothran, D.J., & Regualos, R. (2006). Teachers' reports of student misbehavior in physical education. *Research Quarterly for Exercise and Sport, 77* (1), 32-40.

Masser, L.S. (1990). Teaching for affective learning in elementary physical education. *Journal of Physical Education, Recreation and Dance, 61* (7), 18-19.

Moone, T. (1997). Teaching students with respect. *Teaching Elementary Physical Education, 8* (5), 16-18.

Rosenthal, M., Pagnano-Richardson, K., & Burak, L. (2010). Alternatives to using exercise as punishment. *Journal of Physical Education, Recreation and Dance, 81* (5), 44-48.

Sander, A.N. (1989). Class management skills. *Strategies, 2* (3), 14-18.

Siedentop, D., & Tannehill, D. (2000). *Developing teaching skills in physical education* (4th ed.). Palo Alto, CA: Mayfield.

Timmreck, T.C. (1978). Will the real cause of classroom discipline problems please stand up! *Journal of School Health, 48* (8), 491-497.

Tousignant, M., & Siedentop, D. (1983). A qualitative analysis of task structures in required secondary physical education classes. *Journal of Teaching in Physical Education, 3* (1), 47-57.

Watson, D., & Lounsbery, M.F. (2000, July/August). D.A.P.S.I.S.: Strategies for phoning home. *Strategies,* 16-18.

Williams, E.W. (1995). Learn student names in a flash. *Strategies, 8* (5), 25-29.

11

Building Critical Thinking Skills

> During a lesson with students in kindergarten, they were practicing pencil rolls. I saw a student who was doing the pencil roll with his legs and arms bent. When I went over to provide feedback on how to do a pencil roll correctly, the student replied, "Oh, I am not trying to do a pencil roll. This is the broken pencil roll!"

Rich Wood,
Paddy Hill Elementary School,
Rochester, New York

Reprinted with permission from PE Central
(www.pecentral.org).

After reading this chapter, you should be able to do the following:

- Explain the value of critical thinking activities in physical education.
- Describe the differences between convergent and divergent problem solving.
- Analyze the skills and characteristics of teachers who provide quality critical thinking learning experiences.

It's time to switch gears. The first 10 chapters assumed that you were mostly using a direct style of teaching (Mosston & Ashworth, 2002), in which you tell the students what to do and when to do it, and they comply (Lee, Landin, & Carter, 1992). Our sense is that the majority of teachers use this style for the majority of their lessons. Some lessons, however, may be taught using a more indirect style of teaching, involving learners in problem solving as they respond to questions posed by the teacher (Mosston & Ashworth, 2002). In these lessons students explore, discover, create, and generally experiment with a variety of ways of moving—both for enjoyment and to stimulate their critical thinking abilities as they relate to physical activity and sport (SHAPE America, 2014). In fact, physical activity is an excellent medium for providing critical thinking opportunities (Blitzer, 1995; Cleland & Pearse, 1995; Cone et al., 1998; Hautala, 1996; Johnson, 1997; Lodewyk, 2009; McBride, 1992; Mosston & Ashworth, 2002; Schwager & Labate, 1993).

This chapter describes and analyzes the teaching skills of questioning and presenting problems as alternatives to more direct styles of teaching. Proficient movers frequently need to make decisions when participating in physical activities. For instance, a high school student playing soccer constantly must make decisions about rules, the best strategy (offensive or defensive move) in the moment, and how to perform the skills necessary to accomplish the task. Ideally, promoting critical thinking skills begins early for children, not only in physical education but also in other subject areas such as science, reading, and math.

Value of Critical Thinking Experiences

In physical education, critical thinking experiences involve movement to stimulate the higher-order thinking skills of learners as they are challenged to explore and create solutions to movement problems (Blitzer, 1995; Cleland & Pearse, 1995; Hautala, 1996; Johnson, 1997; Lodewyk, 2009; McBride, 1992; Metzler, 2000; Mosston & Ashworth, 2002; Schwager & Labate, 1993). As students grow accustomed to these types of learning activities, it is fascinating to observe their concentration and interaction as they work through their responses. It is especially interesting and rewarding to see youngsters work cooperatively in these types of lessons.

Learning to use a questioning or problem-solving approach well requires time and practice. Used adeptly, this method provides students with an intellectually challenging learning environment. Used ineptly, it often results in puzzlement, which leads to bewilderment and eventually off-task behavior. Good teachers ask questions and pose problems that are productive and thought-provoking and that provide worthwhile experiences that the students understand and enjoy.

Like any method or teaching strategy, this approach works better with some classes and students than it does with others. Alyssa, a middle school student in one study, offered the following insight about alternatives to direct instruction: "I think this would be good. They [teachers] usually make us sit there and lecture you, like 'So try this and this and this', and then they are talking too much and they don't let you get a chance to try it. But if they just simply ask you and then you go on to then do it that would be good because you are thinking about it, and you are more focused, and it gives you a chance to try it" (Cothran & Kulinna, 2006, p. 176).

An indirect approach to teaching using questioning and problem solving stimulates students' curiosity, decision-making ability, and creativity. The physical education environment is naturally conducive to promoting critical thinking skills because it easily allows for decisive expression through movement. Movement in a lesson that uses a student-focused, indirect approach makes students' thinking visible. By providing adequate support to your students, teaching and modeling critical thinking, and giving them multiple opportunities to solve problems and develop answers, you foster the development of critical thinking skills they will use in other academic areas and throughout their lives (Lodewyk, 2009).

Children With No Bodies

From time to time I (GG) become involved in a discussion about the value of physical education in schools—especially when budgets are being cut. One argument I use to stress the importance of physical education is that schools are responsible for educating the whole child, not just the child's head. If this weren't the case—I argue facetiously when I am losing the discussion—just think of the money that could be saved in busing and classroom space if parents and guardians just sent their children's heads to school and kept their bodies at home. This argument can be turned around to make the point that when children come to physical education, both their bodies and their heads are present. Clearly, our unique responsibility as physical educators is to focus primarily on the physical, but we certainly do not want to neglect students' cognitive and affective development (SHAPE America, 2014). A questioning and problem-solving approach might require more time to implement, but it is a valuable tool in the toolbox of master teachers for use at appropriate times throughout the year.

Using knowledge and skills to solve problems in a physical education class requires that students think and act critically. This chapter addresses both convergent and divergent problem solving, including specific teaching behaviors used in each approach. In addition, the teaching skills of asking questions and presenting problems are discussed, along with some recent thinking about verbal, rather than movement, problem solving.

Convergent Problem Solving

In a convergent problem-solving lesson, students are guided to discover one or more solutions to a problem. There is a right answer, sometimes several. But rather than simply telling them the answer, you lead them to discover it gradually (Blitzer, 1995; Johnson, 1997). For this reason, convergent problem solving is also referred to as guided discovery (Mosston, 1981; Mosston & Ashworth, 2002). The learnable piece in problem-solving lessons can be movement related (e.g., what happens to the flight of a kicked ball when your plant foot is behind the ball rather than next to the ball; S1.E21.1) or in the affective domain (e.g., when more than one of your group members had solutions for the team to try, how did you decide which one to try first? S4.M4.7 [SHAPE America, 2014]).

Our favorite example of convergent problem solving is Mosston's (1981) now-classic slanty rope lesson. (This concept was also discussed in chapter 8 as a way to design tasks to accommodate different skill levels.) Imagine a class of students organized into small groups. Each group has two ropes placed parallel on the ground about 12 inches (30 cm) apart. The students are challenged to jump the imaginary river formed by the two ropes without getting wet or being swallowed by the alligators. They all succeed. Now they are asked to widen the river so that it is 24 inches (60 cm) apart and see if they can still jump it. They continue to widen the river until some can no longer jump it. Now the groups are ready to hear the problem: Is there a way to set up the ropes so that everybody in the group can jump the river?

There are at least two solutions to this problem. One is to arrange the ropes so that at one end they are close together and at the other end they are farther apart (see the cartoon in chapter 8). The other solution is to keep one rope straight and curve the other so that the river is narrower in the middle and wider at the ends.

This is one example of a convergent problem-solving lesson. Here are some others:

- What are the five basic ways to take off and land when jumping?
- What are the most balanced and least balanced positions you can make?
- How do you land from a jump so that the landing is soft and quiet?
- What is the quickest way to mount the bench (box, table, beam, bars)?
- How can you stand so that you are ready to move quickly?
- What is the best way for a defender to position herself when playing defense in a game such as soccer or lacrosse or speedball?
- Where is the best place to look when traveling at a specific bearing using a compass?
- In disc golf, when the disc is behind a tree, what is the most advantageous place to throw the disc to set up the next throw to the hole?

TECH TIPS Student-Created Workouts

In a fitness unit with seventh-graders, consider having your students work in small groups to develop CrossFit-style workouts. They can then share them with the class and participate in other groups' workouts. Using the iMuscle 2 app on iPads, they can record the exercises they are doing and the muscles they are using on their team worksheets.

Never Give the Answer

The most obvious guideline in convergent problem solving is that the teacher never gives the answer. If you give the answer, students become less willing to explore the solutions, knowing that you will eventually provide the answer. In fact, it can be productive to finish a lesson when the students have not yet discovered the answer. Wonder and curiosity are valuable mental processes that can be readily stimulated through physical activity. And, after all, what's so bad about leaving a class and still not knowing the answer you had in mind? Some students may return to the next PE class having discovered the solution!

Responding to Incorrect Solutions

In convergent problem solving, there is at least one correct answer, and sometimes more. When students reach a conclusion that is incorrect, rather than telling them they are wrong, you might ask, "Do you need more time?" or "Have you checked your answer?" or "Can you explain your answer to me?" Try to ask questions that reveal errors in an incorrect solution to lead them to making corrections on their own. This preserves the atmosphere of discovery and problem solving.

Using the disc golf example listed earlier, students may believe that they can "thread the needle" between eight trees and throw right to a hole, when the safer route is to throw just around the side of a group of trees and set up the next throw. You can ask questions such as "How big of a window do you have to throw through?" and "If you don't make it through, how many more throws will it likely take you to get to the hole?" Such questions may help them identify a safer play.

Look at It This Way

My (GG) experience is that children have a much more creative and mirthful way of interpreting questions. I remember asking one class to make a narrow shape with their bodies. As I looked at one child, she definitely had a wide shape: arms and feet spread wide apart. When I queried her about her "narrow" shape, she said, "You're looking at it the wrong way. Look at it from the side." She was right! Viewed from the side, her shape was narrow. Asking children to balance with a certain number of body parts touching the floor is also fascinating. Some children, for example, view a foot as one part; others count each toe, so a one-foot balance, for them, is a five-part balance. Some count the rear end as one part; others, as two.

Convergent problem solving is probably easier with young children who have little or no knowledge or habits related to the problem. They are eager to explore movement. Older children, unfortunately, often have had some of their curiosity dampened and may be more interested in finding correct answers. Upper elementary and secondary students benefit most from this approach when the problem is relevant and interesting to them, especially when they can work in groups. For example, challenging middle school students to create and reduce open space in invasion games (S2.M4.6-8; S2.M5.6-8) (SHAPE America, 2014) presents some excellent opportunities for convergent problem solving. In a soccer unit, a convergent lesson might be organized to help students discover that, when playing goalie in soccer, they can often stop more shots by moving away from the goal to cut off shooting angles.

 Checking for Understanding The web resource provides a video example of a teacher asking children to describe concepts of bound and free flow as they exit the gym.

Discussing Solutions

During closure (chapters 7 and 13) and often between problem-solving activities, many teachers discuss responses with students. Some do not. Some want their students to be able to verbalize their movement responses (e.g., verbally describe a stable or unstable balance); others are satisfied if their students can provide movement answers (e.g., how to create and reduce open spaces in an invasion game). Team-building activities often require a discussion, or debrief, following an attempt at solving a challenge.

TECH TIPS Backchannels

Using a mobile device and a backchannel can be an excellent way to give every student a voice while working in groups to find a solution. A backchannel is a digital conversation that runs concurrently with a face-to-face activity. Even the youngest child can record ideas on a backchannel such as a Padlet wall on an iPad. (The Padlet app is $5 per month with unlimited free student accounts.) For example, you give students the problem. They type their ideas on the Padlet wall, discuss the strategy (or strategies) they might use to solve the problem, and then, together or individually, they solve the problem through movement.

Divergent Problem Solving

In contrast to convergent problem solving, divergent problem solving asks students to explore alternatives and discover many different ways to solve a problem (Cleland & Gallahue, 1993; Mosston & Ashworth, 2002). Convergent problem solving results in one or perhaps a few correct answers; divergent problem solving can result in an infinite number of responses. There is no limit to the diversity and range of answers. Whereas convergent problem solving leads students to focus on the depth of an answer, divergent problem solving emphasizes a breadth of responses. The exciting part of divergent problem solving is the ability to create a variety of unique solutions while exploring answers to questions you pose.

Lessons using divergent problem solving might address different ways to do the following:

- Travel in general space
- Balance on the floor or on an apparatus
- Mount or dismount safely from a bench, table, or vaulting box
- Outmaneuver opponents in a game
- Pass a ball when guarded by an opponent
- Create sequences of gymnastics or dancelike movements
- Pass a ball from player A to player B
- Create a game
- Create a playbook for a sport

 Problem Solving The web resource includes examples of several teachers showing students in a problem-solving process as they design their own games.

Asking Divergent Questions

There are many ways of asking questions leading to divergent movement. Some are better than others. Mosston (1981) suggested that two frequently used questions might be counterproductive:

- The question "Can you . . . ?" might result in the response "No, I can't."
- The question "How many ways . . . ?" might lead some students to respond with only one movement or become intimidated because they can hardly think of one response, let alone several.

He recommended that divergent questions take the following form: "What are three possible ways to . . . ?" When (if) students discover three ways, you can then ask for several more. This format of questioning helps students find three solutions.

The way you ask the question is more important when you are beginning to teach using a divergent problem-solving approach. In time, when your students have become accustomed to problem solving in the gym, the way you ask the question (not the content) becomes less crucial. Youngsters enjoy the uncertainty of exploring and discovering movement alternatives. They also trust you to provide interesting, fun problems to solve.

Learning Atmosphere

For divergent problem solving to work, you must create a supportive environment in which students feel comfortable exploring new concepts and ideas. Most of your feedback statements should be neutral (chapter 9) as you encourage your students to continue exploring alternatives. For example, you might say to a child who has found two ways to move at a low level: "That's two different ways. Can you find a third?" When a student's response simply does not address the question, explain why the response is inappropriate so that she is clear about the problem she is to solve.

Pinpointing

Pinpointing (chapter 7) can be helpful for showing students the diversity of responses that you encourage. In the beginning, students are often looking for the right answer and fail to understand that you are not looking for a single answer. You can pinpoint several students who are making appropriate responses so the others can see the type of diversity you are encouraging.

If you have asked for different ways to travel in general space, for example, many students might be traveling on their feet. You might pinpoint those who are traveling at low levels on their hands and knees or those transferring weight (as in a cartwheel) to encourage all students to explore alternatives. In this instance, you should explain that you are looking for ways to move other than those that were just pinpointed. If this is not clear, the students will mimic the movements previously pinpointed—the opposite of what you are searching for in divergent problem solving.

In game situations, offensive patterns (creating open spaces) provide a virtually infinite number of possibilities for innovation (S2.M1.6; S2.M2.6-8) (SHAPE America, 2014). Coaches especially are noted for creating new offensive possibilities (divergent thinking) for their teams to give them an advantage. Secondary students, as well as upper elementary students, enjoy the challenge of creating their own offenses and then trying them out against opponents in physical education classes.

Verbal Problem Solving

Up to this point, we have assumed that students' responses involve movement rather than being verbal. Clearly, however, you will sometimes ask for verbal responses to questions.

We have devised two guidelines, based on classroom research, about verbal responses to questions. One involves students calling out answers; the other involves waiting for an answer.

Callouts

One clear finding is that callouts (situations in which students respond immediately and simultaneously) are not as effective as calling on youngsters who have their hands raised. We have all asked questions to a class of children only to have eight children answer at once. Children in another class at the same school—when asked the same question—might respond by raising their hands but remaining silent. Clearly, the way they respond is based on the protocol the classroom teacher established at the beginning of the year (chapter 2).

Generally, many educators agree that asking students to respond by raising their hands to be recognized by the teacher is more effective than allowing them to call out (Johnson, 1997). The exception is for those truly unmotivated classes that seem to respond better in a rapid-fire question-and-answer setting—the type often depicted in movies about teachers who work in difficult teaching situations.

Wait Time

One of the reasons students are taught to raise their hands is so the teacher can pause for several seconds (three is suggested) before calling on a student (Johnson, 1997). This allows the class to think about the answer while waiting to see who will be called on. It seems that once a teacher calls out a name, the others tend to relax and stop thinking. The three seconds or so of wait time also allows students to formulate better responses. We have all observed kindergarten and first-grade classes in which all children raise their hands to respond to every question the teacher asks. When no time is allowed for thought (and even sometimes when it is), it is common to call on a child only to realize that he doesn't have an answer but just wanted to see if he could be the one chosen from the field of waving hands.

Waiting three seconds or more before calling on a student is an interesting teaching behavior to adopt. Initially, three seconds might seem like an eternity. Over a series of lessons, however, both you and your students will become accustomed to the wait time, and they benefit more from waiting than from being called on immediately. It's obviously even less productive to name a student to answer a question before it is asked.

TECH TIPS Word Clouds

Have students create wordles or word clouds. There are several free sites that allow students to choose a shape or image and fill that image with words specific to a topic (e.g., wordle.net). This can be used as a pretest before students come to physical education class to initiate a conversation about a topic or a new unit.

Necessary Teacher Characteristics

As with any aspect of pedagogy, a variety of related teacher behaviors and characteristics blend together to create an effective method or technique. Asking questions and presenting problems are no different. Teachers who challenge and motivate students to think about movement in creative and intellectually challenging ways have patience, have a good knowledge of the content and the developmental level of their students, and are positive and accepting.

Patience

Developing lessons using a problem-solving approach requires patience. Problem solving takes time; it's a much slower process than simply telling students the answers. This might be why we see problem solving less often than we see other types of lessons—the process takes longer, and most programs are severely limited in time.

Initially, students need time to learn how to explore solutions to a problem. They aren't instantly terrific problem solvers. Naturally, this depends on what they are accustomed to in the classroom. If problem solving is used in the classroom, it is reasonable to expect the students to be adept at the process. In contrast, a class that is taught using only a direct approach will take much longer to learn to solve problems well.

Once a class of students has learned the process, it still takes them a while to discover a solution or explore alternatives on their own. Obviously, however, certain content lends itself to problem solving, and this is the reason many teachers use a critical thinking approach. It might take longer, but students benefit from the process.

One indicator of how well students are adapting to the problem-solving approach is the amount of time they are involved in a problem. Initially, they may be satisfied with a sequence, game, or offense that they create in just a few minutes. As they have more experience with the process, however, it seems that they always need more time. As students expand their movement repertoires, they often need more time to refine their gymnastics sequences or games to make them truly satisfying. The fifth-grade class that initially created a group dance (S1.E5.4) (SHAPE America, 2014) in five minutes might need two or three class periods once they understand all that is involved in creating and polishing a routine so that it is interesting and satisfying.

Knowledgeable About Content

In addition to having patience, you will need a thorough knowledge of the lesson content. Ideally, this is true for every lesson you teach, but it seems that it is even more important with a problem-solving approach because you are gradually leading learners to one or more solutions. An example of teaching the concept of balance to a class of young children will help illustrate (Mosston, 1981, p. 176):

- "What does the word *balance* mean?"
- "Right. It means that you are not falling down and that you are able to remain steady."
- "Show me one way to balance with your body."
- "Now let's see how you can make that balance even steadier."
- "Is this your most balanced position?" (In time, with your guidance, the children will realize that the lower and wider the position is, the more stable the balance will be. A few children may actually lie flat on the floor.)
- "Now let's see how you can change your balance to make it less steady."
- "Even less steady?"
- "Show me your least-balanced position."

During closure (chapters 7 and 13), you can discuss ways students changed from most to least balanced (i.e., the characteristics of balance). This basic concept is one example of content that lends itself well to problem solving because the students easily and accurately grasp the essence of balance through this process.

The next example uses problem solving with content (the overhand throw) that leads to a possible misunderstanding by students. This lesson uses problem solving to help students understand the concept of using the opposite foot when forcefully throwing overhand.

- "Using an overhand throw, throw the ball hard against the wall." After a number of tries, you might ask, "Which foot do you step with? The one on the same side as the throwing hand? Or the one on the opposite side?"

- "Try some throws now and use the other foot—the one you haven't been stepping with. Does the ball travel faster when you step with one foot or the other?" This process might continue for some time as you continue to ask the students to change feet, sometimes using opposition, sometimes an ipsilateral step.

- During closure you might then ask, "Which foot do you step with to make the ball go faster—the one on the same side as the throwing arm or the one on the opposite side?"

Our experience and observations of other teachers suggest that in the previous example you would probably receive a mixed response. Some students would argue for opposition; others would not. Unlike the concept of balance, opposition might not be a good topic to use in a guided discovery lesson. The reason is that the child who does not use opposition when he throws is not quickly comfortable doing so. He is also not convinced that opposition improves his throwing ability. Because it is a new and awkward feeling for the child, his throw doesn't necessarily go farther or harder, and the child concludes that a unilateral stepping pattern results in better throws for him. You are then faced with a dilemma: whether to tell the child he has drawn the wrong conclusion, causing him to distrust his ability to discover, or to allow that solution to stand until a lesson later in the year (Ainsworth & Fox, 1989).

Obviously, some ways of guiding children to discover the effectiveness of opposition are not counterproductive. Over the years, however, we have observed this lesson taught by enough teachers to conclude that some content lends itself well to problem solving, whereas other content does not. The important point is that, in addition to patience, you need to know the content well to design and implement an effective problem-solving lesson.

Knowledgeable About Students' Developmental Level

Along with knowing the content, you should be familiar with the age and developmental level of your students. You also should know what types of questions or problems are interesting and provocative at various grade levels (figure 11.1). The two examples related to balance and opposition are appropriate for primary-grade children. With intermediate-grade children, however, they won't be of much interest. If children don't already understand these concepts, they probably aren't interested in spending much time exploring solutions.

Older students are often interested, however, in working in small groups to design and synchronize a series of movements (as in gymnastics or dance) or to design a game. Identifying strategies used to escape from a defender is another problem that fascinates many older students. The following examples are often interesting to students in upper elementary and middle school (S1.E3.5) (SHAPE America, 2014):

FIGURE 11.1   Critical-Thinking Skills: Levels of Complexity

Teachers can ask questions that promote critical thinking at various cognitive levels from lower-order thinking (level 1) to more complex or higher-order thinking (level 3) (Schwager & Labate, 1993). The three levels of complexity are as follows:

- **Level 1:** Count, describe, match, name, recite, recall, select, and tell. *Examples:* "Did you hop, jump, or leap over the rope?"; "Describe how high you need to toss the ball to serve it overhand."

- **Level 2:** Analyze, compare, contrast, classify, distinguish, explain, infer, reason, sequence, solve. *Examples:* "Sarah, what was the difference between your way of traveling over the rope and Tom's?"; "How does the height of your toss compare with the toss Joachim and Stian just demonstrated?"

- **Level 3:** Apply a principle, estimate, evaluate, forecast, hypothesize, imagine, judge, predict, make an analogy, speculate (S2.E3.5c) (SHAPE America, 2014). *Examples:* "Can you think of a way of traveling over the rope that would get you high into the air?"; "Why do you think you would get higher with a leap than a hop?"; "Why do you think most of your serves are hitting the net? Do you think you need to adjust the swing of your racket, the height of your toss, or both?"

Adapted, by permission, from S. Schwager and C. Labate, 1993, "Teaching for critical thinking in physical education," *Journal of Teaching in Physical Education* 64(5): 24-26.

- "With a partner, design a sequence that has at least one roll, one balance, one weight transfer, and a beginning and ending shape. Repeat it three times, each time varying the speed of the sequence."

- "In a group of four to six, make up a game. The game must involve kicking a ball. Use cones to define your boundaries."

- "In groups of three or four, see if you can find at least three ways to form a counterbalance. Everyone must keep at least one foot on the floor. When it is finished, I will take a picture of it for other classes to see. I will also put some pictures on our school website for your parents and guardians to see."

Problem Solving The web resource includes a video of children designing a game that focuses on dribbling with the hands.

Being Positive and Accepting

In addition to being patient and having a good knowledge of the content and the developmental level of your students, you need to create an environment in which students feel comfortable trying out new ideas and solutions without fear of failure. You can do so by being positive and accepting with students.

As youngsters offer solutions, either verbally or in movement, they are bound to present some ideas that you will recognize as counterproductive—silly or uninventive, or lacking in much effort. What is important to remember, however, is that you are a more sophisticated problem solver who knows many solutions. The students do not. Thus, part of the process is encouraging students to continue to work and try even though they might appear to be a long way from the solution.

When a teacher isn't positive and accepting, students, especially older ones, might sense it and become unwilling to genuinely participate in the process. This is especially true when the teacher makes youngsters feel as if their responses are not worthwhile or appropriate. The challenge for you, of course, is to distinguish between the student who is off task and just goofing around and the student who is creatively working at solving the problem. The off-task youngster needs to be refocused; the creative one needs to be reinforced for her efforts.

When students appear to not be involved in the process, perhaps talking to friends or simply playing with a ball, but not really on task and certainly not moving, questions such as the following can involve them in the process:

- If the student says, "How?" you can say, "How do you think? Think about it; then show me."

- If a student is just standing around, ask, "What ideas do you have? I am interested in hearing what you are thinking about."

- If you see a student getting frustrated, don't solve the problem for him, but say, "Let me give you a little more information to help you think of an answer."

- To encourage students to continue to work on the problem, you may ask, "What other ideas do you have?" or "Can you think of a few more solutions?"

Highly Skilled Students as Problem Solvers

My (GG) experience has been that highly skilled students often have more difficulty solving problems in physical education than lower-skilled students do. This might be because highly skilled youngsters already have a movement repertoire that they have polished and refined through practice. They have a series of responses to questions and thus see no need to search for alternatives. I am particularly reminded of youngsters who are excellent gymnasts. Many of them, when asked to create a sequence, rely totally on their predesigned stunts so that their sequences appear very similar to Olympic gymnastics floor exercise routines. Personally, I find these routines far less interesting than those of the less-skilled students who discover creative solutions to movement problems. When I work with gymnasts who rely on traditional rolls, balances, and weight transfers, I am often tempted to tell them that they can't use any of these movements in their sequences. I remind myself, however, that that's *my* need, and I try to remain patient and accepting of their efforts.

Direct or Indirect: Which Approach Is Best?

Successful teachers are always searching for better ways to help and motivate students to learn. Choosing the teaching approach is one decision they continually face: would a direct approach (providing the answers) or an indirect approach (problem solving) be better with this lesson?

Some questions to consider relate to the role of the teacher and the students. Ainsworth and Fox (1989) developed a helpful analysis that compares what they termed a traditional (direct) approach and a cognitive processes (indirect) approach to learning in physical education. Ainsworth and Fox (1989) indicate that a traditional approach is subject centered. The teacher often tells students what to do and ignores the students' movement experience. In such traditional approaches, the students play a relatively passive role in the classroom while the teacher identifies errors and prescribes corrections. In a cognitive processes (indirect) approach, the class is learner centered and students explore the class topic. Students are able to pull from their own movement experiences while assuming a major responsibility for their own learning. The students learn to identify errors and make adjustments. Learner-centered approaches may be more time consuming in early stages, but the result is often students that are more engaged in the classroom and more interested in their own learning. Although the analysis doesn't fit exactly with the approaches discussed in this chapter, it is a helpful summary to use when you are deciding which approach to use in your classes, and when.

We hope that you seriously consider involving your students in the process of critical thinking related to sports and physical activity as suggested in the national standards (SHAPE America, 2014). How often you will be able to do this in your program depends on how often you meet with your classes and your willingness to develop the skills to guide youngsters in this process.

Summary

Master teachers are adept at various styles of teaching, both direct and indirect. Critical thinking experiences are valuable for students, and questioning and problem solving can promote higher-order thinking in movement (an indirect style of teaching). Two important teacher behaviors that encourage convergent problem solving (discovering the answers to a problem) are to never reveal the answer and to respond appropriately to incorrect responses. Teacher guidelines for divergent problem solving (searching for a variety of alternatives rather than one or more answers) include asking divergent questions, creating a learning atmosphere conducive to divergent problem solving, and using pinpointing (discussed in chapter 7) to encourage divergent thinking. Teacher characteristics for encouraging problem solving (both convergent and divergent) include being patient, having knowledge of the content and the developmental levels of the students, and being positive and accepting. Ainsworth and Fox's (1989) comparison of traditional behavioral (direct) and cognitive processes (indirect) approaches can help you decide whether to use a direct or indirect teaching approach.

Questions for Reflection

1. List five concepts or skills typically taught in physical education. Which of them might be taught using a divergent problem-solving approach? Which might be taught with a convergent problem-solving approach?

2. Do you think problem solving is widespread or barely used in physical education classes today? Explain the reasons and why this might be the case.

3. Why does problem solving require more time than a direct teaching approach?

4. Considering your characteristics as a teacher, are you more or less apt to use a problem-solving approach? Why do you think this is so?

5. Classroom teachers appear to be reluctant to use problem-solving lessons that involve students in movement. What would you say to convince a classroom teacher that higher-order thinking skills can be developed in the gym as well as at a desk?

References

Ainsworth, J., & Fox, C. (1989). Learning to learn: A cognitive process approach to movement skill acquisition. *Strategies, 3* (1), 20-22.

Blitzer, L. (1995). It's a gym class . . . what's there to think about? *Journal of Physical Education, Recreation and Dance, 66* (6), 44-48.

Cleland, F.E., & Gallahue, D.L. (1993). Young children's divergent movement ability. *Perceptual and Motor Skills, 77* (2), 535-544.

Cleland, F., & Pearse, C. (1995). Critical thinking in elementary physical education: Reflections on a yearlong study. *Journal of Physical Education, Recreation and Dance, 66* (6), 31-38.

Cone, T.P., Werner, P.H., Cone, S.L., & Woods, A. (1998). *Interdisciplinary teaching through physical education.* Champaign, IL: Human Kinetics.

Cothran, D.J., & Kulinna, P.H. (2006). Students' perspectives on direct, peer, and inquiry teaching strategies. *Journal of Teaching in Physical Education, 25,* 166-181.

Hautala, R. (1996). Gym class with "Coach Piaget": How cognitive development theories can be used in PE. *Teaching Elementary Physical Education, 7* (1), 20-22.

Johnson, R. (1997). Questioning techniques to use in teaching. *Journal of Physical Education, Recreation and Dance, 68* (8), 45-49.

Lee, A.M., Landin, D.K., & Carter, J.A. (1992). Student thoughts during tennis instruction. *Journal of Teaching in Physical Education, 11* (3), 256-257.

Lodewyk, K. (2009). Fostering critical thinking in physical education students. *Journal of Physical Education, Recreation and Dance, 80* (8), 12-18.

McBride, R. (1992). Critical thinking—An overview with implications for physical education. *Journal of Teaching in Physical Education, 11* (2), 112-125.

Metzler, M. (2000). *Instructional models for physical education.* Boston: Allyn & Bacon.

Mosston, M. (1981). *Teaching physical education.* Columbus, OH: Bell & Howell.

Mosston, M., & Ashworth, S. (2002). *Teaching physical education* (5th ed.). New York: Benjamin Cummings.

Schwager, S., & Labate, C. (1993). Teaching for critical thinking in physical education. *Journal of Teaching in Physical Education, 64* (5), 24-26.

SHAPE America. (2014). *National standards & grade-level outcomes for K-12 physical education.* Champaign, IL: Human Kinetics.

Building Positive Feelings

12

> My first grade class was learning to dribble. As they practiced in their space, I reminded the class to try to control the ball and not let it get away. A little girl responded, "I'm trying, my ball won't listen!"

Carmen M. Gonzalez,
Academy of Arts and Letters,
Brooklyn, New York

Reprinted with permission from PE Central
(www.pecentral.org).

After reading this chapter, you should be able to do the following:

- Identify inappropriate practices in physical education thought to lead to negative feelings toward sport and physical activity.

- Discuss the intentional and unintentional actions of teachers that contribute to how students feel about themselves and physical activity.

- Analyze games and activities taught in physical education in terms of how they influence students' feelings.

- Explain how to modify games to de-emphasize competition.

- List ways to avoid making students feel bad about testing and test results in physical education classes.

- Describe ways to help students get in touch with and understand their feelings about their involvement in physical activity.

As we begin this chapter, Funky Winkerbean, the cartoon character created by Tom Batiuk, is hanging from a climbing rope. He can't get down. He's been stuck on the rope all day. Now everyone is gone except the janitor, who's sweeping the gym floor. Cartoon readers will have to wait until tomorrow to discover how Funky solves his dilemma.

Last week the cartoon focused on the overweight, sweatshirted, bewhistled coach who filled class time by showing movies. One day the principal was commenting on the fact that the coach had already burned out three movie projectors during the year. Another day the students were discussing why the windows in the coach's classroom had been painted black—they concluded it was because the coach did nothing but show films.

These are funny scenarios—to some. For us, however, they hurt more than amuse. That's our profession, and those are our colleagues he is mocking. Obviously, Tom Batiuk, the creator of the Funky Winkerbean cartoon, had some unpleasant experiences in physical education. Unfortunately, he's not the only one. All too many adults share his feelings about physical education classes.

This chapter focuses on those feelings and their development related to physical activity, including the following:

- Feelings about self
- Feelings about others
- Feelings of joy
- Feelings of satisfaction
- Feelings of pleasure
- Feelings of self-accomplishment
- Perceptions of competence

The list could continue. All of these feelings fall into the category of the affective domain: how people feel about themselves and about physical activity. There's a lot we don't know or understand about feelings. We do know, however, that participation in physical activity has the potential to create powerful and lasting impressions—both painful and joyous.

Our goal as physical educators is to create environments that are pleasant, warm, and caring—and that result in youngsters developing positive attitudes. Perhaps if Tom Batiuk had been in such classes, Funky Winkerbean might find physical education more enjoyable, and the coach would be depicted as a caring, sensitive, and respected teacher.

This chapter focuses on pedagogical skills physical education teachers use to create environments that lead to students developing positive attitudes toward physical activity and their involvement in it. We address the everyday things we do as teachers and how they influence students' feelings.

Inappropriate Practices

We would hope that teachers would see Funky Winkerbean struggling in class and then change the environment so that no student would feel singled out or left to hang on a rope without any support. We have learned much from our past practices. In fact, it is quite possible that many of the things you experienced when you were a student in physical education are now known to be inappropriate and ineffective. Unfortunately, in many gyms across the United States, you may still witness even the most obviously inappropriate practices. As a result, youngsters feel uncomfortable about themselves and their abilities and find physical activity and sports less than enjoyable.

This section addresses seven inappropriate practices in physical education, which are often called hall of shame practices (SHAPE America, 2015a, 2015b, 2015c; Williams, 1994, 1996, 2015): singling students out, having unreasonable expectations of all students, using elimination games, having long waiting times, emphasizing competition, using exercise as punishment, and not having a clear learning purpose. We describe the practices in this first section; the remainder of the chapter presents alternatives to engender positive attitudes that can lead youngsters toward a lifetime of physical activity.

Singling Students Out

The first inappropriate practice is singling students out. Imagine being asked to perform a skill that you were not very good at in front of 30 of your peers. Would you feel self-conscious? Would you enjoy the experience, or would you want to never have to do that again? How about if you could try the skill on your own without everyone watching? Youngsters who are not confident about performing a skill and are singled out and put in the spotlight rarely enjoy the experience. Following are a few examples of ways students have historically been singled out in physical education:

- Like Funky Winkerbean, trying to climb a rope while the rest of the class watches.
- During fitness testing, performing the flexed-arm hang or pull-up test while the entire class watches while waiting in line.
- Using shirts versus skins to identify teams during game play (Williams, 2015).
- Setting up relay races. Inevitably, the poorly skilled or overweight students end up at the back of the relay lines. They are the ones still lumbering along when the race has already been decided and they become the target of ridicule and are often blamed for the loss—even though the other team members may also have been slow (Williams, 1994).
- Using the mile run. Once again, the overweight, slow, or less-skilled student is left to struggle to finish while the rest of the class watches.
- Publicly posting or displaying test results (e.g., written tests, fitness tests).
- Having captains pick teams. This practice is excruciatingly painful and creates lasting, haunting impressions that those picked last are inept at sports and physical activities, even into adulthood (Graham et al., 1992; National Association for Sport and Physical Education [NASPE], 2008; Williams, 1996).

These are only a few examples; you may recall others.

They Have to Learn Sometime

I (SP) remember visiting a teacher who had selected two captains, athletic boys, to pick teams. When I asked the teacher why she used that approach, she replied, "Kids have to learn to get picked last sometime." My jaw hit the floor. We all have tough lessons to learn in life, but is it the PE teacher's responsibility to intentionally set up a class so that a child "learns" how to be hurt? This is straight up abusive, and there is no excuse for it. This process should be banned from schools—even be against the law. It simply hurts too much to stand and wait, only to be picked last or next to last. Sadly, children don't understand that they are being picked last because they are unskilled; they think that they are picked last because they are unpopular, or bad, or ugly, or because of any number of self-imposed, harmful perceptions.

Unreasonable Expectations

A second inappropriate practice is requiring youngsters to perform tasks and activities that are unreasonable for their skill or ability levels. Picture a young child, say, four years old, trying to catch a ball. Arms are eagerly outstretched, the ball is lightly tossed, and it passes between the arms. After a slight delay, the arms come together. Developmentally, this child is unable to track the ball and catch it.

An example of unreasonable expectations in physical education is a traditional approach to teaching a sport. Let's use basketball. Historically, teachers might spend the first couple of days of a unit working on static skills such as dribbling with no opposition and practicing shooting and passing—again, with no defense. These static skill practices would then be followed by two or three days of game play (e.g., 3v3 half-court basketball games)—even though the students never had a chance to practice their dribbling and shooting skills against opponents.

We've already discussed how long it takes to learn and improve motor skills in the planning chapters (3, 4, and 5), so believing that one or two days of dribbling or shooting practice will result in skillful dribblers or shooters is clearly unrealistic. Once games start, often a tournament, some of the students become frustrated because they have virtually no success when they need to dribble or shoot the ball when closely guarded. On the flip side, those students who are skillful enough for game play are also inappropriately challenged during the isolated skill practice. Unfortunately, this scenario also occurs in sports such as soccer, softball, lacrosse, and speedball. Clearly, these frustrations can lead to youngsters disliking, even hating, sports and physical activity—hardly the path to physical literacy discussed in chapter 1.

Elimination Games

A third inappropriate practice is elimination games. Basketball knockout is a classic example. This game is played with a line of students and two basketballs. The first student in line shoots the ball at the hoop and continues to shoot until either she makes the shot and returns to the end of the line, or the player behind her in line makes his shot first, resulting in the first player being eliminated from the game. Who is eliminated first? The student who needs the most practice, of course. This is simply a prehistoric practice that needs to be stopped in schools, and not only in physical education (Graham et al., 1992; NASPE, 2008; Williams, 2015). Alternatives to this inappropriate practice, and the others in this section, are provided in the second half of this chapter.

Waiting Time

Elimination games are also inappropriate because they lead to a tremendous amount of waiting time, particularly for those who are less skilled. As described in chapter 3 (planning), time is limited in physical education, and you must make the most of every available second. Critically analyzing your own teaching may help you increase your efficiency. For example, where you place equipment and how students get equipment can make a big difference in how long it takes to get activities started. Instead of having one bin containing 30 balls, you could have six bins with five balls each or spread the balls (or rackets or beanbags) throughout the space.

Relay races are another practice that results in a lot of waiting time (Williams, 1992). Try this: Choose one student from the class and start the stopwatch every time the student performs the activity (e.g., dribbling a basketball down and back); stop the watch when the student is not performing the task (e.g., waiting in line for a turn). You'll quickly realize that if eight minutes of class time is dedicated to the relay, the student you watched may only be dribbling a basketball for less than one minute. Is this a good use of class time, especially given the recommendation that students spend at least 50 percent of a lesson in moderate to vigorous physical activity (Centers for Disease Control and Prevention, 2010b)?

Overemphasis on Competition

Competitive games can also be damaging to students' perceived self-competence (Bernstein, Phillips, & Silverman, 2011). At various times in your physical education classes, students will participate in competitive games. Scores will be kept and winners determined. An overemphasis on competition on your part, however, may put pressure on youngsters, especially the poorly skilled. Lower-skilled students, who are less likely to remain physically active as adults, are often hurt the most by competitive activities (Sidwell & Walls, 2014; Spencer-Cavaliere & Rintoul, 2012) when winning becomes more important than enjoyment and improvement.

Exercise as Punishment

Another inappropriate practice is using exercise as punishment (NASPE, 2009; Williams, 1996). Consider the purpose of physical education—to encourage youngsters to become and remain physically active for life. You spend hours planning lessons, designing tasks, and organizing your classes, all to instill a love of physical activity in your students. Let's

Competition for Children: Convincing the Skeptics

Occasionally, I (GG) encounter the view that competition for children is good for them. "They need to learn how to lose!" is the battle cry often emitted by the frustrated ex-athlete or wannabe superstar. There might be a grain of truth to the idea that children need to learn how to lose gracefully and with understanding, but I remain convinced that cooperating with others is a far more important skill to learn than how to lose. An occasional loss might not be harmful to children. Losing every day, however, is certainly unpleasant, if not harmful. And if we're not careful and sensitive, some children can easily experience virtually every physical education class as a losing experience.

When people confront me on my views of competition for children, I refer them to classic books: *Winning Is Everything: And Other American Myths* (Tutko & Bruns, 1976) and *Joy and Sadness in Children's Sports* (Martens, 1978). I don't know whether they read them, but I hope they do, because these books create a powerful and sensitive portrayal of the damage an overemphasis on competition can do to a child's emerging self-concept.

now say that a student breaks a rule and you tell him to run two laps as punishment. Using the very thing you're trying to promote as punishment reinforces many students' feelings that running or physical activity is bad. One word describes this practice: hypocrisy.

Another example of using physical activity as punishment is taking away physical activity time for not completing work or misbehaving in class. Let's think back to chapter 10. With a good behavior management system in place that students know well and that you reinforce and practice daily, you will have much less need for instilling punishment and negative consequences. But when it is necessary to take disciplinary action during physical education, make sure to use appropriate disciplinary measures (e.g., time-out zone) rather than prescribing a form of physical activity that doesn't even address the behavior problem at hand. It is important to not take away valuable physical activity time that will only enhance learning in the classroom (Centers for Disease Control and Prevention, 2010a).

No Clear Purpose

A final inappropriate practice is not having a clear purpose for a lesson or program (Williams, 1996). Student learning is what separates physical education from physical activity. Without a clear learning purpose for playing games or performing tasks or activities in physical education classes, students are left with "busy, happy, good" or "roll out the ball" programs (Placek, 1983). These may be fun, but without a focus on learning, they are missing an opportunity to develop an appreciation for physical activity.

Intentional and Ever Present

The seven inappropriate practices just described are at best counterproductive and at worst, many believe, turn youngsters off to sports and physical activity. When youngsters come to physical education class, they should look forward to the experience, not be apprehensive or fear being embarrassed. They should feel that physical education class is a warm and caring environment that encourages and supports them in learning new skills and activities. They should also understand that mistakes will be made and that they are an important, and necessary, part of learning. These feelings translate into positive attitudes about themselves and physical activity, ideally contributing to the enjoyment of physical activity for a lifetime.

You can help create positive attitudes in your students by doing the following:

- Making an intentional effort to create positive attitudes every day for every class you teach. These attitudes don't just happen by accident.
- Make your effort "ever present"—consistent in all your actions, not just during a few games or activities from time to time.

A number of texts (e.g., Flugelman, 1976; Glover & Midura, 1995a, 1995b; Grineski, 1996; Hichwa, 1998; Orlick, 1978a, 1978b; Rohnke, 1984; Turner & Turner, 1984) describe games and activities that promote cooperation and cooperative experiences. It seems, however, that developing positive attitudes involves more than simply playing hug tug, frozen beanbag, lap sit, cooperative musical chairs, or long, long jump. It's an environment that you create that says: *You're OK; I'm glad you're here even if you aren't very skilled or very fit. This class is to help you improve and enjoy physical activity, not to make you feel bad because you can't do something.* A variety of tools are available to help you create such a positive environment and avoid using inappropriate practices. Some are subtler than others, but together they say to the students, *You belong here, and my goal is to help you feel good about yourself as you participate in physical activities.*

Values of Physical Activity

One part of the definition of a physically literate person (chapter 1) relates specifically to that person's feelings about the value of physical activity. Programs that are positive and considerate of students' feelings help them learn to value physical activity and its contributions to a healthy lifestyle. A physically literate person "recognizes the value of physical activity for health, enjoyment, challenge, self-expression and/or social interaction" (SHAPE America, 2014, p. 1).

Techniques and Strategies

It is often easier to point out inappropriate teaching practices than to offer alternative, appropriate practices. Several techniques and strategies can help you assist every student, not just the highly skilled, to enjoy physical activity (Reeve & Jang, 2006). The strategies presented in previous chapters can help you avoid the inappropriate practices discussed earlier in this chapter. By clearly designing and articulating classroom rules and expectations, as well as the consequences for misbehavior (chapter 2), you can avoid using exercise as punishment. Carefully planning lessons for students at a variety of ability levels (chapters 4 and 5) and maximizing activity time (e.g., giving each student a ball rather than having them take turns) avoids high waiting time, overemphasizing competition, singling students out, and not having a lesson purpose. Adjusting instruction for students' individual needs (chapter 5) helps you avoid having unreasonable expectations.

This section presents additional general strategies that you can use to build positive feelings in the gym and on the playing field, including providing choices, actively teaching responsibility, analyzing your interactions with students, asking about students' feelings, and analyzing your teaching behaviors via audio or video. To be a successful teacher, you need to work hard to create an environment that says *It's OK to make mistakes in this class* and to help youngsters understand that learning sport skills and becoming physically fit take hours and hours—not just one or two classes.

TECH TIPS Student PSAs

Student PSAs (public service announcements) publicizing what you are doing in your classes allow students to take pride in what they are doing in physical education and inform other teachers and staff about your program. Students can create weekly podcasts (with a program such as Podbean, approximately $3 per month) to be linked to the school website on topics such as fitness tips and information about your program and upcoming events. Having students and staff excited about what's happening in your classes creates a positive school climate, especially when the students produce the news.

Providing Choices

Poor Funky Winkerbean! His teacher provided no choice but for him to climb to the top of the rope, and he got stuck. A caring teacher would have given Funky several choices so that he could have avoided the embarrassment of trying to do something he knew he couldn't do—but was required to do anyway (chapter 7).

Here is an example of providing students with a choice: "We are going to play two games. In this game we are going to keep score; that game is just for fun—no score will be kept." Although you might think that having two games going on simultaneously (intratask variation) would be difficult, the practice is becoming increasingly common in physical education classes (chapter 8).

Providing choice avoids students being singled out in front of the class where they are embarrassed by their awkwardness. Activities are designed and taught so that youngsters have an alternative to playing in competitive games and are appropriately challenged (e.g., every student has a ball to dribble; there are three or four batters in several minigames; or there are three or four "its" in a game of tag). Teaching by invitation and intratask variation also avoids placing youngsters in uncomfortable situations by providing choices (chapter 8). Funky Winkerbean, for example, might have been invited to see if he could climb higher than he did last time—or climb to one of several sections on the rope marked by different-colored tape.

Teaching Responsibility

How the students in the class treat one another (social interaction) also strongly influences the enjoyability of physical education (Wallhead, Garn, & Vidoni, 2013). The national physical education standard 4 states that students should "exhibit responsible personal and social behavior that respects self and others" (SHAPE America, 2014). This includes following rules but also learning to respectfully give and receive feedback, work with others, and take responsibility for one's own actions. Hellison's (2011) levels of affective development (chapter 10) provide a sample rubric of the levels of responsibility.

You can intentionally plan opportunities for your students to learn how to work with others, and then reinforce responsible behavior. Try using an alternative system of scoring such as awarding points for good sporting behavior (e.g., "Two points for the yellow team because I heard Viviana tell Troy 'Good try'"). Youngsters initially may find it difficult to adjust to alternative scoring systems, but these are often the youngsters who need to develop a perspective on their behavior in competitive situations.

TECH TIPS Badges

Awarding badges for academic success, positive behavior, or other accomplishments promotes self-efficacy. ClassBadges provides free access to a large bank of badges and allows you to load your students by class.

Another strategy for teaching responsibility is to have students design their own games, dances, or gymnastics sequences (chapter 11). Although the activities they design will often be different from yours, they will derive satisfaction and enjoyment from creating new activities—and they often adjust their activities for differences in abilities. Youngsters who are not highly skilled are often terrific at inventing enjoyable sequences, games, and dances.

You should decide when it is appropriate to include student-designed activities. Obviously, youngsters need some background information before they can begin to design successful activities. Here are three examples of student-designed tasks:

- "Make up a game with your partner. It needs to have kicking in it. You may use one or two foam soccer balls. There are also hoops and cones if you need them."
- "Your game [e.g., batting, shooting baskets, throwing a football] can be played with three or four people. The equipment is limited to . . . ."
- "In groups of three, your challenge is to make up a dance [or gymnastics sequence] that incorporates three of the skills we worked on this week. It can be no longer

than one minute." [Music could also be incorporated into the sequence if there is an appropriate 60-second cut of music.]

Grouping With Care

Grouping in physical education can be a time-consuming nightmare or a quick reorganization that leads into the next activity with little waiting time. Ideally, having one half of the class compete against the other should be a rare occurrence in physical education classes. At times, however, it is developmentally appropriate to divide a class into two teams. There are several ways to do so that are relatively quick and do not damage students' self-esteem.

TECH TIPS Apps for Selecting Teams

Using your smart device, download an app for choosing teams such as Team Shake. Projecting this on a wall or screen lets students know that you are not choosing teams or picking favorites. This app is a great way to quickly divide your class into the number of teams you want.

One of the easiest ways is to ask students to find partners (don't tell them that you are about to organize them into teams). Ask one partner to stand on the blue line and face his partner, who is standing on the red line. All students will be standing on two lines, facing one another. The students on the blue line comprise one team; the ones on the red line, the other team. Interestingly, this is one of the quickest and easiest ways to form teams of equal ability because youngsters often pick partners of similar ability. Here are some other strategies:

- Jigsaw: Tell students to get into groups of five. In each group, they number off 1 through 5. Reorganize so that the 1s are in one group, the 2s are in another group, and so on.

- Ask students with birthdays in the first six months of the year (January through June) to stand on one line; those with birthdays in July through December stand on the other line. This should come out reasonably even in numbers. Birthday months can also be used to divide into two to six groups.

- Quickly have students count off (1s and 2s). The 1s are on one team; the 2s are on the other. Or you can ask them to count off in fours—1s and 3s, for example, are on one team, and 2s and 4s are on the other.

Line Up and Count Off

Be prepared for students to forget their numbers, skip spots in line, or not know what their birth months are so that they can team up with their friends. Just quickly move a couple of students to another team and begin the next task. Changing the grouping strategy regularly to keep the students guessing helps them get used to working with random classmates.

Be aware of situations that might lead to students being hurt by peers. For example, having students select their own partners is a common grouping strategy. A student can be hurt, however, if not picked by a classmate. Sometimes you may need to anticipate that a given student is likely to be hurt, and proactively partner this student with someone in as unobtrusive way as possible (e.g., call the paired students over right after giving the partnering direction). Changing the grouping strategies frequently helps, as does having clear expectations of students when they are selecting partners and groups (chapter 2).

Finally, teaching responsibility is similar to teaching motor skills: it involves planning a progression of tasks that will lead to students learning personal and social responsibility. Table 12.1 displays a progression of team-building skills that can be used for designing learning outcomes. Note that these are not intended for use within a single lesson but are provided as an example of what can be covered throughout a year or an entire program. Just as learning motor skills takes a long time, teaching students to exhibit responsible personal and social behavior also takes a long time.

TABLE 12.1   **Progression of Team-Building Skills**

Category	Description
Ice breakers	Games and activities that require class interaction, often switching partners frequently by chance. Simple tag and other get-to-know-you games.
Communication	Tasks that require participants to communicate (speaking, listening, other means of communicating).
Problem solving	Partner to large group activities that challenge groups to develop a plan, come to a consensus, and collectively carry the plan out.
Trust and risk	Includes individual challenges with group support such as partner trust falls or experiences on a challenge course.

Adapted from Rohnkie-Butler 1995.

Performing Interaction Analyses

Another way to avoid contributing to the development of negative attitudes toward physical education is to become aware of who you interact with, and how. If you interact differently with the skilled or attractive students than you do with the unskilled or unattractive students, you send a subtle message to the students, reinforcing any tendency toward feelings of incompetence. You may tend to interact differently with boys and girls; students of different ethnic groups such as Latinos, American Indians, or African Americans; or students with differing sexual orientations. You might not be aware of your interaction patterns, but the students are! When you meet several hundred students a day, it's hard to make the hundreds, perhaps thousands, of interactions all ideal.

We hope that a single embarrassing or unfortunate incident won't instantly create a negative attitude in a youngster. However, several years of negative interactions and experiences will certainly contribute to feelings of inadequacy and incompetence. Figure 9.1, the feedback analysis form (available in the web resource), can give you some insights about which students you are interacting with and how. You can easily modify it to answer a number of questions related to your interactions with individual students.

Taking Emotional Temperatures

Another helpful pedagogical tool is assessing students' feelings about physical education by simply asking them how they feel about what and how you are teaching—that is, checking the emotional temperature of the class (McCaughtry, 2004). Jan, the teacher in McCaughtry's (2004) study, had this to say about teaching students to throw a football (American football): "How students feel about, say, throwing a football matters as much as whether they can throw it well. You see, if they hate football, or feel embarrassed at their throwing, or are continually bad, they will quit trying to learn . . . and if they learn how to throw it, but just don't care about it, then what's the reason for teaching it? They're never going to use it if they don't have that emotional bond" (p. 41).

Jan described another example of checking the emotional temperature of a class when she asked a group playing a small-sided game of touch football how they felt about their game. They told her that they were bored. Jan watched their games for a few minutes and realized that the receivers were running too far downfield and the quarterbacks were unable to throw the ball that far. She used play-teach-play (chapter 7) to have them practice shorter pass routes before they returned to the game. She employed techniques from her pedagogical toolbox to assess her students' emotional state to better match the lesson and unit contents to their interests and abilities.

Recording

You can ascertain the type of environment you are creating by recording a class using either audio or video. You might record a video by setting up an iPad in the corner of the gym, strapping a small audio recorder on your belt, and attaching the microphone to your shirt. When you listen to the recording, try to hear what you communicate to students about what is important to you. Answer the following questions:

- Do you provide feedback about knowledge of results (the ball went into the goal) or knowledge of performance (critical elements related to the movement)?
- Do you sound too demanding or too critical?
- Do you communicate a tone of warmth and caring to the students?
- Do you sound supportive? Encouraging? Understanding?
- Do you interact differently with boys than with girls? With high-skilled students than with low-skilled students? With students who have physical disabilities than with those who don't?

When you listen to (or watch) the recording, consider how you sound in relation to how you want to sound. You might want to ask someone you trust to listen to part of the recording to help you interpret the affective messages you are communicating. Do not be too hard on yourself. Remember that teaching is a complex and difficult job.

Allowing for Mistakes

Students feel good about themselves when they realize that learning inevitably involves mistakes. You can help them by explaining that making mistakes is how we learn. We try not to make mistakes, but they happen—and that's OK.

Consider declaring the playground or gym a mistakes-are-OK-here zone. Explain that everyone, yourself included, will make mistakes from time to time. It's normal—an important part of learning. When a mistake does occur, encourage students not to laugh at, ridicule, or single anyone out. Help them accept it and understand.

Obviously, you can describe the mistakes-are-OK-here zone, but a description is not enough. When a youngster does make a mistake and is ridiculed or laughed at, immediately stop the class and focus on the idea of a mistakes-are-OK-here zone—to let everyone know that criticism and sarcasm are not acceptable in your class.

The mistakes-are-OK-here zone is also created when students see you making mistakes when you are trying to learn something you have yet to master. Obviously, how and when this is done will depend on you, the class, and other factors, but letting your students witness your mistakes is an important way of communicating the idea that learning involves trial and error. Students learn a great deal from watching someone they respect try to learn something. They begin to realize that skills are learned, not inherited, and that mistakes are part of the learning process, not something to become upset about.

PE Teachers Are Superheroes

Many children, especially the youngest, regard their PE teachers as superheroes. They believe you can do everything. They don't realize that your physical adeptness came from lots of practice and hard work. They just assume that you were born that way. You will reinforce this perception if you demonstrate only the skills you can do well. Are you willing to let your students know that there are some skills you don't do so well? Or do you want to preserve your superhero image?

Using the "Yet" Intervention

Agnes Stillman (1989) described one of the ways she helps students feel positive about physical education. She has humorously titled it the Stillman two-part "yet" intervention.

Part 1—When a student forgets and says "I can't," Stillman adds "yet" on the end of the comment. She concluded after 21 years that the phrase "I can't" will never be totally eliminated from the vocabulary of students.

Part 2—She makes a deal with the student. She asks him to try the skill 37 times, and if he still can't do it, then she accepts that he can't do it.

The number 37 is arbitrary. Stillman's point is that she wants students to try—and try hard. But if they truly try and still can't do it, she accepts that and suggests something else for them to try. A conversation might go something like the following:

I can't!

Hearing Ralph's voice attached to that, I turn to him and say (with my finger up), "Ralph, what did I hear you say?"

"I can't . . . yet."

"Thank you. Now, how many tries have you made?"

"Eleven."

"So, how many more tries do you have?" (We can integrate math skills!)

"Twenty-six."

I give him some encouragement and then move on to Sarah and Sam. Sure enough, I look over at Ralph in time to see him execute the skill well enough that he is actually smiling about it. I've got him now.

I eventually get back around to Ralph.

"Well, what are we up to now?"

We both know he lost count. He creates a number—33. He could have said 37, but he's an honest kid. By saying 33, he knows he has only four more tries to close our deal. By now, however, he's not trying to prove me wrong. He has had some success, although he hates to admit it. I ask if I may watch his last four tries, which I point out should be his best efforts. And, of course, they're successful enough to bring praise, pats on the back, and high fives.

Ralph heads for the locker room with a feeling of accomplishment and I say a quiet "thank you" and prepare for the next Ralphs to arrive.

"The 'yet' intervention," A. Stillman, *Strategies*, 1989, 2(4): 17, 28, adapted by permission of Taylor & Francis (Taylor & Francis Ltd, http://www.tandfonline.com).

Decision Making by the Loudest

Have you ever watched a class of students respond to the question What game do you want to play today? Invariably, a few children respond quickly and loudly—"Kickball" or "Dodgeball" or "Killerball." Especially to beginning teachers, it sounds as though the whole class is in agreement. In fact, the loud response is made by a few students—often the highly skilled, and they are forceful. Needless to say, those who really don't want to play those games keep quiet.

Testing

In addition to the hall of shame practices just discussed, another arena in which students can feel inferior and physically inept is testing situations. In the classroom, tests are relatively private affairs—only the teacher and student know about mistakes on a math test. In physical education, however, results are public. All students know who came in last in the mile or who can't catch a ball. You need to be sensitive to this fact and be careful to minimize harmful effects that might influence students' feelings. Fortunately, we have developed some ways to avoid placing youngsters in uncomfortable situations, including ways to help them understand test results and set their own goals.

TECH TIPS Creating and Sharing Movies

A great way to share the good things going on in your physical education class is to create a video montage of lesson snippets to share with parents and guardians or other teachers in the school. Using iMove on your iPad is a great way to record clips and create a fun and professional-looking movie that will help tell your story.

Interpreting Test Results

If you choose to share test scores with students, how you do so is important. Posting scores on a wall for everyone to see can quickly lead to ridicule and magnify feelings of incompetence in unskilled students. Certainly, you can ask students not to discuss others' scores, but that's naive. Students do compare scores.

It also seems that standardized norms and criterion scores are harmful to students who know that they are less skilled than many others in the class. What good does it do to reinforce feelings of inadequacy?

The most humane and sensitive approach to reporting test scores to youngsters is to encourage them to compare their current scores with their past scores. Are they improving? That's the truly important score, and the one they have the most control over. Probably the only advantage of being poorly skilled is that practice can rather quickly result in drastic improvements on tests (i.e., it's easier for the poorly skilled child to show improvement than it is for the highly skilled youth). Computers make it easy to provide students with reports of their test results and to show them how they have improved since the last test.

Setting One's Own Goals

Another way you can help students feel good about themselves is by helping them set their own goals (Grineski, 1993). This works better with older students who are beginning to understand that improvement takes time and practice. No matter how old the students are, at the beginning they will need help in setting realistic goals that they can accomplish in a relatively short period of time. Increasing the number of times they can jump a rope or dribble a ball or do sit-ups in 30 seconds is readily achievable. If you're not careful, however, students will set goals that are simply unreachable, even in a year. For example, making 9 of 10 free throws or running a mile in under six minutes are goals that are difficult to attain, even for highly skilled or fit students.

Over time, more difficult goals can be set as students realize what is required to achieve various goals. If you have asked your students to set their own goals, you must devote time to explaining the process of goal setting—including the meanings of success and failure and the idea that goals are for the students themselves, not to impress teachers or friends.

Understanding Feelings

One of the advantages of aging is that we can better understand our feelings. Children have a difficult time separating their feelings from their self-worth (e.g., *I can only do a few push-ups and I miss the ball a lot when I am batting, so I must not be a very good person*). Over time, they begin to realize that athletic prowess does not equate to self-worth, but this process can take a while. You can promote this understanding in physical education by having students keep logs or journals and by implementing discussion circles.

Student Logs and Journals

Asking students to write about the feelings that arise from participating in physical education can keep you apprised of their feelings (Cutforth & Parker, 1996; Tjeerdsma, 1997). With the increased emphasis in elementary schools on "writing across the curriculum," more classroom teachers are willing to give students five minutes or so to write in their PE logs immediately after they return from physical education class.

A question such as "How do you feel about dance?" can often be answered better in a paragraph than a single word. The log gives you deeper insights about your students that might otherwise go undetected.

Rather than just asking open-ended questions such as "How do you feel about physical education?" specific questions, prompts, or even sentences that youngsters respond to might more effectively stimulate writing about physical education (Wentzell, 1989). For example, you can prompt 4th through 8th graders to respond to a question such as "I felt prepared or unprepared for the lesson because . . ." (Wentzell, 1989). Other prompts might include "I can't play this sport on my own because . . .," "When I designed a practice with my squad, it was helpful when . . .," or "I really wish my teacher would . . . ." The idea is to encourage students to explain their feelings, accomplishments, or challenges through writing. Providing specific prompts to your students may elicit more thoughtful responses in their logs.

Having only one or two classes at a time keeping physical education logs and then only for a period of several weeks seems to work best. Given that you may teach 400 or more students in a week, it would simply be overwhelming (and not enjoyable) to spend an entire weekend reading logs. The purpose of the logs is to help students get in touch with their feelings and for you to better understand how they feel about your teaching and your program. This can be accomplished by reading the logs of a few students—not all 400. You can also make comments in the logs if you believe it is appropriate and would be of value to the students.

Students' journals should be durable, especially if they will be writing outside. You want them to last several months. Some teachers use manila folders with papers inside. Others use college bluebooks or find ways to laminate covers and bind pages inside the journals (Cutforth & Parker, 1996). The advantage of a bound journal is that it is easier to avoid losing pages, especially outside on a windy day. The disadvantage is that it is hard to add pages. Journals can be kept in cardboard boxes, organized by class, or organized alphabetically. Writing tools can be stored in cups, shoe boxes, or bags (Cutforth & Parker, 1996). As with virtually everything you do in physical education, it is important to teach journal-writing protocols so that your students understand how to get their journals out and put them away.

Discussion Circles

Another way to get in touch with youngsters' feelings is a discussion circle. Again, this can be done occasionally with a class or two. The purpose is to determine how they are feeling about your physical education classes or program.

Sit in a circle with your students and talk about how things are going in class (Tjeerdsma, 1997). Questions such as the following seem to work best:

- "How do you feel about coming into the gym and getting started immediately?"
- "How do you feel about the way I ask you to find partners or form groups?"
- "Do you feel tired when you leave PE class?"
- "Is there some activity that you wish I would teach from time to time?"
- "This week we have been striking with rackets [tennis]. Have you practiced that skill after school? Why or why not?"

If you have never used a discussion circle, several techniques are important to note. First, for a discussion circle to be productive, you need to carefully plan your questions and be certain that the students don't wander too far off during the discussion. It also helps to set a time limit at the beginning.

Second, students need to be encouraged to say what they feel. If you become defensive or angry, the discussion circle will not succeed.

Third, these are youth, and they will say what they think. If you want to hear only good things about the program, then it is probably not a good idea to use a discussion circle. To lead a productive discussion circle, you must be able to remain objective about what youngsters say and help them express their feelings about the program.

Learned Helplessness

Often, youngsters who do poorly in school, in any subject, fall victim to the learned helplessness syndrome (Martinek & Griffith, 1994). They believe that success or failure is beyond their control, so they quickly give up or quit trying because they believe they can't do anything to improve or succeed.

Learned helplessness can occur as early as third grade (Martinek & Griffith, 1994). The comments that follow are vivid yet painful examples of learned helplessness and show how some youngsters feel about their chances of success in physical education:

> "I always drop the ball because I am too slow." "Serving the ball is always hard for me because I can't hit the thing very well." "I have always been clumsy . . . that's why I have a hard time doing gymnastics." (Martinek & Griffith, 1994, p. 119)

Clearly, these youngsters believe that they can't succeed in these activities because of their lack of ability. When these statements are contrasted with the following statements made by children who are "mastery oriented" (Martinek & Griffith, 1994), the concept of learned helplessness becomes even clearer. Youngsters who are mastery oriented make self-critical but positive statements:

> "I did not do good on that task, but I think I can do it if I keep practicing at it." "I did terrible on this (the bump). I would miss it at first, but after a while I started trying . . . it started to come." "I had trouble with the headstand last week. I am trying to strengthen my stomach muscles so I can do it." (Martinek & Griffith, 1994, p. 119)

Concluding Thoughts

The examples of teaching strategies to build positive feelings in this chapter don't require a new curriculum. You don't necessarily have to change what you teach, although you may want to alter the way you teach certain activities.

The message of this chapter is that you need to be sensitive to all students in your classes so that they are comfortable and feel your support. When youngsters come to physical education class, they should feel secure. They should trust that you will try not to embarrass them or put them in uncomfortable situations. Physical education class should be a special place where youngsters feel good about themselves—and about physical activity.

Funky Winkerbean got down from the rope with the help of the custodian. He was embarrassed, but he made it. The coach is still showing movies to his classes. In some schools, physical education is still being taught the way it was 30 years ago, but there is a growing revolution in physical education. We hope this chapter will contribute to these changes so that the Funky Winkerbeans of the future will no longer be placed in embarrassing situations that lead to a dislike of physical activity and contribute to the development of a poor self-image.

Summary

Physical activity has a powerful influence on how youth feel about themselves. You must do everything you can to be sensitive to how your students feel and help them build positive feelings about their involvement in physical activity. Be aware of inappropriate practices such as singling students out, having unreasonable expectations, using elimination games, having too much waiting time, overemphasizing competition, using exercise as punishment, and not having a clear instructional purpose for every lesson. To help youngsters build positive attitudes, you should be constantly aware of their feelings and consciously modify and select activities that are considerate of both the highly skilled and the poorly skilled, the enthusiastic and the reluctant, and the physically fit and less fit. Techniques and strategies to help you do this include providing students with choices, actively teaching responsibility, analyzing your interactions with students, asking students about their feelings, and analyzing your interactions using audio and video. You can also establish a positive learning environment by establishing a mistakes-are-OK-here zone and using the "yet" intervention.

Testing should be conducted in a way that does not single students out or lead to comparisons between students. You can have a better understand of students' feelings by using student logs and journals as well as discussion circles. Finally, design your learning activities to help students become mastery oriented so that they don't develop feelings of learned helplessness. Overall, make sure that all students leave physical education feeling good about themselves and physical activity so that they choose to remain active for the rest of their lives.

Questions for Reflection

1. Think back to your experiences in physical education classes. Try to recall three examples of teachers being unpleasant or even harmful to the poorly skilled or unfit students in your classes. Why do you think teachers weren't sensitive to them?

2. What games and activities do you remember from physical education that would belong in the hall of shame? What can you do to modify them to make them appropriate?

3. Reflect on your own teaching. Do you think you tend to favor any certain group of students—high- or low-skilled? Attractive or unattractive? Boys or girls? What can you do, as you teach, to be sensitive to your tendency to favor a certain group?

4. Think about your friends or acquaintances who have been turned off to physical activity. Do you know why? Why do they find it so hard to exercise regularly? Can any of these feelings be traced back to their experiences in physical education classes?

5. In physical education, keeping testing private is difficult. What are some ways you could test in physical education to ensure the relative privacy of your students? Do you think students can test one another? Why or why not?

6. Youth have different levels of experience and understanding than adults do. Can you recall two examples of how you saw something differently as a child or adolescent and now as an adult? Briefly describe the change in your feelings or attitude.

References

Bernstein, E., Phillips, S.R., & Silverman, S. (2011). Attitudes and perceptions of middle school students toward competitive activities in physical education. *Journal of Teaching in Physical Education, 30* (1), 69-83.

Centers for Disease Control and Prevention. (2010a). *The association between school based physical activity, including physical education, and academic performance.* Atlanta: U.S. Department of Health and Human Services.

Centers for Disease Control and Prevention. (2010b). *Strategies to improve the quality of physical education.* Atlanta: U.S. Department of Health and Human Services.

Cutforth, N., & Parker, M. (1996). Promoting affective development in physical education: The value of journal writing. *Journal of Physical Education, Recreation and Dance, 67* (7), 19-23.

Flugelman, A. (Ed.). (1976). *The new games book.* Garden City, NY: Doubleday.

Glover, D.R., & Midura, D.W. (1995a). *More team building challenges.* Champaign, IL: Human Kinetics.

Glover, D.R., & Midura, D.W. (1995b). *Team building through physical challenges.* Champaign, IL: Human Kinetics.

Graham, G., Castenada, R., Hopple, C., Manross, M., & Sanders, S. (1992). Developmentally appropriate physical education for children: A position statement of the Council on Physical Education for Children (COPEC). Reston, VA: National Association for Sport and Physical Education.

Grineski, S. (1993). Achieving educational goals in physical education—A missing ingredient. *Journal of Physical Education, Recreation and Dance, 64* (5), 32-34.

Grineski, S. (1996). *Cooperative learning in physical education.* Champaign, IL: Human Kinetics.

Hellison, D. (2011). *Teaching personal and social responsibility through physical activity* (3rd ed.). Champaign, IL: Human Kinetics.

Hichwa, J. (1998). *Right fielders are people, too: An inclusive approach to middle school physical education.* Champaign, IL: Human Kinetics.

Martens, R. (Ed.). (1978). *Joy and sadness in children's sports.* Champaign, IL: Human Kinetics.

Martinek, T.J., & Griffith, J.B. (1994). Learned helplessness in physical education: A developmental analysis of causal attributions and task persistence. *Journal of Teaching in Physical Education, 13,* 108-122.

McCaughtry, N. (2004). The emotional dimensions of a teacher's pedagogical content knowledge: Influences on content, curriculum and pedagogy. *Journal of Teaching in Physical Education, 23,* 30-47.

National Association for Sport and Physical Education (NASPE). (2008). *Appropriate practices for elementary physical education.* Reston, VA: Author.

National Association for Sport and Physical Education (NASPE). (2009). Physical activity used as punishment and/or behavior management [Position statement]. Reston, VA: Author.

Orlick, T. (1978a). *Cooperative sports and games books.* New York: Pantheon.

Orlick, T. (1978b). *Winning through cooperation.* Washington, DC: Acropolis Books.

Placek, J.H. (1983). Conceptions of success in teaching: Busy, happy and good? In T. Templin & J. Olson (Eds.), *Teaching in physical education* (pp. 46-56). Champaign, IL: Human Kinetics.

Reeve, J., & Jang, H. (2006). What teachers say and do to support students' autonomy during a learning activity. *Journal of Educational Psychology, 98* (1), 209-218.

Rohnke, K. (1984). *Silver bullets: A guide to initiative problems, adventure games, stunts and trust activities.* Dubuque, IA: Kendall/Hunt.

Rohnkie-Butler, K. (1995). *Quicksilver: Adventure games, initiative problems, trust activities and a guide to effective leadership.* Dubuque, IA: Kendall Hunt.

SHAPE America. (2014). *National standards & grade-level outcomes for K-12 physical education.* Champaign, IL: Human Kinetics.

SHAPE America. (2015a). Appropriate instructional practice guidelines for elementary school physical education. Retrieved from www.shapeamerica.org

SHAPE America. (2015b). Appropriate instructional practice guidelines for high school physical education. Retrieved from www.shapeamerica.org

SHAPE America. (2015c). Appropriate instructional practice guidelines for middle school physical education. Retrieved from www.shapeamerica.org

Sidwell, A.M., & Walls, R.T. (2014). Memories of physical education. *Physical Educator, 71* (4), 682-698.

Spencer-Cavaliere, N., & Rintoul, M.A. (2012). Alienation in physical education from the perspectives of children. *Journal of Teaching in Physical Education, 31* (4), 344-361.

Stillman, A. (1989). The "yet" intervention. *Strategies, 2* (4), 17, 28.

Tjeerdsma, B.L. (1997). A comparison of teacher and student perspectives of tasks and feedback. *Journal of Teaching in Physical Education, 16* (4), 388-400.

Turner, L.F., & Turner, S.L. (1984). *Alternative sports and games for the new physical educator.* Palo Alto, CA: Peek.

Tutko, T., & Bruns, W. (1976). *Winning is everything: And other American myths.* New York: Macmillan.

Wallhead, T.L., Garn, A.C., & Vidoni, C. (2013). Sport education and social goals in physical education: Relationships with enjoyment, relatedness, and leisure-time physical activity. *Physical Education and Sport Pedagogy, 18* (4), 427-441.

Wentzell, S.R. (1989). Beyond the physical—Expressive writing in physical education. *Journal of Physical Education, Recreation and Dance, 60* (9), 18-20.

Williams, N.F. (1992). The physical education hall of shame. *Journal of Physical Education, Recreation & Dance, 63* (6), 57-60.

Williams, N.F. (1994). The physical education hall of shame, part II. *Journal of Physical Education, Recreation and Dance, 65* (2), 17.

Williams, N.F. (1996). The physical education hall of shame, part III: Inappropriate teaching practices. *Journal of Physical Education, Recreation and Dance, 67* (8), 45-48.

Williams, N.F. (2015). The physical education hall of shame, part IV: More inappropriate games, activities, and practices. *Journal of Physical Education, Recreation & Dance, 86* (1), 36-39.

13

Assessing and Reporting Student Progress

DO YOU KEEP TRACK OF WHAT THE CHILDREN HAVE LEARNED?

" When talking about ways to make our muscles stronger with our kindergartners today, I asked my students if they knew the names of any muscles in their body. With a straight face, a student raised his hand and answered with "the guns" while pointing to his bicep. "

Steve Condon, Bernice A. Ray Elementary School, Hanover, New Hampshire

Reprinted with permission from PE Central (www.pecentral.org).

After reading this chapter, you should be able to do the following:

- Explain why assessment is an important part of a quality program of physical education.
- Discuss the differences between alternative and standardized assessments.
- Describe approaches to evaluating students such as checklists, rating scales, and rubrics.
- Discuss realistic and practical approaches to assessing students' improvement in and understanding of motor skills.
- Explain practical ways of assessing students' understanding of physical education concepts.
- Describe practical ways to assess students' attitudes and feelings related to physical education.
- List ways of reporting progress to parents and guardians based on student assessments.
- Provide examples of assessing youngsters using checking for understanding and during closure.

Each chapter since chapter 5 (Teaching From the Lesson Plan) has presented active teaching skills for your pedagogy toolbox—the skills you can use when you are actually with your students. This chapter focuses on another aspect of teaching, one that you carry out both with your students and in your office or home. Essentially, you want to answer the question, "How can I realistically determine whether my students are learning what I want them to learn as a result of my teaching?"

Why Assess?

Assessment is quite simply the gathering of information about student skills, knowledge, and dispositions. To teach any lesson well, you must continually assess your classes and students. The three general reasons for this are to determine the extent to which your students are meeting (or not meeting) your instructional outcomes, guide your instruction, and evaluate your physical education program.

Student Learning

First of all, assessment forces you to look carefully at every student in a class, at least for a few moments, to determine what he or she knows and the extent to which he or she has learned what you're teaching. This allows you to briefly reflect on all the youngsters and how well they can perform a skill, demonstrate a learnable piece (movement cue), or explain a concept. Most of the time, you will probably be reasonably accurate about your subjective (informal) assessments of your students' abilities. There will be surprises, however, and formal assessment helps you uncover them.

Assessment, as described in this chapter, also becomes a self-imposed accountability measure. When you teach, you'll often find yourself surprised by what your students don't know—even after a lesson that you believe you taught so well and so clearly that no one could possibly have not learned the content. Testing what you have taught, rather than what someone else thinks you have taught, can be a real eye-opener.

TECH TIPS Heart Rate Monitors

The U.S. national physical education content standards include "calculating target heart rate and applying that information to a personal fitness plan" for high school students (S3.H10) (SHAPE America, 2014). Many teachers use heart rate monitors to teach students how to measure heart rate and calculate target heart rate. Polar heart rate monitors display student heart rates in real time in color-coded boxes with beats per minutes and the percentage of maximal heart rate—all on a big screen!

Similarly, performance assessments also provide opportunities for student accountability and for reporting student learning. To really assess skill or knowledge, you must have clearly articulated learning expectations. For example, you might expect your fourth-graders to kick a ball in the air with mature form (S1.E21; SHAPE America, 2014). Mature kicking form can be described as follows (Graham, Holt/Hale, & Parker, 2012):

- Approaching with one or more steps
- Taking a leap to plant the nonkicking leg next to the ball
- Bending the knee on the backswing
- Extending the leg on follow-through

- Leaning the upper body slightly backward just before and during contact
- Dispersing momentum with a slight hop on the support leg in the direction of the target

You can use your recordings of students' demonstrations of these critical elements of kicking to provide feedback to students and reports to their parents or guardians. This is in contrast, for example, to being asked by a parent about a student's progress and having no recorded evidence, only what you can remember about the student—and you may not remember anything.

Informed Instruction

Second, when you have an assessment system in place with some recorded evidence about the progress your students are making, you can make more informed, sounder instructional decisions about the individual students in your program. For example, you might learn from an assessment that all students except Brooke, Evan, and Tuan consistently move to open space when they don't have the ball when playing modified soccer. You can then use this information to select a new task for those three students (intratask variation; chapter 8) to help them practice moving without the ball. Assessment data can be used for unit and daily lesson planning, as well as to adjust instruction during a lesson.

Program Evaluation

A third purpose of assessment is program evaluation. Assessments done in fifth or sixth grade in elementary schools, eighth grade in middle schools, and 12th grade in high schools provide overall analyses of the success of physical education programs. They reveal whether a program is truly instructionally aligned and answer the all-important question of "Am I meeting the goals and objectives for my program?" Assessment provides insights into what your students have and haven't learned over the years they've spent in your physical education program (assuming you have been teaching at that school the entire time). It also increases your credibility as a professional (Arbogast & Griffin, 1989; Collier, 2011a, 2011b; Doolittle, 1996; Hopple, 2005; Schiemer, 2000). Parents and guardians, as well as administrators, expect you to be able to assess, and report, student progress.

Alternative and standardized assessment methods are used for the three purposes just discussed. Alternative approaches are frequently teacher developed and align with the student learning outcomes or goals of local programs. Standardized assessments are most frequently developed to align with national or state standards, or to evaluate the outcomes of a specific curriculum. These two general categories are described in the following sections.

What to Assess?

In chapters 3 and 4, we described instructional alignment (designing down, or backward design) to identify what to teach. This is an obvious starting point for thinking about the purposes and goals of your physical education program (chapter 3) and answering the question "What are the outcomes I want to accomplish in my physical education program (Cave & Dohoney, 2009; Hopple, 2005)?"

The next step is to decide which of those outcomes to assess, because given the limited amount of time allocated for physical education in most districts, it is unrealistic to believe that you can assess every one (Graber & Locke, 2007). Guides and standards published by national associations, in all subject areas, are good places to start when making these decisions—but these are typically wish lists because of the lack of time. When deciding which outcomes to assess, consider the following:

- New topics
- Fundamental motor skills that are highly valued
- Key learning outcomes for program evaluation
- Selecting a variety of psychomotor, cognitive, and affective assessments
- Value orientation (which outcomes you consider most important)
- District or school curriculums
- Using the same outcomes from year to year to track student progress
- New outcomes to capture a broad range of achievement spanning multiple years

Once you have decided what to assess, the next step is to choose an assessment approach. As mentioned earlier, assessments are generally categorized as either alternative or standardized.

Alternative Assessment

Alternative assessments give both you and your students insights about their progress. Alternative assessment techniques have the following six characteristics (Lund, 1997):

1. Alternative assessment tasks are designed to be meaningful and genuine to young-sters, not contrived. Multiple choice tests, for example, do not meet these criteria. Nor do traditional physical fitness tests. Good alternative assessments are more like interesting problems for youngsters to solve.

2. Alternative assessments require youngsters to use higher-order thinking skills because tasks are often complex and require critical thinking (chapter 11) to solve a problem.

3. Students know the scoring criteria in advance of the assessment. The criteria are called rubrics and allow them to evaluate their performance progress because they understand what they are expected to learn (NASPE, 1995). Teachers typically create a variety of rubric categories depending on the concept or skill to be assessed (Schiemer, 2000). Ardovino and Sanders (1997), like Shellhase (1998) and Smith (1997), use three categories in their rubric for assessing the underhand throw: achieving, developing, and not yet. Westfall (1998) suggested achievement levels for degrees of quality, frequency, and expertise on a four-point scale for recording student progress.

4. Alternative assessments assess the curriculum the teacher is actually teaching. For this reason, assessments often seem to the students to be a part of regular lessons. When assessments truly reflect what is being taught in a program, teachers literally teach to the test—to the benefit of students.

5. Because students know the criteria for alternative assessments in advance (scoring rubric), the teacher can assume the role of coach or ally as opposed to test administrator. Although this is a subtle difference, many teachers enjoy this role because they can actively root for youngsters to succeed.

6. Finally, when alternative assessments are authentic, many of them also become public. It is understood that they will be shared with others.

Fortunately, you have a plethora of performance or alternative assessments to choose from (Hopple, 2005; Schiemer, 2000; SHAPE America, 2010, 2011, 2014; see also chapter 8) in addition to standardized written, fitness, and skill tests. The assessment used often depends on the learning outcomes. Motor skill outcomes require a form of psychomotor assessment involving teacher observation, video, or other performance assessments and tasks (Hopple, 1997; Young, 2011). Cognitive and attitude assessments can take the form of observation (e.g., checking for understanding, teacher observation) or written forms (exit slips, exams, worksheets) as well as projects, portfolios, or other written work (Hopple, 1997; Young, 2011). The following sections provide more thorough descriptions of strategies for motor skill, cognitive, and affective assessments.

Motor Skill Assessments

At times you may find yourself asking, *Do the students seem to be grasping this concept? Should I move on or stay with this task or cue?* In this case you are not attempting to assess the progress individual students are making, but rather asking a broader question about the progress of the entire class (chapter 5). Scanning, video recording, and digital media, along with performance tasks, can help you answer these questions.

Scanning

One method of scanning involves providing a task for students and then observing a single critical element during a 10- to 15-second visual scan (chapter 5). The task might be to see how many times students can strike a ball against a wall using a racket. Once students begin, scan to see whether they are turning the appropriate side to the wall (forehand or backhand) as they strike. Using this technique, you can obtain in a short time a rough estimate of the number of students who are turning their sides appropriately.

Some qualitative components are more easily assessed than others with observation. For example, observing whether, when catching, students use their hands appropriately (thumbs together for high-level catches; little fingers together for low-level catches) is

relatively easy. Other critical elements, such as sequential hip and shoulder rotation, are harder to observe in live settings unless you have a lot of practice doing so.

Video Recording

Recording a class can help you observe how well students are grasping a critical element, especially one that is difficult to observe in a live setting (Doering, 2000; SHAPE America, 2010, 2011). A camera using a wide-angle setting can be placed in one corner of the gym or playground and turned on for several minutes during a lesson. Later you can view the video and assess student use of the critical elements. This is especially interesting when students are playing games, because some tend to forget some of the critical elements during the excitement of a game. You can replay the video in a later class to show students what they are forgetting during game play. This has to be done carefully, however, to avoid embarrassing youngsters who are not skillful.

Digital Media

You can use digital media (iPads, iPhones, tablet PCs, digital cameras, smartphones) to illustrate assessment stations or learning centers; to help you memorize students' names; and to enhance student portfolios, posters, and bulletin boards, and school websites (Ryan, Marzilli, & Martindale, 2001). Smartphones can now be used to make short videos or take photos to review for assessment purposes (make sure you have permission from parents or guardians, and follow school policies).

TECH TIPS Evernote

Evernote is a great app that students can use to take pictures and express their knowledge in one place. For example, if you create stations for skills practice, they can work in groups to take pictures of each other performing the skills and type in the key skill cues. Students can log into your Evernote account (if you are using a school device, it will already be set), and all of their responses will be available to you immediately if you are in a Wi-Fi zone. Or you can sync later. With Evernote you can monitor students' activity throughout the class to ensure on-task behavior.

Performance Tasks

A fourth approach to assessing student motor skills is organizing performance tasks, such as musical or dramatic performances; dance, gymnastics, or movement sequences; game officiating; fitness and skill tests; debates and interviews; oral presentations and reports; skill checks during game play; skits or dramatizations; and peer tutoring (Hopple, 1997; SHAPE America, 2010, 2011). The strength of performance task assessments improves when student performance can be video recorded.

One interesting example of a performance assessment is a system for assessing improvement in 13 fundamental motor skills (Shellhase, 1998). Shellhase (available at www.pecentral.org) provided performance standards for grades K through 6 in a logical progression based on U.S. national standards (NASPE, 1995) and skill themes (Graham, Holt/Hale, & Parker, 2012), along with teaching cues for each skill. She devised a reporting system, using the assessment rubric for each motor skill, which she sent home to apprise parents and guardians of their children's progress. *PE Metrics* also outlines a number of performance tasks intended to be video recorded for teacher evaluation (SHAPE America 2010, 2011).

Student performance assessment results, such as the two just discussed, can be stored on an iPad, tablet PC, or other electronic device (or on paper and transferred to a computer). This lets you modify as necessary and download or use Mail Merge (a function in Microsoft Word) to avoid the plethora of paperwork that is so difficult to manage when teaching several hundred students a week (Wegis & Van der Mars, 2006).

Assessments on PE Central

As mentioned earlier, PE Central (www.pecentral.org), a website for K-12 physical educators, contains a wealth of information, including assessments that can be downloaded for free and adapted for use with all grade levels (Werner, 1997). The table of contents on the front page of the site will guide you to the assessments.

Cognitive Assessments

As we know, accomplished physical educators focus on youngsters' cognitive understanding of concepts, in addition to their physical abilities (SHAPE America, 2010, 2011). Quick written tests and checking for understanding are two techniques to help you informally assess whether youngsters are grasping critical concepts.

Quick Written Test in the Gym

The standard paper-and-pencil test comes to mind when we think of assessing cognitive understanding. The process, however, need not take a long time (Cave & Dohoney, 2009; Griffin & Oslin, 1990; Lipowitz, 1997).

One technique that is easily done on a cafeteria floor or blacktop playground is to ask the students to help their friend Murgatroid. Here's how it works: Before one or two classes (not necessarily every class taught that day), set out papers and pencils in an area away from the activity. Five-by-eight-inch index cards may work better if you are outside. At some point in the lesson, ask the students to go to this area and respond to a scenario, such as this: "Your friend Murgatroid doesn't know how to dribble a ball. List up to five things (cues) you would tell her so that she can become a good dribbler." As soon as the students are finished, they can resume activity. This takes less than five minutes and provides valuable information on what the students have learned. The list in figure 13.1 was provided by a group of fourth-graders several days after they had finished

1. To use the fingerpads of your hand not the palm

2. Not to hit the ball down, push it so you will stay in control

3. Don't have your wrist like a piece of metal but don't have it so loose you can't control it

4. Keep your eyes looking in front of you to make sure you don't run into anything

5. Don't bash the thing so hard it goes above your head, keep it at your waist

Figure 13.1 Response of fourth-graders to the teacher's directive: "Your friend Murgatroid doesn't know how to dribble a ball with her hands. List five things to help her become a good dribbler."

a sequence of lessons on dribbling with their hands. The information gave the teacher a measure of how effective he had been in teaching his students the critical elements (cues; chapter 4) of dribbling.

Secondary students can complete task sheets or other written materials during class. These can also serve as assessments. For example, reviewing a student's written pass patterns or plays in flag football (American) provides information regarding how well students are grasping the concepts.

PE Central provides a quick paper-and-pencil catching assessment for young children (Werner, 1997). Children fill in drawings of blank faces to indicate how well they can perform certain skills (figure 13.2).

Checking for Understanding

Another quick way to learn how well students understand a concept is to use the technique of checking for understanding. When used at the end of a lesson, or during closure, this method is called closure assessment (Marks, 1988). Ask students to show you their understanding of a cue (critical element) or concept you have taught. For example, when students are assembled around you, ask them to do the following:

- "Show me how your hands should look when you are trying to catch a ball at a high level."
- "Show me one good way to stretch your lower back muscles."
- "Show me how your knees should look after you land from a jump."

A quick visual survey will tell you how well students have understood the concept. Of course, simply because they can show you they understand doesn't mean that they will always do it, but understanding is a necessary first step. This is also an excellent way to

 Checking for Understanding   The web resource includes video clips of teachers checking for understanding.

Student name_____ Grade_____

Fill in faces by drawing a happy face if you feel good about or you agree with the sentence, a straight line if you are unsure, or a frown if you don't feel good about or disagree with the statement.

1. I am a good catcher.

2. I think I could help someone else learn how to catch better.

3. My classmates are good catchers.

4. I always put my pinkies together when catching at a low level.

5. I always put my thumbs together when catching at a high level.

6. To be a better catcher, I need to continue practicing.

This is a picture of me "catching" in physical education class:

Figure 13.2 Catching assessment.

Reprinted, by permission, from P. Werner, 1997, "Using PE Central and the National Standards to develop practical assessment instruments," *Teaching Elementary Physical Education* 8(3): 12.

conclude the lesson by reviewing one or two cues (reminder words; chapters 4, 5, and 7) emphasized in the lesson. Some cognitive concepts can be assessed this way; others can't.

TECH TIPS Create Quizzes

At times you may want to do a quick check for understanding with your students. Socrative is a free app that allows you to create a quiz or assessment that can be taken on a smart device. Students log in to your assigned room number, select the assessment, and begin. You control the start and stop times. Students receive immediate feedback, and you can download the results to add to your own grading program.

Projects

Another way to assess cognitive learning is with projects. Student-generated projects that take the form of exhibitions or displays include flag football playbooks, science fair projects, personal fitness plans, drawings (e.g., a map of the neighborhood with routes

to access parks), video and audio recordings, models, posters, slide shows, collages, and banners (Hopple, 1997; Young, 2011). Based on the outcome you are assessing, you might decide to create a rubric describing the criteria for the project. Projects are especially valuable when students can complete them as homework or in another class as art, science, or writing projects.

Portfolios and Other Written Work

Because written assessments require skills highly valued across the curriculum, portfolios and other written assessments can often be completed in classrooms (Fortman-Kirk, 1997). In fact, some classroom teachers welcome the opportunity to have students write essays or reports on topics of special interest to them. Written assessments include essays, stories, poems, research papers, portfolios, learning logs, personal fitness and activity plans, self-assessments reported in writing, advertisements, brochures, checklists of cues or critical elements, editorials or opinion pieces, and newspaper articles or article proposals (Hopple, 1997; Melograno, 2006).

TECH TIPS Create Student Portfolios

Creating online portfolios with Google Sites by importing files from Google Drive is a great way to showcase student learning and advocate for your program. Three Ring is another great online student portfolio app that works across all platforms; you can easily update it from a mobile device.

Affective Assessments

In addition to assessing physical performance and cognitive understanding, you can gain insights into the attitudes of your students toward physical activity and toward themselves through affective assessments. The attitudes of youngsters are important barometers for determining their proclivities for developing active, healthy lifestyles that endure into adulthood (SHAPE America, 2014). Affective assessments can be done using exit polls, which take little time, or with paper and pencil.

Exit Polls

One simple, albeit somewhat imprecise, way to learn how students feel is to conduct an exit poll. For example, you can laminate a number of faces: smiley, neutral, and frowny. As students leave the gym, ask them to pick a face that best represents their feelings about their ability, their enjoyment, or the lesson from one of the three shoe boxes by the door (one contains the smiles, another the neutrals, and a third the frowns) and deposit it in the ballot box. Another approach is to ask the students to cover their eyes with one hand and then use the fingers on the other hand to show on a scale of 1 to 5 their responses to your question. Following are some sample questions:

- "How do you feel about your ability to strike a ball with a bat?"
- "How do you feel about doing sit-ups over the weekend?"
- "How do you feel about continuing to work on designing your own dances next class?"
- "How do you feel about today's lesson?"
- "How well do you feel your group worked together today?"

Paper-and-Pencil Attitude Assessments

Like the questions assessing cognitive understanding, attitude questions can also be asked as part of paper-and-pencil tests. These assessments can be very revealing.

In one study (Graham, Metzler, & Webster, 1991), students were asked to circle one of three faces to indicate their feelings about various subjects taught in physical education (questions 6 through 11 in figure 13.3). They consistently circled smiley faces until they came to the question about their feelings about dance and gymnastics. Then many circled neutral or frowny faces. This suggested that the dance and gymnastics programs needed to be reevaluated because, apparently, they were turning students off to these activities. Unfortunately, boys tended to circle frowny faces on the questions related to dance. A number of questions are provided in figure 13.3 to suggest ways to assess the feelings and attitudes of your students.

Logs, journals, and discussion circles also provide valuable insights into how and what students are learning in physical education classes—or whether they are learning at all (chapter 12).

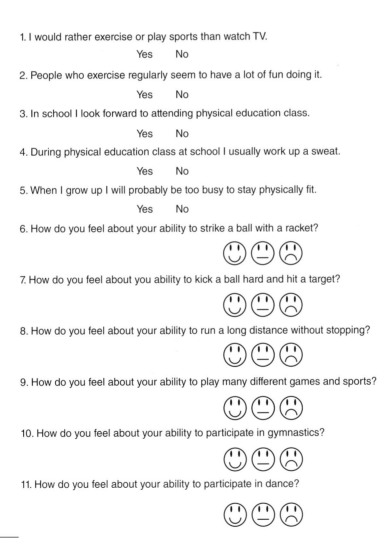

1. I would rather exercise or play sports than watch TV.

        Yes   No

2. People who exercise regularly seem to have a lot of fun doing it.

        Yes   No

3. In school I look forward to attending physical education class.

        Yes   No

4. During physical education class at school I usually work up a sweat.

        Yes   No

5. When I grow up I will probably be too busy to stay physically fit.

        Yes   No

6. How do you feel about your ability to strike a ball with a racket?

7. How do you feel about you ability to kick a ball hard and hit a target?

8. How do you feel about your ability to run a long distance without stopping?

9. How do you feel about your ability to play many different games and sports?

10. How do you feel about your ability to participate in gymnastics?

11. How do you feel about your ability to participate in dance?

Figure 13.3 Questions for helping you understand students' feelings and attitudes toward physical activity.

Recording Student Performance

When recording student performance data, you may find yourself spending more time looking at the paper or an iPad rather than actually observing your students. One suggestion is to initially mark what you expect of all students (e.g., meeting the standard), and then spend your time identifying those who are above or below the standard and changing their scores.

Evaluating Assessment Data

Remember that assessment is the collection of information about knowledge, skills, or attitudes. Making a value judgment about the quality of a student's work or performance is called evaluation. There are many approaches to evaluating assessment data. Many resources are available that explore evaluation and assessment in physical education in more detail than we have space for in this book (see Assessment and Evaluation Resources in Physical Education). We do, however, want to briefly focus on three approaches used by physical educators: checklists, rating scales, and rubrics.

Assessment and Evaluation Resources in Physical Education

Hopple, C. (2005). *Elementary physical education teaching and assessment* (2nd ed.). Champaign, IL: Human Kinetics.

Hopple, C.J. (1997). The real world process of assessment. *Teaching Elementary Physical Education, 8* (4), 4-7.

Lund, J., & Kirk, M. (2010). *Performance-based assessment for middle and high school physical education* (2nd ed.). Champaign, IL: Human Kinetics.

Lund, J., & Veal, M.L. (2013). *Assessment-driven instruction in physical education.* Champaign, IL: Human Kinetics.

National Association for Sport and Physical Education. (2010). *PE Metrics: Assessing national standards 1-6 in elementary school.* Reston, VA: AAHPERD.

National Association for Sport and Physical Education. (2011). *PE Metrics: Assessing national standards 1-6 in secondary school.* Reston, VA: AAHPERD.

PE Central (www.pecentral.org)

Schiemer, S. (2000). *Assessment strategies for elementary physical education.* Champaign, IL: Human Kinetics.

Checklists

One of the simplest assessment forms is a checklist—a list of items that you mark yes or no. For example, as you watch a student throw a ball, you indicate whether or not he starts with his side to the target, steps with the opposite foot, transfers weight from the back to the front leg, and follows through (figure 13.4). Figure 13.5 is a checklist focused on assessing offensive strategies.

You can also create checklists using the movement cues you teach throughout a unit or school year. In an end-of-unit assessment, each student can be assessed on each cue listed on the checklist. These are easier to build and use but often lack sufficient detail including whether the criterion was met one time, met by chance, or demonstrated consistently.

FIGURE 13.4 Overhand Throw Checklist (S1.E14.4a)

	Side to target		High elbow		Step with opposite foot		Throw ball forward		Point to target	
Aisha	Yes	No	Yes	No	Yes	No	Yes	No	Yes	No
Ali	Yes	No	Yes	No	Yes	No	Yes	No	Yes	No
David	Yes	No	Yes	No	Yes	No	Yes	No	Yes	No
Jamal	Yes	No	Yes	No	Yes	No	Yes	No	Yes	No
Miguel	Yes	No	Yes	No	Yes	No	Yes	No	Yes	No
Sasha	Yes	No	Yes	No	Yes	No	Yes	No	Yes	No
Tisa	Yes	No	Yes	No	Yes	No	Yes	No	Yes	No

Adapted, by permission, from S. Westfall, 1998, "Setting your sights on assessment: Describing student performance in physical education," *Teaching Elementary Physical Education* 9(6): 7.

FIGURE 13.5 Checklist for Offensive Tactics in Invasion Ultimate (S2.M2.8)

Name _____

Criteria	Yes	No
Moves to open space when doesn't have the disc.		
Uses at least two types of throws (e.g., forehand, backhand).		
Fakes to get to open space.		
Uses a give-and-go.		

Rating Scales

Rating scales, in contrast to checklists, add a measure of how well a criterion is met. Standards-based report cards that are commonly used in elementary schools in the United States today are a form of rating scale. For example, a brief description of how frequently or how well the criterion or standard is met can be added. Figure 13.6 includes criteria for a gymnastics sequence. In this case the checklist has been replaced with four levels of competence, which are described above the recording sheet. Figure 13.7 is a rating scale to assess mountain biking skills in grade 8.

Rubrics

A third approach to defining expectations is rubrics—narrative descriptors of the essential elements of a task or movement that include levels of competence. Rubrics can be either holistic or analytic. Holistic rubrics include a description of an entire performance or multiple criteria as a whole. Analytic rubrics keep components of a product separate and have rich descriptions of performances at various levels. Think of analytic rubrics as rating scales that have more detailed descriptions of the expectations at each level. Rubrics are very common in many subjects (e.g., in language arts to evaluate writing) and can be used just as effectively in physical education. Two physical education rubrics are provided in figures 13.8 and 13.9.

FIGURE 13.6 Rating Scale for Gymnastics Sequences (S1.E10.3)

Name _Cody McIlroy_

☐ Level 1 = Does not demonstrate action.

☐ Level 2 = Demonstrates action less than half of the time.

☐ Level 3 = Demonstrates action half to three quarters of the time.

☐ Level 4 = Demonstrates action more than three quarters of the time.

Criteria	Level 1	Level 2	Level 3	Level 4
Moves into a balance position using a combination of twisting, curling, and stretching actions.	X			
Maintains static balance for at least three seconds.				X
Moves out of a balance position using a combination of twisting, curling, and stretching actions.		X		

FIGURE 13.7 Rating Scale for Mountain Biking

Class _3rd period_

☐ Consistently (C) = 90% of the time or more

☐ Usually (U) = 75 to 89% of the time

☐ Sometimes (S) = 50 to 74% of the time

☐ Rarely (R) = <50% of the time

Student	Rolling over obstacles Uses the sit position until the front wheel clears the obstacle; moves to a set position when rear wheel goes over obstacle; feet flat; arms with slight bend.	Shifting Prepares to shift by quick push on cranks; free spins when clicking shifter to new gear; pushes or pulls shifter correct way to appropriately move to higher or lower gear; anticipates and shifts to new gear before a climb.	Braking Uses two fingers on left-hand, three fingers on right-hand brake lever; maintains appropriate body position (sit position for braking on descent, set position or on saddle while braking on flat ground).
Jamal	C	R	C
Miguel	U	S	R
Sasha	R	U	R
Tia	S	C	R

FIGURE 13.8   Analytic Rubric for the Underhand Throw

Student	Achieving - Always faces target when throwing underhand - Always swings arm back ("tick") - Always swings arm forward ("tock") - Always steps with the opposite foot - Always watches the target	Developing - Sometimes faces target when throwing underhand - Sometimes swings arm back ("tick") - Sometimes swings arm forward ("tock") - Sometimes steps with the opposite foot - Sometimes watches the target	Not yet - Does not face target when throwing underhand - Does not swing arm back ("tick") - Does not swing arm forward ("tock") - Does not step with the opposite foot - Does not watch the target
Aisha		X	
Ali	X		
David		X	
Jamal		X	
Miguel			X

Adapted, by permission, from L. Ardovino and S. Sanders, 1997, "The development of a physical education assessment report," *Teaching Elementary Physical Education* 8(3): 24.

FIGURE 13.9   Holistic Rubric for Floor Hockey

Assessment task: Play a modified game of 3v2 floor hockey.

Level	Basic skills	Offensive skills	Movement without the puck	Defensive skills
4	Consistently uses effective* passing, receiving, and shooting skills.	When initiating play, effectively* passes puck and moves to open space to receive a pass 3 times.	Consistently moves to open space with good timing and clear intent to create a passing lane.	Consistently moves to intercept puck or make passing difficult for offensive players.
3	Usually uses effective passing, receiving, and shooting skills.	When initiating play, effectively passes puck and moves to open space to receive a pass 2 times.	Usually moves to open space to create a passing lane.	Usually moves to intercept puck or make passing difficult for offensive players.
2	Sometimes uses effective passing, receiving, and shooting skills.	When initiating play, passes puck and moves to open space to receive a pass 1 time.	Sometimes moves to open space.	Sometimes moves to intercept puck or make passing difficult for offensive players.
1	Seldom uses effective passing, receiving, and shooting skills.	When initiating play, passes puck and never moves to open space to receive a pass.	Seldom moves to open space.	Seldom moves to intercept puck or make passing difficult for offensive players.
0	Violates safety procedures, does not complete the assessment task, or both.			

* *Effective(ly)* is defined as receiving or sending a playable pass, accurate shooting on goal.
Scoring: Consistently = 90% or above; usually = 75 to 89%; sometimes = 50 to 74%; seldom = <50%
Adapted from *PE Metrics* – secondary page 60

TECH TIPS Analyzing Assessments

Google Forms is a very popular way to assess and analyze both formative and summative assessments. Google Forms are very easy to create, and they provide immediate feedback. You can grade quizzes and tests using Google Forms and other add-ons (Flubaroo or Super Quiz) in Google Sheets. Use the summary of responses in Google Forms to assess your students' learning and then analyze what you need to do to modify upcoming lessons.

Standardized Assessments

The majority of assessments that you use will be alternative, often designed by you. In contrast, standardized assessments are designed and tested to ensure that they accurately measure the intended learning outcomes (validity) and lead to reliable results. The SAT and ACT examinations are common standardized tests in the United States. K-12 youngsters take standardized tests in every state in the United States. The Common Core State Standards, which have garnered tremendous debate and discussion in U.S. news over the past few years, are simply national standards to be adopted by states. Examinations that test student achievement of the Common Core State Standards are standardized assessments.

Standardized assessments exist in physical education as well. In 2010-2011, the National Association of Sport and Physical Education (NASPE) published *PE Metrics*, a collection of standardized performance and written tests that align with the national standards in physical education (NASPE, 2005). You can still use *PE Metrics*, although the national physical education standards were updated in 2013 (SHAPE America, 2014), making the *PE Metrics* assessments out of date. SHAPE America is in the process of revising *PE Metrics* to reflect the updated standards.

In the United States the most common form of standardized testing in physical education has to be fitness testing. This form of assessment, whether appropriate or not, has been used in physical education for decades.

Fitness Testing

Although an increasing number of teachers use alternative or other standardized assessments, as suggested by SHAPE America (2014), many states and districts in the United States still require physical fitness tests. If you aren't careful, however, such tests can make for unpleasant and meaningless student experiences (Hopple & Graham, 1995). Typically, fitness tests include a cardiorespiratory health assessment, such as a pacer test or a distance run, and a measure of flexibility and upper-body and abdominal strength. Regardless of the version you use, there are ways to save time administering the tests and to make them more valuable for your students.

Self-Testing

One way to save time is to teach upper-grade and secondary students to test themselves or one another. Yes, you will need to spend some time teaching the proper way to administer and perform the tests. Will this work with every class in every school? No. Will it work with many classes? Yes, depending on the students and how well they are taught the process of self-testing.

Ultimately, the most important part of any test is letting students know how they are improving in relation to their past performances—their progress. When youngsters measure their own progress, be sure to emphasize the importance of recording honest scores. This is most likely to happen when there is no pressure to compare scores with other students in the class (chapter 12). Self-measuring also allows you to test items throughout the year rather than only once a year in the spring, for example. In some cases, youngsters can be responsible for entering their own scores into a class computer. Needless to say, having youngsters handle this responsibility saves you a lot of time and also teaches them responsibility.

Sometime during the year, you might need to turn in an official set of scores. These scores might need to be administered by you or at least be more closely supervised than the more informal tests done by students.

Another advantage of teaching students to test themselves is that they can do it on days when the classroom teacher is responsible for physical education. This allows more time for instruction and practice during the days scheduled with you, the specialist (Parker & Pemberton, 1989). When the fitness sheets are kept in the classroom, you have less bookkeeping to do.

Broad Categories

An easy way to streamline the fitness testing process is to insert scores into broad categories. For example, whether a student runs a mile in 9:15 or 9:25 is important to the student but not very important to your assessment of her cardiorespiratory fitness (based on the assumption that the mile run is a valid measure of that component of fitness). Categories of fitness require a lot less bookkeeping and yield much quicker assessments. For example, as students complete a mile run, their times can be placed in three categories: under 7:30, between 7:31 and 9:30, and 9:31 and over. Sit-up scores might be recorded as fewer than 10, 11 to 40, and over 40.

Outside Help

A third method of saving time in fitness testing is not new, but it is effective. Recruit parents and guardians, classroom teachers, high school or university students, or retirees to volunteer to help with testing (East, Frazier, & Matney, 1989). Once you have contacted and trained volunteers, you will save a lot of time on the days the tests are administered.

● ● ● ●

Any of these ideas will save time and probably be more effective than administering an entire fitness test battery by yourself. They also give you more time to use other types of assessment. The most recent standards have in some ways de-emphasized fitness testing primarily because it is difficult to make measurable changes to fitness through physical education alone. Moreover, focusing on improving fitness during physical education often comes at the expense of spending time working on many of the other critical learning outcomes identified in the national standards (SHAPE America, 2014). Most programs, however, do more than simply try to enhance fitness performance scores; many teachers and students want to know about the progress they are making in other areas.

Reporting and Grading

Assessment is the collection of student performance information; evaluation is making a value judgment about student performance. Grading is a way to tell parents and guardians how well their children are doing in your class. Of course, youngsters also pay attention to their grades (some more than others!).

Many schools provide relatively limited opportunities for physical educators to inform parents and guardians about how their children are doing. Some elementary physical educators, for example, report student progress by checking one of three categories:

- Excellent
- Satisfactory
- Needs improvement

Secondary physical education teachers are often required to present grades (e.g., A, B, C, D, F, including – and +) that summarize student work during class. This is often all the information parents and guardians receive on how their children are doing in physical education.

Is Grading in PE Different From Grading in Math?

Imagine a student who comes to math class every day; brings his pencil, textbook, and calculator; and turns in all of his homework. Let's also say that this student gets virtually all of his answers wrong. Should he pass math, or should his grade reflect his learning? Unfortunately, grading in physical education has historically been based on dressing out, good behavior, and perceived effort (which may very well mean being well behaved) rather than learning (Young, 2011). Such grading practices have contributed to the perception that no learning occurs in physical education, that grading is pointless because all students have to do is show up, dress out, and not cause problems (Collier, 2011b; Young, 2011).

We hope that you choose to base grades on student learning. If you do, you will have many decisions to make regarding how to calculate grades. For example, how much should daily and end-of-unit assessments contribute to the overall grade, or do you value certain standards or outcomes more than others? Do you value or weight psychomotor performance more than cognitive or affective performance? Do you include fitness scores in grades? The resources in the Assessment and Evaluation Resources in Physical Education sidebar earlier in this chapter provide more information regarding grading in physical education.

Needless to say, many teachers regard reducing student performance to a single letter grade as unsatisfactory, although they are required to do so. The ideal way of reporting is to provide parents and guardians with information about the progress their children are making—what they have accomplished and what they need to work on (evaluation information). The ideal approach is to report assessments of student progress directly to parents and guardians (Shellhase, 1998). The Mail Merge function in Microsoft Word and similar functions in other grading programs are tremendous tools for quickly sending personalized detailed reports home from the assessment data collected during a semester or school year. Because criteria for each assessment are spelled out in a rubric, you can give parents and guardians, and administrators, clear descriptions of what you expect from your students and the progress they are making.

The recent move in the United States toward standards-based report cards is another example of providing additional information to parents and guardians regarding what their children have or have not learned, and how this leads to an earned grade (Melograno, 2007). Melograno (2007) described using the physical education standards to create

Student name _____ Teacher _____

School _____ School year _____

Rating Scale for Achievement Standards

☐ 4 Exceeds expectations of grade-level indicator

☐ 3 Meets expectations of grade-level indicator

☐ 2 Progressing toward expectations of grade-level indicator

☐ 1 Limited progress toward expectations of grade-level indicator

☐ — indicates not assessed at this time

Standard	Performance indicators	Quarter			
		1st	2nd	3rd	4th
1. Demonstrates competency in a variety of motor skills and movement patterns.	Throws a lead pass to a moving partner off a dribble or pass (S1.M5.8).				
	Executes the following offensive skills during small-sided game play: pivot, give-and-go, fakes (S1.M7.8).				
	Demonstrates correct technique for basic skills in at least two self-selected individual performance activities (S1.M24.8).				
2. Applies knowledge of concepts, principles, strategies, and tactics related to movement and performance.	Opens and closes space during small-sided game play by combining locomotor movements with movement concepts (S2.M1.8).				
	Varies the speed, force, and trajectory of the shot based on the location of the object in relation to the target (S2.M9.8).				
3. Demonstrates the knowledge and skills to achieve and maintain a health-enhancing level of physical activity and fitness.	Participates in physical activity three times a week outside of physical education class (S3.M2.8).				
	Participates in a self-selected lifetime sport, dance, aquatic, or outdoor activity outside of the school day (S3.M5.8).				
4. Exhibits responsible personal and social behavior that respects self and others.	Accepts responsibility for improving one's own levels of physical activity and fitness (S4.M1.8).				
	Provides encouragement and feedback to peers without prompting from the teacher (S4.M3.8).				
5. Recognizes the value of physical activity for health, enjoyment, challenge, self-expression, and/or social interaction.	Analyzes the empowering consequences of being physically active (S5.M2.8).				
	Identifies and participates in an enjoyable activity that prompts individual self-expression (S5.M5.8).				

> continued

FIGURE 13.10   *> continued*

A	Outstanding; well exceeds achievement standards
B	Good; above achievement standards
C	Satisfactory; meets achievement standards
D	Improving; below achievement standards
F	Unsatisfactory; well below achievement standards

	Quarter		
1st	**2nd**	**3rd**	**4th**

"Grading and report cards for standards-based physical education," V.J. Melograno, *Journal of Physical Education, Recreation & Dance*, 2007, 78(6): 45-53, adapted by permission of Taylor & Francis (Tayler & Francis Ltd, http://www.tandfonline.com).

a standards-based report card (figure 13.10) that uses a four-point scale (rating scale approach): *Exceeds, Meets, Progressing*, and *Limited progress*.

Alternative assessments lend themselves to comprehensive reports that parents and guardians can easily understand and appreciate (Allen, 1997; Ardovino & Sanders, 1997; Doolittle, 1996; Fox, 2012; Hopple, 1997; Melograno, 2007; Shellhase, 1998). Figure 13.11 contains Ardovino and Sanders' parent report titled "Just to let you know what

FIGURE 13.11   Progress Report to Parents of Young Children

Name _____ Date _____

This week we learned the *underhand throw*. The underhand throw should include the following components:

- Face the target (K-2).
- Swing your arm back "tick" (K-2).
- Swing your arm forward "tock" (K-2).
- Watch the target (K-2).
- Step with the opposite foot (1-2).
- Bend the knees as you step (3-4).
- Point your fingers to the target (3-4).

Helpful hints for the underhand throw include: Make sure the arm comes just past the knee ("tick") and forward ("tock"); to make the ball go straight toward the target, point the hand right at the target.

Your child has

- not yet developed the skill.
- developed the skill.
- achieved the skill.

Next week we will be working on the *overhand throw*. Some helpful hints for the overhand throw include:

- Throw hard.
- Bring arm way back just near the ear.
- Step with opposite foot.
- Follow through.

Please discuss this skill with your child and return this to me.

Parent's signature _____

Reprinted, by permission, from L. Ardovino and S. Sanders, 1997, "The development of a physical education assessment report," *Teaching Elementary Physical Education* 8(3): 23-25.

we are doing in physical education." Hopple (1997) suggested three criteria for parent and guardian reports:

- M—Child has *mastered* the skill or concept.
- P—Child is *practicing on/working toward* mastering the skill or concept.
- B—At the present time, child is *below developmental level* regarding this skill or concept.

Hopple's parent report includes concepts of body awareness and space awareness, as well as kicking skills, punting skills, and behavior.

It is easy to get lost in assessment and reporting and want to give up. Once again, begin with what you expect your students to learn. From there, identify a way to figure out how they're progressing. The final step is reporting progress to students and their parents or guardians. These same assessment data can be used to design and offer better lessons as well as to determine the quality of your physical education program. In our dream world, physical education teachers would be held to the same expectations as math, language arts, and science teachers. Because that isn't always the case today, it's up to you to value and apply student assessment.

A Frightening Thought

Increasingly, schools are being held accountable for what students are or are not learning. We are concerned that if we don't design our own ways of assessing our classes, a physical education test battery will be handed to us, similar to the standardized tests used in many classrooms today, and we will have to administer those tests to every student. In some districts and states in the United States, this has already happened with physical fitness tests. Although fitness is an important part of what we teach in physical education, good programs certainly do more than just attempt to improve fitness (SHAPE America, 2014). We need to discover ways of assessing our students in all domains, not only fitness; otherwise, the success of our programs will be measured only by how many pull-ups students can do, how fast they run a mile, or the number of minutes they spend in physical activity. Are those the important measures of a physical education program?

Summary

The examples in this chapter are more than any teacher could use in a year. Some you might never use. Others you might use occasionally or frequently or virtually every day. In any case, you need to be smart about assessment. Assessment is strictly collecting information about your students. You assess to measure student motor skill, cognitive learning, and attitudes. Techniques include scanning, digital media and video, written work and exit polls, checking for understanding, and designing performance tasks. How well students perform is often described using checklists, rating scales, and rubrics. In addition to alternative assessments, standardized tests such as fitness tests are often used in physical education. If you must use fitness tests, use appropriate practices and methods such as self-testing and peer testing and recruiting volunteers.

When it is time for reporting student learning, the age-old practice of grading for dressing out and participation must be replaced with evaluating student learning. In addition to grades, you need to commit to providing additional evaluation data to parents and guardians regarding what their children have learned. Fitness testing is not emphasized today as much as it was in the past, but it is the focus of many programs.

Although it's easy to become overwhelmed with assessment, keep in mind that the purpose is to deliver a better physical education program that leads to youngsters learning important skills. These skills are intended to lead them to becoming physically active for life. Without evaluating your own teaching, how well your students are learning, or whether your program is effective, you cannot make any meaningful difference in the lives of your students.

Questions for Reflection

1. It is generally agreed that elementary school physical education teachers do not typically test their students to any great extent. In this era of accountability, why do you think this is? Do you have any evidence that this is changing?

2. Students can learn to test themselves on various fitness and motor skills. Discuss the pros and cons of this process and the circumstances under which it would (and wouldn't) work.

3. Typically, we have relied on a few standardized items to test physical fitness. Describe several other ways, beyond the current methods used, that we might assess physical fitness.

4. Is it important to assess the critical elements of motor skills? Why or why not?

5. This chapter describes a variety of ways you might realistically assess the progress students are making in physical education. Of all the ways, which ones do you think you are most likely to use? Which ones are you least likely to use? Why?

6. What do you think are the potential consequences of simply not assessing students?

7. How do you think grades should be calculated in physical education? Should dressing out be included? How much do you value psychomotor, cognitive, and affective learning? Would you include fitness in your grades? Why or why not?

References

Allen, V. (1997). Assessment: What to do with it after you've done it. *Teaching Elementary Physical Education, 8* (6), 12-15.

Arbogast, G.W., & Griffin, L. (1989). Accountability: Is it within reach of the professions? *Journal of Physical Education, Recreation and Dance, 60* (6), 72-75.

Ardovino, L., & Sanders, S. (1997). The development of a physical education assessment report. *Teaching Elementary Physical Education, 8* (3), 23-25.

Cave, C.C., & Dohoney, P. (2009). Assessment strategies that motivate students to learn: A success story. *Strategies: A Journal for Physical and Sport Educators, 22* (6), 8-12.

Collier, D. (2011a). Increasing the value of physical education: The role of assessment. *Journal of Physical Education, Recreation and Dance, 82* (7), 38-41.

Collier, D. (2011b). The marginalization of physical education: Problems and solutions—part 2. Increasing the value of physical education: The role of assessment. *Journal of Physical Education, Recreation and Dance, 82* (7), 38-41.

Doering, N. (2000). Measuring student understanding with a videotape performance assessment. *Journal of Physical Education, Recreation and Dance, 71* (7), 47-52.

Doolittle, S. (1996). Practical assessment for physical education teachers. *Journal of Physical Education, Recreation and Dance, 67* (8), 35-37.

East, W.E., Frazier, J.M., & Matney, L.E. (1989). Assessing the physical fitness of elementary school children: Using community resources. *Journal of Physical Education, Recreation and Dance, 60* (6), 54-56.

Fortman-Kirk, M. (1997). Using portfolios to enhance student learning and assessment. *Journal of Physical Education, Recreation and Dance, 68* (7), 29-33.

Fox, C. (2012). How teachers can use PE Metrics for grading. *Journal of Physical Education, Recreation and Dance, 83* (5), 16-22.

Graber, K.C., & Locke, L.F. (2007). Chapter 7: Are the national standards achievable? Conclusions and recommendations. *Journal of Teaching in Physical Education, 26* (4), 416-424.

Graham, G., Holt/Hale, S., & Parker, M. (2012). *Children moving: A reflective approach to teaching physical education* (9th ed.). New York, NY: McGraw-Hill.

Graham, G., Metzler, M., & Webster, G. (1991). Specialist and classroom teacher effectiveness in children's physical education [Monograph]. *Journal of Teaching in Physical Education, 10* (4), 321-426.

Griffin, L., & Oslin, J. (1990). Got a minute? A quick and easy strategy for knowledge testing in physical education. *Strategies, 4* (2), 6-8.

Hopple, C. (2005). *Elementary physical education teaching and assessment* (2nd ed.). Champaign, IL: Human Kinetics.

Hopple, C., & Graham, G. (1995). What children think, feel and know about fitness testing. In G. Graham (Ed.), Physical education through students' eyes and in students' voices. *Journal of Teaching in Physical Education, 14*, 408-417.

Hopple, C.J. (1997). The real world process of assessment. *Teaching Elementary Physical Education, 8* (4), 4-7.

Lipowitz, S. (1997). Integrated assessment: Sue Schiemer makes assessment a regular part of her program. *Teaching Elementary Physical Education, 8* (3), 16-18.

Lund, J. (1997). Authentic assessment: Its development and applications. *Journal of Physical Education, Recreation and Dance, 68* (7), 25-28.

Marks, M. (1988). A ticket out the door. *Strategies, 2* (2), 17, 27.

Melograno, V.J. (2006). *Professional and student portfolios for physical education* (2nd ed.). Champaign, IL: Human Kinetics.

Melograno, V.J. (2007). Grading and report cards for standards-based physical education. *Journal of Physical Education, Recreation and Dance, 78* (6), 45-53.

National Association for Sport and Physical Education (NASPE). (1995). *Moving into the future: National standards for physical education.* St. Louis: Mosby.

Parker, M., & Pemberton, C. (1989). Elementary classroom teachers: Untapped resources for fitness assessment. *Journal of Physical Education, Recreation and Dance, 60* (6), 61-63.

Ryan, S., Marzilli, S., & Martindale, T. (2001). Using digital cameras to assess motor learning. *Journal of Physical Education, Recreation and Dance, 72* (8), 13-16, 18.

Schiemer, S. (2000). *Assessment strategies for elementary physical education.* Champaign, IL: Human Kinetics.

SHAPE America. (2010). *PE Metrics: Assessing National Standards 1-6 in elementary school.* Reston, VA: Author.

SHAPE America. (2011). *PE Metrics: Assessing National Standards 1-6 in secondary school.* Reston, VA: Author.

SHAPE America. (2014). *National standards & grade-level outcomes for K-12 physical education.* Champaign, IL: Human Kinetics.

Shellhase, K. (1998). Grades K-6 assessment system: A complete assessment package for the K-6 physical education teacher. Blacksburg, VA: PE Central. www.pecentral.org

Smith, T.K. (1997). Authentic assessment: Using a portfolio card in physical education. *Journal of Physical Education, Recreation and Dance, 68* (4), 46-52.

Wegis, H., & Van der Mars, H. (2006). Integrating assessment and instruction. *Journal of Physical Education, Recreation and Dance, 77* (1), 27-35.

Werner, P. (1997). Using PE Central and the national standards to develop practical assessment instruments. *Teaching Elementary Physical Education, 8* (3), 12-14.

Westfall, S. (1998). Setting your sights on assessment: Describing student performance in physical education. *Teaching Elementary Physical Education 9* (6), 5-9.

Young, S. (2011). A survey of student assessment practice in physical education: Recommendations for grading. *Strategies, 24* (6), 24-26.

Continuing to Develop as a Teacher

> "I was walking down the hall eating a fun size Kit Kat after lunch. One of the 5th grade boys looked me up and down and said, "Ms. Wilson, why are you eating chocolate? Aren't you supposed to be a fitness teacher?""
>
> Allison Wilson,
> The Academy of Leadership at
> Millcreek Elementary,
> Lexington, Kentucky
>
> Reprinted with permission from PE Central
> (www.pecentral.org).

After reading this chapter, you should be able to do the following:

- Describe the three stages of a teaching career and their influence on the way you teach.
- Discuss ways to improve and learn throughout your teaching career.
- Explain why it is important to continually strive to remain current and improve your teaching ability.

We began this book with the quote from George Bernard Shaw—"Those who can, do. Those who can't, teach"—and even mentioned what some believe to be true: "Those who can't teach, teach physical education"! We hope that, by now, you have been stimulated to think about many of the ways teachers have found to avoid turning kids off to physical education—and on to learning and enjoying physical activity.

We hope, too, that you have recognized many of the skills and approaches you already use as a teacher and that you have been stimulated to expand your pedagogical toolbox with some of the skills presented. Good teaching, as described in the last 13 chapters, isn't easy. It's hard work! The purpose of this final chapter is to describe some of the ways teachers have found to maintain their enthusiasm for teaching and continue to develop as professionals. Why is that important? Your students deserve the best practices you can bring, and that includes new content, better pedagogical skills, and new technological tools. Also, *you* deserve to love your job! Teachers who stay current and continue to develop professionally are typically more enthusiastic about their subjects and their students. Professional development helps you avoid the stagnation and fatigue that eventually come to any professional who settles into a comfortable routine that remains unchanged year after year.

Stages of Teaching

As a teacher of children or adolescents, you need to understand how youth develop so that you are familiar with the skills or movements they can learn at various ages and stages. Knowing that, you can design and implement developmentally appropriate experiences.

Understanding the developmental stages of teaching is also important so that you can better understand your own feelings, attitudes, and professional growth. You may be wondering:

- Why is the first year of teaching typically the most difficult?
- Why do experienced teachers seem to know so much?
- Why do beginning teachers seem to have more discipline problems than veterans?
- How do teachers improve and develop?

- How can teachers retain their freshness and eagerness throughout a career?
- Are there actually stages in a teaching career?

This chapter is the only one in the book that is not directly about teaching youngsters. It is a significant chapter, however, because it addresses you, the person doing the teaching.

Feiman-Nemser (1983) suggested three stages of teacher development. Her analysis provides a starting point for a discussion of the types of things teachers do to remain current and enthusiastic about their teaching and to improve over the course of their careers.

In a rather simplified overview, Feiman-Nemser (1983) suggested that teachers pass through two stages on the way to mastery (the third stage in her developmental analysis). The initial stage is induction, and the second stage is consolidation.

Induction Stage

Undergraduate practicum experiences in schools, student teaching, and the first year of teaching are all included in the category of induction. For many, the first year of teaching is the most challenging for three reasons:

- In most cases, you are alone with little or no collegial support.
- Much of what you do is brand new: discipline, students, school and colleagues, boss (principal), and content development in long-term and short-term planning (chapters 3 and 4).
- The daily schedule demands a great deal of time and energy.

One challenge of the induction year is simply to learn how to talk to students of various ages so that they will listen and understand. You may quickly learn, for example, that telling a class of kindergartners to form a circle outside on the grass is futile—for both you and the children. So is a direction such as, "Stand with your right side facing the wall," or "Read the directions written on the board." As you watch their perplexed faces and disorganized responses to statements they are not yet ready for, you learn a lot about teaching.

During the induction year, you also begin to learn how to develop tasks that help students meet the grade-level outcomes; how long to spend at various tasks; what to do when one student refuses to partner with another student; how to deal with tattling,

cussing, and fighting; how to quickly organize students to avoid pushing and shoving; and how to explain the qualities of various movements and skills. For these reasons and numerous others, the first year of teaching is often considered a survival year.

Wet Blankets and Mentors

In the first year of teaching, often during the first few days of school, you might encounter at least one veteran teacher who wants to tell you "what it's really like teaching today." Often, these veterans are dissatisfied with their careers and quickly proceed to tell you all that they see wrong with kids today, the principal, and the parents. They also quickly add all the reasons that what is currently being taught at universities won't work in the real world. Be ready for these wet blankets. They are the type of people who doubted that airplanes could fly, that televisions would be in every home, and that the Internet would become part of daily life. My recommendation is that you listen politely to the wet blanket, refrain from arguing, and then continue to do what you were doing.

Not all experienced teachers are wet blankets, however. In fact, most are not. It is wise to find one, or more, that you really connect with and use him or her as a mentor for the countless questions that arise in the first few weeks of school: How do you complete this form? Which meetings are important to attend? How does the school deal with parent and guardian complaints? In elementary schools, your mentor may not be another physical educator, but his wisdom and experience about youngsters, how schools work, and getting along with the principal and parents might prove invaluable. And you will need a mentor—no matter how well you are prepared for your first year of teaching, questions will always arise. It is comforting to be able to ask a mentor you can trust, who is also positive, for the answers that you need right now—not tomorrow or next week.

Throughout induction, especially toward the beginning, two questions addressed in chapters 2 and 10 may seem to dominate your thoughts about teaching:

- Do the students like me?
- How can I find better ways to ensure that students do not misbehave?

Consolidation Stage

During the next phase of teaching, the consolidation stage, these questions become less common and are replaced by concerns related to learning how to accommodate the varying skill levels of students in a single class and how to make the best of the time available to enhance learning. This holds especially true if you see your students only once or twice a week.

During this stage, your knowledge of pedagogical content truly begins to develop— knowledge that cannot be learned at universities but is attained only through years of working in schools with children and adolescents. This is when you begin to learn to use many of the tools in your pedagogical toolbox. Following are some of the changes that occur during the consolidation stage:

- You begin to understand how a 5-year-old is different from an 8-year-old, who is different from an 11-year-old; and that middle school students are not mini high school students. Your lessons become more developmentally appropriate.
- You begin to recognize tasks that will succeed with sixth-graders and those that won't, and you no longer have to rely on the first one or two lessons of the day to adjust the lesson (chapter 4) (Graham et al., 1993).

- The "functional fixedness" of the induction phase dwindles, and you become comfortable exploring different ways to use the equipment and facilities (Housner & Griffey, 1985). For example, you may no longer be devastated when you discover, five minutes before a class is scheduled to begin, that the indoor facility is in use for the winter play rehearsal.

- You learn that youngsters still like and respect you even when you are firm and demanding (chapters 2 and 10).

- Your observational skills become much sharper (chapter 5); you can quickly scan a class and analyze what is (or isn't) going on (Housner & Griffey, 1985).

- You know the content better because of the lessons you have taught and reflected on; you change tasks less and focus more on student learning. You become adept at making small task changes to actively involve students in practicing tasks and skills (Graham et al., 1993).

As a result of your experience and hard work, the satisfying feeling that you are doing a good job comes more frequently in the consolidation stage. You know when an unsuccessful lesson was a result of poor teaching and when it was a result of external circumstances (a substitute teacher, Halloween, or dogs or bees on the playground) (Tjeerdsma, 1995). You realize that you still have a lot to learn, but you also recognize how much you have learned since the induction stage.

Mastery Stage

Feiman-Nemser (1983) suggested that after several years, some teachers begin to approach mastery. They effectively orchestrate and use many of the teaching skills described in the previous 13 chapters.

Master teachers have learned through experience and hard work to develop lessons that are enjoyable and beneficial for students. Their lessons have definite and clear purposes that mesh with the long-term goals of their programs (chapter 4). Whether they're teaching dance, games, gymnastics, or fitness concepts, they have mastered the process of presenting the content (chapters 4 and 7) so that students are interested, challenged, and successful (chapters 5, 8, and 11). Master teachers observe and understand students as they move (chapter 5) and improvise appropriately based on their vast storehouses of knowledge and information accumulated in earlier years of teaching (Borko & Livingston, 1989). Discipline problems are minimal, and when they do occur, they are dealt with effectively and humanely (chapters 2 and 10). Feedback is both useful and pervasive (chapter 9). Students view physical education class as a warm and supportive experience that they enjoy and look forward to (chapter 12).

In contrast to the consolidation-stage teacher, the majority of the lessons taught by a master teacher are effective and satisfying for both teacher and students. There are surprises, but a master teacher's past experience and hard work help her to deal with many of the problems that every teacher encounters—and to deal with them in ways that are beneficial to the students and personally fulfilling to the teacher.

People aren't born master teachers. They might have many characteristics that will help them succeed at teaching, but they gain mastery only through experience and constant effort. One prevalent characteristic of highly successful teachers is their inquisitiveness and ability to analyze and reflect on their own teaching (Schon, 1990). When they might be satisfied, they are instead constantly trying to improve their teaching and their programs. David Hawkins made this point poignantly when observing a veteran teacher of 35 years and a student teacher:

The veteran teacher commented that what held her to teaching after all these years was that there was still so much to be learned. The student teacher responded in amazement that she thought it could be learned in two or three years. (Feiman-Nemser, 1983, p. 150)

Teaching is a dynamic journey that never ends. Although it's possible to teach the same content, using the same process, essentially repeating the first year 30 times, most of us desire more from our careers. We want to improve, learn, develop, change; we want to explore new ideas and approaches—to become better teachers than we were the year before. How do physical education teachers do this?

Techniques for Continuing to Improve as a Teacher

Good teachers work at it! They purposely search for ways to remain refreshed and excited about their teaching year after year. It is saddening to meet teachers who haven't remained current. They just aren't abreast of recent developments. They know it. Their older students know it. And, unfortunately, the principals of their schools and the parents and guardians of their students know it. Needless to say, this hurts our profession because it reflects on our image as physical educators. Insulting jokes by comedians and illustrations by cartoonists are testimony to these poor teachers' ineffectiveness and the harmful effects of being in their classes.

So how do you continue to develop as a teacher? This section briefly describes some of the techniques you can use to remain current in and energized about your profession (Docheff, 1992; Markos, Walker, & Colvin, 1998; Raxter, 1992): reading and researching, joining support groups, engaging in professional development, sharing your expertise, serving your profession, and continuing your education.

Reading and Googling

One way to remain current is to read. Consider purchasing a new book every year related to physical education, physical activity, or teaching in general to keep up with new or different teaching strategies, techniques, and content. Journals such as *Strategies* and the *Journal of Physical Education, Recreation and Dance* are great resources as well. If you prefer to learn through visual resources, consider watching DVDs and video podcasts. And

now with a plethora of web-based books, visual resources, and informational websites, you can find new information on just about any topic in a matter of seconds. Having all this information at your fingertips regularly gives you no reason not to stay current with new information that can help you upgrade your teaching.

Disconnected Curriculum

Although there may be easier ways to teach, many experts are convinced that the process we have described in the previous 13 chapters has the potential to lead youngsters to become physically active for a lifetime (SHAPE America, 2014).

If you are just entering the profession of physical education, we sincerely hope that you become a physical educator who teaches with a purpose—that you want your students to develop the confidence that leads to a lifetime of enjoyable participation in sports and physical activity. If you don't already know it, not every physical educator teaches for learning. Some simply try to provide their students with a series of games, perhaps dances, that may be enjoyable for some but that are disconnected from other activities—their programs lack a sequential progression.

Spotting these teachers is easy. They are always searching for new, fun activities to keep their kids busy, happy, and good. You may encounter them at conferences or workshops. They may be excited to discover a new game to teach that they think their classes will love. If the game doesn't address varying skill levels or maximize students' active time, we often wonder how it connects to their curriculums. Do these teachers simply wake up in the morning and ask themselves, *What can I do today that will keep my students entertained?*

Our genuine hope is that you are, or will become, a physical educator with an inner filter to screen the activities you present to your students. Some activities you find on the Internet, in books, or at conferences and workshops are a waste of time. They may appear fun, but they don't lead to youngsters becoming physically literate. We hope this book along with the national standards and grade-level outcomes of SHAPE America (2014) make you an informed consumer. Our hope is that your curriculum is connected from lesson to lesson, theme to theme, and year to year, and that you make an impact on the thousands of youngsters you will be fortunate enough to teach throughout your career.

Joining a Support Group

Establishing professional learning communities within a school gives teachers an opportunity to learn from one another, work collaboratively to find solutions, and apply learning to the physical environment of their schools (Armour & Yelling, 2007; Beddoes, Prusak, & Hall, 2014). Sharing ideas and concerns with others seems especially important for PE teachers because they are often alone and isolated. Classroom teachers, on the other hand, have chances throughout the day to vent their emotions, celebrate their small victories, and generally be sociable with other teachers in similar situations. For many PE specialists, the majority of their adult interactions during a school day are with the cooks in the cafeteria or custodians.

Recent studies have shown that professional learning communities in which teachers select supportive colleagues promote professional learning and colleague collaboration and support (Armour & Yelling, 2007). Of course, because physical educators also need to collaborate with other teachers in their field, some form support groups with other specialists across their districts (Beddoes, Prusak, & Hall, 2014). They meet monthly, sometimes weekly, in person or over the phone, to share ideas and provide emotional

support. We have become increasingly convinced that opportunities to gain and give support are vital for teachers to reach their full potential. The support might come from a spouse or a friend, but given the challenges of teaching physical education, teachers who remain enthusiastic about teaching seem to find ways to get support.

The Internet offers a plethora of ways to communicate with other teachers in your field. Interestingly, when the first edition of this book was published in 1992, the Internet was not even mentioned. How differently we view the world and our options now! Many social networking sites (e.g., Facebook, Twitter) facilitate teacher communication and support. Some sites provide teacher discussion forums that are monitored by registered users. One of the newest and best is the SHAPE America All Member Forum. It includes new discussion threads daily and is an excellent example of a group of professionals offering advice, support, and resource recommendations. This is another perk of becoming a member of the U.S. national professional organization, SHAPE America!

TECH TIPS Connecting With Others

Many teachers enjoy using social media to create online professional learning networks (PLNs). On Twitter you can use hashtags to search for groups such as #physed and #pegeeks. Facebook has many physical education groups, and Google Plus has physical education communities. Using social media to develop your professional learning network can connect you to physical educators you would not have had the chance to meet in person.

As we have mentioned, probably the most comprehensive and widely used Internet site for K-12 physical educators is PE Central (www.pecentral.org). The site includes hundreds of lesson ideas, examples of assessments, and descriptions of best practices. PE Central is also an excellent source for publications and music related to physical education. Sign on to PE Central's Facebook and Twitter sites to connect with colleagues everywhere.

Engaging in Professional Development

To develop into a quality PE teacher, engagement in ongoing professional development opportunities is a must (Bechtel & O'Sullivan, 2006). Continuing professional development (CPD) increases your content knowledge and improves your pedagogical skills and technology skills; most important, it helps you positively affect student learning. In the past, one-day in-service trainings at the beginning of the year, and teachers' own desire to improve by reading books and journals, were about the extent of CPD opportunities for many teachers. Now, more teachers and administrators are recognizing the value of CPD for physical education teachers, including attending state and national conferences and workshops as well as CPD in their own districts that is specific to the PE content area. For CPD to truly be meaningful, it should involve gaining new information from experts and collaborating with colleagues to exchange ideas and share stories (Armour & Yelling, 2007; Keay, 2006; O'Sullivan & Deglau, 2006).

Hopefully, as a preservice teacher, you have been or were encouraged (or better yet, required) to be involved in state or national conferences for ongoing professional learning. Documented evidence shows that becoming involved in national and state professional organizations early in their careers keeps teachers involved throughout their careers (McPhail et al., 2014). Engaging in a variety of roles in a learning community facilitates learning and motivation—not just presenting at a conference, but also attending, observing, and assisting. The relationships you build will contribute to your role in becoming a part of a learning community. You may speak with the president of the sponsoring organization and realize that her leadership skills were the result of much hard work and commitment to the profession, something you see yourself doing in the future. Or you may attend a presentation by the author of an important book from one of your courses, and the book may become more relevant and more real—and more important! You may also meet other first-year teachers like yourself who are struggling with the same issues and experiencing some of the same joys. All of these experiences make attending conferences invaluable.

We hope that you will be (or are) teaching in a school led by a principal who values conferences and workshops as a way for you to grow and become more inspired to be a quality teacher. Unfortunately, when CPD initiatives are not seen as a valuable use of time or money, teachers may come to view them the same way (McCaughtry et al., 2006). Don't let that happen!

In addition to attending workshops and conferences, you can attend weekly webinars on timely topics. Many are free and can be viewed at any time once they have been delivered live. For example, SPARK (www.sparkpe.org) has free webinars for PE teachers and administrators on current trends in physical education, and SHAPE America offers webinars on demand that can be used to fulfill teacher licensure renewal requirements for a small fee. Teachers, schools, and districts can take advantage of these online CPD opportunities when they best fit into their schedules.

TECH TIPS **Organizing Web-Based Resources**

With so many web-based resources at your fingertips, it is helpful to have a way to organize them so that you can find them quickly and on multiple devices. Portaportal is a bookmarking utility that will save you time and help you access the information you need in a flash. You can also use Portaportal to bookmark websites for students to access (e.g., for an out-of-class assignment).

Sharing Your Expertise

As discussed in the previous sections, the Internet allows physical educators throughout the world to share the latest information. You can ask and answer questions related to your teaching, participate in support groups, and share your lesson ideas on PE Central and other websites. The following sections offer a few more ideas on how to share your expertise with others. We all have something to share, no matter what stage of teaching we are in. What do you consider your expertise? How will you share it with others?

Teachers Visiting Teachers

In addition to sharing your ideas virtually, you may be fortunate to have colleagues close by. If so, a visit to observe them teaching can be especially valuable. In fact, some teachers find a visit more valuable than attending conferences or reading. Such visits may reinforce some of what you already do while also stimulating new ideas. One teacher said, "I think it would be brilliant to go into other schools. . . . I think so much of PE, or so many PE teachers pick up on things in a practical way, rather than sitting in a lecture theatre and being told how to do something" (Armour & Yelling, 2007, p. 189). Unfortunately, many school administrators have yet to see the value of teachers' visiting teachers, so release time may be hard to obtain.

Videos

Sharing video of lessons is another way to gain fresh approaches to teaching. You can exchange recorded lessons on dance, task sheets, or intratask variation with other teachers. An advantage to this approach is that you don't need to be close by—discussions and questions can be shared via e-mail, phone, or social media. There are even video clubs for teachers in which members solve problems collaboratively; teachers learn from each other and add to their teaching repertoires (Sherin & Han, 2004).

If you have viewed several video clips and developed a support group, you might be willing to take a risk and explore a new way of teaching. Many veteran teachers, for example, find it difficult to use a scattered formation in which every student has a ball and students are all moving at the same time. The transition from lines to scattered formations is not an easy one. A teacher who has watched a video, for example, and developed a relationship of trust with a colleague might be more willing to experiment with a scattered formation or another new method.

You may read about an idea or hear it described at a conference but are unwilling to try it. If you see the idea come to life on video, however, and know that you can call a friend to ask about it, you may be more willing to try it. PE Central has a library of PE-related video clips. The videos are hosted by SchoolTube, which most schools allow you to access. A number of other websites allow teachers to upload video clips to share.

Presentations

Making presentations is motivating for some teachers. Others hate even thinking about it. Although presentations can be nerve racking and time-consuming, an occasional one about an idea or activity that you have found successful can be a stimulant for personal growth. Teachers have told us countless times that they have nothing of value to share. After some prodding and encouragement, they realize that they have an idea or two that just might benefit others. As mentioned earlier, conferences are important to your professional development, regardless of your role. But making a presentation alone or with other teachers is a rewarding experience, and a benefit to your audience. Hopefully, as a preservice or beginning teacher, you will have or have had an opportunity or two to join one of your professors and perhaps other colleagues to design and deliver a professional presentation.

In addition to conference attendees, consider others who would find your expertise helpful, such as parents and guardians, other teachers in your school, and community organizations that support the health culture of your school. Remember, you are the physical activity expert. You have important information to share.

TECH TIPS **Presentation Software**

In addition to PowerPoint, try some other presentation software options such as PowToon (mentioned in chapter 6) and Prezi. Prezi is web-based and allows you to include video clips, text, and images. Prezi also has a collaboration feature that allows you to work remotely with a colleague. It does require a monthly fee to make your presentations private.

Supervising Student Teachers

Supervising student teachers and mentoring beginning teachers are other opportunities to gain new ideas and insights by working with those who are fresh out of college. If you are conscientious as you work with a student teacher, you will find yourself reflecting on how you teach, what you teach, and why you have done it that way over the years—a learning experience in itself. Good supervision is time-consuming; it's also professionally stimulating.

Sharing Your Lesson Ideas Online

Here are great websites for sharing lessons ideas (and you will get credit for your contributions!):

- PE Central (www.pecentral.org)
- Active Academics (www.activeacademics.org)
- Share My Lesson (www.sharemylesson.com)

Serving Your Profession

Another important element of professional growth is engaging in professional service. In addition to those previously discussed, service to your profession can be carried out in your school and community, as well as in state and national organizations.

Committees

You can remain current by serving on physical education committees within your district or at the state or national level. Occasionally, the committee work itself is stimulating; more often, the interaction with other teachers is the valuable part of committee work. The value, of course, is that it exposes you to other viewpoints and ideas. A little committee work may go a long way in helping to open new horizons. Not surprisingly, it's usually easy to serve on a committee—volunteers for committee work are about as rare as lottery winners.

School and Community Leadership

Another professional service that can keep you current and allow you to share your expertise, even though it may not be part of your job, is providing leadership for your school's comprehensive school physical activity program. All schools should have one, and no one knows physical activity better than you! If your school is a Let's Move! Active

Schools participant, it needs a champion to be the school's physical activity leader. Your role may simply be to lend your expertise in helping the school wellness team provide more physical activity opportunities for students throughout the school day, to help ensure 60 minutes of physical activity a day for all school-age youth.

Continuing Your Education

Continuing your education is the final technique we will discuss to help you improve as a teacher. Although you may think of it as a way to make more money or have a better job title, the real benefit comes from gaining a new set of skills and knowledge, strengthening old skills, networking, and perhaps doing research-based work to establish yourself as an expert in your field. Even though continuing education credit is required to keep your teaching certification, graduate school is a decision to make based on the benefits mentioned earlier, or maybe just because you find learning fun and enjoy challenging yourself.

TECH TIPS Staying Current

Flipboard is a great app that allows you to follow current events related to your profession. Set up your account, choose your interests, and let the app do the work for you. Flipboard pulls all current articles related to your topics and houses them under one roof. You can also share them with others.

Graduate School

The degree of stimulation you will find in graduate courses depends on the content of the course, the professor, and your personal motivation for taking the course. It seems that teachers who have been instructing for several years derive more benefits from returning to school than do those who have just finished their undergraduate degrees. They seem to know the questions they want to ask and to appreciate being back in school. If they discover ways to apply the course work to their teaching, they often notice an improvement. One barrier to returning to school to seek a graduate degree is the commitment to being away from home. One alternative is to pursue an online degree.

Online Education

Many universities now offer all online master's degrees, or hybrid degrees, in which students take online courses during the school year and then go to the university campus for a few weeks in the summer for face-to-face courses. The advantage, obviously, is that you can do your work from home and conduct action-based research in your own school. The disadvantage is the lack of social support from a community of learners, or at least having a different kind of social support.

Continuing Education Credit

Many states in the United States are increasingly providing alternatives to graduate courses for teachers wanting to obtain recertification. This provides some interesting ways of recharging batteries (e.g., some states give recertification credit for attending conferences, writing articles, or participating on state committees). The temptation, of course, is to take the easy way out and simply do what's quickest and requires the least amount of work. This is understandable but certainly doesn't lead to career improvement.

Seven Habits of Highly Effective Teachers

You might have read the best-selling book by Stephen R. Covey called *The 7 Habits of Highly Effective People* (1989). The book is about how successful people lead their personal and professional lives. Martin (2004) applied the habits described by Covey to physical educators, as follows:

1. Be proactive. Base your work on your goals and accept responsibility for the outcomes; don't blame others when things don't work out. Instead, ask what you might do differently in the future.

2. Begin with the end in mind. Ask the key question "What type of teacher do I want to be remembered as at the end of my career?" and then work toward the answer throughout your years in the profession.

3. Put first things first. Be clear about your goals, and be certain that you make time to work toward them. This can be especially difficult given the busy schedules of teachers, but it is an important part of becoming the teacher you want to become.

4. Think win–win. Try to engineer solutions to problems so that everyone involved feels good about the solution. This can be especially important when working with other teachers and administrators so that you all feel that you are on the same team.

5. Seek first to understand, then to be understood. This habit involves learning to listen to others so that you understand them and, in turn, they understand you. This is a crucial part of the previous strategy of win–win.

6. Synergize. This habit can be summarized as the whole being greater than the parts. It involves working with others to accomplish common goals that could not be accomplished individually—or at least not as well.

7. Sharpen the saw. This final habit involves taking good care of yourself, including your physical, mental, social, emotional, and spiritual dimensions. This will enable you to be effective and productive.

What Type of Teacher Will You Become?

Teachers who do the hard work necessary to develop and improve their careers are naturally inclined to participate in some of the activities we have described to enhance their teaching. No doubt, they also find other ways to improve. Obviously, not every suggestion will be worthwhile for every teacher.

In our profession, as in most others, it is essentially up to the individual to remain current and continue to develop. There are easy ways to satisfy professional growth requirements imposed by a state accrediting agency that might be of virtually no worth to your professional growth as a teacher. The same is true for physicians, attorneys, and accountants. However, to be truly successful, you must continue to study and learn and try new ideas throughout your career—not because you have to, but because you want to (Martin, 2004). Those who don't, decline in effectiveness or perhaps simply never become very adept at teaching. Some teachers even become lifetime members of physical education's hall of shame (Williams, 1996). Others are known for rolling out the ball rather than for being role models for youngsters (Spencer, 1998). Others are touted as great coaches but not-so-great teachers (Konukman et al., 2010).

IT'S SO IMPORTANT TO HELP CHILDREN GET STARTED IN THE RIGHT DIRECTION.

Parting Thoughts

Good teaching is hard work. Part of the hard work is continuing to grow and develop as a teacher. There are times when we all ask these questions: "Is it worth it?" and "Why am I working so hard when others don't seem to care?"

Three quotes might help inspire you to do the best job you can for your students. One is from John F. Kennedy: "Children are our most important natural resource and our best hope for the future." We hope this reminds you of the importance of your job—and what you have dedicated your life to professionally. Reflecting on these words, you may realize that no job, no matter how much it pays or what status it carries, is more important than teaching.

A second quote may help remind you that you are not alone if you find yourself wondering: *What the heck? Why work so hard?* When serving as a U.S. senator, Bobby Kennedy wrote:

Sometimes it seems to me that it doesn't matter what I do, that it is enough to exist, to sit somewhere, in a garden, for example, watching whatever is to be seen there, the small events.

At other times, I'm aware that other people, possibly a great number of other people, could be affected by what I do or fail to do, that I have a responsibility, as we all have, to make the best possible use of whatever talents I've been given, for the common good.

It is not enough to sit in that garden, however restful or pleasurable it might be. The world is full of unsolved problems, situations that demand careful, reasoned, and intelligent action.

The final quote accompanies a photograph of a young boy looking out over a lake.

A hundred years from now it will not matter what my bank account was, the sort of house I lived in, or the kind of car I drove. But the world may be different because I was important in the life of a boy. (Witcraft, 1950, p. 2)

As a physical education teacher, you influence, or will influence, hundreds of young people every year. When you're successful and work hard, you do your part in making the world a better place for children and adolescents to grow up in. We hope that by writing this text, we have helped you become a better teacher and a positive influence on many students throughout your career in teaching.

Summary

This final chapter is the only one in the book that is not directly about teaching students. Rather, it is about you, the teacher, and how to continue to grow professionally. Understanding the three stages of teaching (induction, consolidation, and mastery) can help. Techniques to help you improve as a teacher include reading and researching, continuing professional development, joining support groups, sharing your expertise, providing service to your profession, and continuing your education. The chapter concludes with the seven habits of highly effective teachers and how these can help you determine what type of teacher you will become.

Questions for Reflection

1. Why is it important to continue to work at improving throughout your career? What are the consequences of not remaining current and enthusiastic?

2. This chapter describes three stages of teaching: induction, consolidation, and mastery. Do you agree with these divisions? Why or why not? How might you expand them to include five or six stages?

3. The cartoon about a teacher who hasn't read a PE book in years depicts a hypothetical teacher expressing her views on how things change in physical education. What might you say to her?

4. This chapter addresses a variety of techniques for remaining current and enthusiastic about teaching. Which ones appeal to you most? Least? Why? Do you think your view might change over your career?

5. Given the many resources on the Internet, what are the most important things to consider when using web-based resources? How can you determine whether you are reading a credible article or an appropriate lesson idea?

6. Seven habits of highly effective teachers are described near the end of the chapter. Select three and give examples from your personal life that illustrate how you exemplify these habits—or what you might do differently to do so.

7. In the final section of this chapter, we shared three quotes that we have found personally motivating. Do you have any quotes that you find encouraging? Would you want to share them with other teachers?

References

Armour, K.M., & Yelling, M. (2007). Effective professional development for physical education teachers: The role of informal, collaborative learning. *Journal of Teaching in Physical Education, 26* (2), 177-200.

Bechtel, P.A., & O'Sullivan, M. (2006). Effective professional development: What we now know. *Journal of Teaching in Physical Education, 25* (4), 363-378.

Beddoes, Z., Prusak, K., & Hall, A. (2014). Overcoming marginalization of physical education in America's schools with professional learning communities. *Journal of Physical Education, Recreation, and Dance, 85* (4), 21-27.

Borko, H., & Livingston, C. (1989). Cognition and improvisation: Differences in mathematics instruction by expert and novice teachers. *American Educational Research Journal, 26* (4), 473-498.

Covey, S.R. (1989). *The 7 habits of highly effective people.* New York: Fireside.

Docheff, D.M. (1992). Are you a good teacher? *Strategies, 6* (2), 5-9.

Feiman-Nemser, S. (1983). Learning to teach. In L. Shulman & P. Sykes (Eds.), *Handbook of teaching and policy* (pp. 150-170). New York: Longman.

Graham, G., Hopple, C., Manross, M., & Sitzman, T. (1993). Novice and expert children's physical education teachers: Insights into their situational decision-making. *Journal of Teaching in Physical Education, 12*, 197-217.

Housner, L.D., & Griffey, D.C. (1985). Teacher cognition: Differences in planning and interactive decision-making between experienced and inexperienced teachers. *Research Quarterly for Exercise and Sport, 56* (1), 45-53.

Keay, J. (2006). Collaborative learning in physical education teachers' early-career professional development. *PE and Sport Pedagogy, 11* (3), 285-305.

Konukman, F., Agbuga, B., Erdogan, S., Zorba, E., Demirhan, G., & Yilmaz, I. (2010). Teacher-coach role conflict in school-based physical education in USA: A literature review and suggestions for the future. *Biomedical Human Kinetics, 2*, 19-24.

Markos, N.J., Walker, P.J., & Colvin, A.V. (1998). Professional practice: Elementary "think tank." *Strategies, 11* (4), 7-8.

Martin, L. (2004). The seven habits of highly effective physical educators. *Journal of Physical Education, Recreation and Dance, 75* (2), 47-52.

McCaughtry, N., Martin, J., Kulinna, P.H., & Cothran, D. (2006). What makes teacher professional development work? The influence of instructional resources on change in physical education. *Journal of In-Service Education, 32* (2), 221-235.

McPhail, A., Patton, K., Parker, M., & Tannehill, D. (2014). Leading by example: Teacher educators' professional learning through communities of practice. *Quest, 66*, 39-56. doi:10.1080/00336297.2010.826139

O'Sullivan, M., & Deglau, D. (2006). Chapter 7: Principles of professional development. *Journal of Teaching in Physical Education, 25*, 441-449.

Raxter, L.M. (1992). Keeping your edge: Maintaining excellence. *Strategies, 5* (8), 24-26.

Schon, D. (1990). *Educating the reflective practitioner.* San Francisco: Jossey-Bass.

SHAPE America. (2014). *National standards & grade-level outcomes for K-12 physical education.* Champaign, IL: Human Kinetics.

Sherin, M.G., & Han, S.Y. (2004). Teacher learning in the context of a video club. *Teaching and Teacher Education, 20* (2), 163-183.

Spencer, A. (1998). Physical educator: Role model or roll the ball out? *Journal of Physical Education, Recreation and Dance, 69* (6), 58-63.

Tjeerdsma, B.L. (1995). "If-then" statements help novice teachers deal with the unexpected. *Journal of Physical Education, Recreation and Dance, 66* (6), 22-24.

Williams, N. (1996). The physical education hall of shame, part III. *Journal of Physical Education, Recreation and Dance, 67* (8), 45-48.

Witcraft, F.E. (1950, October 2). Within my power. *Scouting Magazine, 2.*

Index

Note: Page references followed by an italicized *f* or *t* indicate information contained in figures and tables, respectively.

A

activity time 120-122, 121*f*
activity tracking devices and apps 134
Adapted Physical Education National Standards
    (APENS) 73
affective assessment 224-226, 225*f*
alternative assessment 218-226, 222*f*, 223*f*, 225*f*
anticipatory set 97-99
assertive discipline 167-171
assessment
    affective assessment 224-226, 225*f*
    alternative assessment 218-226, 222*f*, 223*f*, 225*f*
    cognitive assessments 221-224, 222*f*, 223*f*
    evaluating data from 226-230, 227*f*, 228*f*, 229*f*
    motor skills assessment 219-221
    outcomes for 217-218
    reasons for 216-217
    reporting and grading 231-235, 233*f*, 234*f*
    resources for 226
    standardized 230-231
    students' self-setting goals 209
    technology for 216, 220, 223, 224, 230
    test interpretation 208
atmosphere 16-17, 187
attendance protocols 21-22
attitude assessments 225, 225*f*
autonomy-supported teaching 129-131

B

back-to-the-wall observation 80, 163
backward design 38, 55-56
BaM Video Delay app 152
basketball goal heights, varied 128
behavior and discipline problems
    assertive discipline 167-171, 168*f*
    back-to-the-wall technique 163
    characteristics of successful discipline systems
        173-175
    disciplinary confrontation 175-176
    discipline systems 167-173
    learning names 165-166
    overlapping 165
    personal and social responsibility model 171-173
    positive pinpointing 166
    proximity control 163-164
    reasons for 162
    selective ignoring 164
    strategies to minimize 162-167
    technology to assist with 165
    with-it-ness 164
behavior protocols 28-32, 31*f*
belittling 19
birth month grouping 27, 204
Blendspace 57
busy-happy-good 12

C

calisthenics 101-102
callouts 188
challenges, in lessons 65-70, 69*t*-70*t*
checking for understanding 115-116, 222-223
checklists 226, 227*f*
choice and motivation 128, 132, 202
ClassBadges 203
ClassDojo app 165
classroom teaching 3-4
class size 40
clothing requirements 21
coaching 6-7, 154
Coach's Eye app 151
cognitive assessments 221-224, 222*f*, 223*f*
cognitive challenges 67
cognitive set 97-99
Common Core State Standards (CCSS) 42
competition 199, 200
component observation 81
comprehensive school physical activity programs
        (CSPAP) 42
consolidation stage of teaching 242-243
content development
    all-task pattern 84-87, 86*f*
    interpreting patterns of 87-90
    observation and content development 83-90, 85*f*,
        86*f*, 88*f*, 89*f*
    sequencing annually 48-50
    task-cue-cue-challenge pattern 87, 89*f*
    task-cue-task-cue pattern 87, 88*f*
    vs. pedagogy 3
content knowledge 41-42, 189-190
convergent problem solving 184-186
critical thinking skills, building
    about 182
    convergent problem solving 184-186
    direct *vs.* indirect approaches 182-183, 193
    divergent problem solving 186-187
    levels of complexity 191
    teacher characteristics for 188-192

critical thinking skills, building *(continued)*
  technology for 184, 186, 188
  value of 182-183
  verbal problem solving 187-188
cross-group feedback 154
cues (critical elements), in lessons 62-65, 63*f*, 64*t*, 69*t*-70*t*, 81
curricula
  coherency of 245
  sample middle school scope 46*t*
  sample scope for 72-lesson program 45*t*

D
deck of cards grouping 27
demonstrating skills 112-114
developmentally appropriate tasks 131-132
digital media 220
discipline problems. *See* behavior and discipline problems
discipline systems. *See also* behavior and discipline problems
  about 167
  assertive discipline 167-171, 168*f*
  characteristics of successful 173-175
  disciplinary confrontation 175-176
  parent support of 175
  personal and social responsibility model 171-173
  rewards and consequences 170-171
  staff support of 175
  student understanding of 174
  teacher consistency 174-175
  time-out 169-170
discussion circles 210-211
divergent problem solving 186-187
Dragon Dictation 55

E
elementary students
  challenges of 6-7
  consequences for misbehavior 169*f*
  curriculum scope 45*f*, 46-47
  entering and leaving gym space 20
  equipment protocols 24
  instant activity posters for 95
  outcomes 38-39
  rewards of working with 7-8, 9
  success-oriented tasks 126-128
  teaching stopping and starting 23
elimination games 199
emotionally safe environments 19
emotional temperature 205-206
entering and leaving gym or outdoor space 20-21
environment, positive 16-17, 187, 192, 200-201. *See also* management protocols
equipment
  budgets 7
  equipment protocols 24-25
  inadequacies in 40
  safety 82, 82*f*
Evernote 56, 220
exchange days 47

exercise as punishment 199-200
exit polls 224
expectancy, teacher 17
extrinsic rewards 170-171

F
Facebook 246
feedback to students
  analyzing 155-158, 156*f*
  biases and 157
  congruent 152
  cross-group 154
  guidelines for effective 155*t*
  knowledge of performance 150
  knowledge of results 150
  negative 154
  positive or neutral 153-154
  research on 158
  simple 152-153
  specific 150-151
  technology for 151, 152, 153
  types of 150-154
field trips 7
Fitbit 134
fitness testing 230, 231, 235
Flipboard 250
fun, as a purpose 90-91

G
gender grouping 27
gender stereotyping 18
Google Drive 56, 139, 224
Google Forms 154, 230
Google Plus 246
grade-level outcomes 39-40
grading assessments 231-235, 233*f*, 234*f*
grouping and selection issues 26-27, 204-205
guided discovery 183-186

H
heart rate monitors 216
high school outcomes 39
homework 117
homework practice 142, 142*f*, 143*f*
Hudl Technique app 151

I
ignoring, selective 164
iMuscle 2 app 184
inappropriate practices
  about 196-197
  competition overemphasis 199, 200
  elimination games 199
  exercise as punishment 199-200
  singling students out 197
  unclear purpose for lessons 200
  unreasonable expectations 198
  waiting time 199
indeterminate zone of practice 5
individualized education plans (IEPs) 71-73
induction stage of teaching 241-242

informational instruction
    based on observations 110-112
    brevity 109
    reminder words and phrases 110, 111*t*
    single concept focus 108-109
instant activity 94-97, 117
instructional alignment 36-38, 55-56
instructional techniques. *See also under* motivation,
    of students
    checking for understanding 115-116
    closure 116-117
    demonstrating 112-114
    informational instruction 108-112, 111*f*
    key development questions 82-83, 82*f*
    observation and content development 83-90, 85*f*,
      86*f*, 88*f*, 89*f*
    observation techniques 80-82
    observing individuals 83
    organizational instruction 106-108
    pinpointing 114-115
    play-teach-play 117-118
    student time use analysis 120-122, 121*f*
    technology tips for 108, 119
    video 81, 108, 119
instruction time 120-122, 121*f*
intimidating 19
intratask variation 133-134
intrinsic reward system 171-173

J

jigsaw grouping 27, 204
journal reading 244-245
Joy and Sadness in Children's Sports (Martens) 200

K

keeping score 68
kinetic sculpturing 140

L

Lambdin, Dolly 16
laps, running 102-103
learned helplessness 211
learning centers 139
lesson plans
    adapting for students with special needs 71-73
    challenges 65-70, 69*t*-70*t*
    content development 55-56
    cues (critical elements) 62-65, 63*f*, 64*t*, 69*t*-70*t*
    example 70-71, 72*f*
    objectives 54-55
    parts of 56-70
    tasks 56-61, 58*t*, 61*t*, 69*t*-70*t*
    tech tips for 55, 56, 57
    writing 54
lessons, teaching
    communicating purpose of lesson 97-100
    instant activity 94-97, 117
    scaffolding 99-100
    technology tips for 95, 97, 101
    traditional starting methods 101-103

Let's Move! Active Schools initiative 42
listening 23-24, 106
locker room rules 30-32
logs and journals 209-210

M

management protocols
    about 19-20
    attendance 21-22
    behavior protocols 28-32, 31*f*
    entering and leaving gym or outdoor space 20-21
    equipment protocols 24-25
    grouping and selection 26-27
    practicing 28
    starting and stopping signals 23-24
    uniforms and dress 21
management time 120-122, 121*f*
MapMyRun 134
mastery stage of teaching 243-244
middle school outcomes 39
mistakes 206-207
motivation, of students
    autonomy-supported tasks 129-131
    developmentally appropriate tasks 131-132
    homework practice 142, 142*f*, 143*f*
    intratask variation 133-134
    music 97
    peer tutors and reciprocal teaching 113, 136-139
    realistic expectations 142-144
    stations (learning centers) 139
    student-designed activities 140, 141*f*
    success-oriented tasks 126-129, 129*f*
    task sheets 135-136, 135*f*, 137*f*, 138*f*
    teacher as cheerleader 144-145
    teaching by invitation 132-133
    techniques for 132-142
    technology and 130, 134, 139, 144
    video recording 140
motor skills assessment 219-221
MOVbands 130
movement experiences, joy in 11
music 17, 97

N

name calling 19
names, learning student 165-166
National Standards for K-12 Physical Education 10,
    11*f*, 37*f*, 38, 43
notebooks, PE 100

O

observation
    and content development 83-90, 85*f*, 86*f*, 88*f*,
      89*f*
    informational instruction based on 110-112
    key development questions during 82-83, 82*f*
    observing individuals 83
    techniques of class 80-82
off-task behavior. *See* behavior and discipline prob-
    lems

optimism 8
organizational instruction 106-108
outcomes, grade-level 39-40, 40*t*
overlapping technique 165
ownership 32

P

Padlet app 186
Pandora 17
patience 189
PE Central 136, 165-166, 221, 246
pedagogical content knowledge (PCK) 41-42
pedagogy. *See also* instructional techniques
    about 4-5, 10
    vs. content 3
pedometers 130
peer modeling 113
peer tutors 136-139
perceived competence 153
performance assessment 220-221
performance check 115-116
personal and social responsibility model 171-173
physical activity promotion 42, 201
physical education programs
    behavior protocols for 28-32, 31*f*
    fun, as a purpose 90-91
    inappropriate practices 196-200
    management protocols for 19-28
    planning program outcomes 44-47, 45*t*-46*t*
    positive techniques and strategies 201-208, 205*t*
    program evaluation 217
    rules 30-32
    technology in 49
    value of 43, 201
physical education teachers/teaching. *See* teachers/
        teaching, physical education
physical literacy 10-11, 11*f*
pinpointing 114-115, 187
Pinterest 50
planning
    about 36-38
    annual plans 48-50
    contextual factors in learning environment 40-41
    formats and components 44-50, 45*t,* 46*t*
    limited teaching time and 39-40
    meeting content standards and guidelines 38-39
    need for 38-43, 40*t*
    overall school goals 42-43
    pedagogical content knowledge 41-42
    program outcomes 44-47, 45*t*-46*t*
    technology for organizing 43, 50
    tendencies to avoid 43
play-teach-play 117-118
Portaportal 50, 247
portfolios 224
positive environment 16-17, 187, 192, 200-201
positive pinpointing 166
positive techniques and strategies 201-208, 205*t*
PowToon 97, 249
praise. *See* feedback to students

Prezi 249
problem solving. *See* critical thinking skills, building
professional development 246-247
professional learning networks 245-246
progress reports 234*f*
project assessment 223-224
proximity control 163-164
public speaking 110

Q

QR codes 95, 108
questioning students 187-188
questions, student 19

R

racial stereotyping 18
rating scales 227, 228*f*
reciprocal teaching 137-139
recognition check 115
repetitions 66-67
replays 68
report cards, standards-based 232-235, 233*f*
responsibility, personal and social, model 171-173
responsibility, teaching 202-203
role models, teachers as 19
rubrics 218, 227, 229*f*
rules 30-32
running laps 102-103

S

safety 82, 82*f*
sarcasm 19
scaffolding 99-100
scanning observation 80, 219-220
schedules 7
school goals, and planning 42-43
selection protocols 26-27
self-adjusting target throwing 127
self-fulfilling prophecies 18
self-testing 230-231
set induction 97-99
SHAPE America 10
shoes and footwear 21
singling students out 197
slanty rope activity 127-128, 184
Society for Health and Physical Educators (SHAPE
        America) 39
Socrative app 223
space awareness 107
SPARK 247
spelling bee model 131
Spotify 17
Sqord Boosters 130
stages of teaching 240-244
standardized assessment 230-231
standards, national 38-39
standards-based report cards 232-235, 233*f*
starting and stopping signals 23-24
static stretching 101-102
stations (learning centers) 139
STEM education 42-43

stereotyping 18-19
stopping and starting signals 23-24
student PSAs 202
students
  age and developmental levels 190-191
  backgrounds of, and planning 41
  choice and motivation 128, 132, 202
  feelings and emotions 209-211
  learned helplessness 211
  learning names of 165-166
  motivation of 97-99, 113
  peer modeling 113
  setting own goals 209
  with special needs 71-73
  student centered *vs.* subject centered 78-79
  student-designed activities 140, 141*f*, 203-204
  student-designed instant activity 96
  students' goals 10
  teachers' impacts on 7-8
  time use analysis 120-122, 121*f*
subject-centered *vs.* student-centered teaching 78-79
successful teaching 10-12, 11*f*
success-oriented teaching 126-129, 129*f*
support group, teaching 245-246

T

tasks, in lessons 56-61, 58*t*, 61*t*, 69*t*-70*t*
task sheets 135-136, 135*f*, 137*f*, 138*f*
teacher expectancy 17, 142-144, 198
teacher-selected groups 27, 204-205
teachers/teaching, physical education
  about 2-3
  analogies of 4
  benefits of 7-8
  challenge of 6-8
  characteristics for building critical thinking skills
    188-192
  content knowledge 41-42, 189-190
  continuing education 250
  describing 5-6
  dynamic nature of 5
  filler speech patterns 110
  improvement techniques 244-250
  interaction analyses 205
  journal and online reading 244-245
  obstacles to 6-7
  patience 189
  pedagogy toolbox of 10
  positivity and acceptance 192
  professional development 246-247
  professional learning communities 245-246
  readiness for 12
  serving the profession 249-250
  seven habits of highly effective 251
  sharing expertise with others 247-249
  stages of teaching 240-244
  student centered *vs.* subject centered 78-79
  successful approaches to 8-9
  successful teaching criteria 10-12, 11*f*

  teacher as cheerleader 144-145
  vs. classroom teaching 3-4
  worth of hard work 252-253
team-building skills 205*t*
Team Shake 204
technology tips
  animated presentations 97
  for assessment 216, 220, 223, 224, 230
  attendance apps 101
  for behavior and discipline problems 165
  for building critical thinking skills 184, 186, 188
  for feedback 151, 152, 153
  for instruction 108, 119
  lesson plans 55, 56, 57
  planning organization 43, 50
  for professional development 246, 247, 250
  QR codes for instant activities 95
  for student motivation 130, 134, 139, 144
  video use in lessons 81
technology use 49
time use analysis, students' 120-122, 121*f*
timing 67-68
Twitter 43, 246

U

understanding, checking for 115-116, 222-223
uniforms and dress requirements 21
unreasonable expectations 198

V

verbal check 115
verbal problem solving 187-188
video
  in instruction 108, 119
  motivating by video recording 140, 144
  for professional development 248
  video analysis apps 151
  video examples 81
  video recording 68, 140, 144, 206, 220
visitor observation 80-81
vocabulary, physical education 100
voice to text app 55

W

waiting time 120-122, 121*f*, 199
wait time 188
walking 21
whistles 23
Winning Is Everything: And Other American Myths
  (Tutko & Bruns) 200
with-it-ness 164
word clouds 188
written assessments 221-222, 222*f*, 224

Y

yearly plans, posting 100
"yet" intervention 207

Z

Zaption 119

About the Authors

George Graham, PhD, is an award-winning university professor and public school physical education instructor who was named to the NASPE Hall of Fame in 2007. He is the author of *Children Moving*, currently in its ninth edition and used in more than 250 universities throughout the United States. Graham has spoken on the topic of positive physical education on *CBS This Morning*, CNN, and National Public Radio. He also has been cited in *USA Today*, the *Harvard Review*, and the *Washington Post*.

Eloise Elliott, PhD, is a Ware Distinguished Professor at West Virginia University, where she leads initiatives to improve the physical activity participation of children. She has developed and taught university physical education teaching courses and conducted teacher training. She developed and oversees a web-based resource to help teachers include physical activity in the pre-K-8 classroom. A former public school physical education teacher, Elliott was appointed to the national President's Council on Fitness, Sports and Nutrition Science Board.

Steve Palmer, PhD, is associate dean at Northern Arizona University (NAU) in Flagstaff. His background includes 15 years in physical education teacher education and research. He also has taught elementary and middle school physical education. Palmer leads and coordinates NAU's physical education teacher education program. He has published numerous papers related to physical education curriculum and teaching.

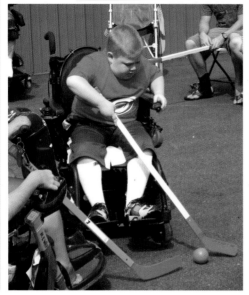